D0004777

PACIFIC
SKIES

PACIFIC
SKIES

AMERICAN FLYERS
IN WORLD WAR II

JEROME KLINKOWITZ

UNIVERSITY PRESS OF MISSISSIPPI / JACKSON

www.upress.state.ms.us

Designed by Todd Lape

The University Press of Mississippi is a member of the
Association of American University Presses.

12 11 10 09 08 07 06 05 04   4 3 2 1
∞
Library of Congress Cataloging-in-Publication Data

Klinkowitz, Jerome.
Pacific skies : American flyers in World War II / Jerome
Klinkowitz.
p. cm.
Includes bibliographical references and index.
ISBN 1-57806-652-2 (alk. paper)
1. World War, 1939–1945—Aerial operations, American.
2. World War, 1939–1945—Campaigns—Pacific Area.
3. World War, 1939–1945—Personal narratives, American.
I. Title.
D790.K563 2004
940.54'25—dc22   2003025097

British Library Cataloging-in-Publication Data available

FOR DICK AND SANDY

CONTENTS

PREFACE

Americans know well the pictures of their country's air war in the Pacific, from the battleship *Arizona* billowing smoke caused by a Japanese bomber's hit and settling to the bottom of Pearl Harbor on December 7, 1941, to the mushroom cloud rising over Hiroshima on August 6, 1945. Between these two events, many know the map like the back of their hand: the enemy's opening thrust, halfway across the ocean toward the continental United States, followed by the long but persistent drive of American forces toward Tokyo. Most know the plot for this action as well, a master narrative intoned by television documentaries such as *Air Power* and *Victory at Sea* that explains the greater sense of these operations even as viewers see the familiar images in motion.

But what of the individuals who fought this war—particularly from the air, where photography was often limited to gun-camera footage and pinpoint air reconnaissance, where maps were a business of navigational specifics and target coordinates, and where war correspondents (with their own master narratives) could only on the rarest occasion fly along? For flyers who fought World War II in the skies over the Pacific, a medium other than picture taking or map making would have to convey the special nature of their experience. Like so many other Army Air Force, Navy, and Marine aviation personnel serving their country, Rowan T. Thomas, a young man from Boyle, Mississippi, turned to the one descriptive asset he had: words. His skills as a heavy bomber pilot helped him survive the war, but his determination to keep a written record of his adventures would win him a place in editor James B. Lloyd's *Lives of Mississippi Authors, 1817–1967*, published in 1981 by the University Press of Mississippi. Here, in the company of such notables as Eudora Welty, Richard Wright, and William Faulkner, Rowan Thomas merits attention for the one book he wrote, *Born in Battle*. Published in 1944, it gives readers a firsthand view of the century's central event, a global war that was reshaping the nature of life on earth, a subject as large as any that Welty, Wright, Faulkner, or any other author would entertain. Not that Thomas hoped to be a professional writer—the son of a cotton buyer, he was trained in the law and hoped for a postwar career in politics. Nor was he writing from an ivory tower or literary artist's garret—as Lloyd describes it, *Born in Battle* was drafted on scraps of paper during flights on the way to action with the enemy. But Rowan Thomas got it down in words and then shared those words with a reading public, a transaction more intimate and more humanly authentic than all the newsreel footage and animated cartography available.

Take *Born in Battle* and more than one hundred other books by or about Pacific theater flyers and you have the subject of *Pacific Skies*. Some of these narratives are by famous aces and bombing leaders—Joe Foss, Pappy Boyington, Paul Tibbets, Curtis LeMay. Most, however, are by individuals like Rowan Thomas: civilians in service for the war's duration and eager only for the world to be made safe afterwards. No one picture is complete—not Thomas's, as he captains a crew of ten, or LeMay's, as he leads an air force numbering in the tens of thousands. But considered together, especially with an eye to the manner in which they are told, these stories form a mosaic with a special sense of comprehension—not what the politicians, or even the historians, have said, but of how the air war was experienced on a very personal basis. Too large for any one participant to sum up, the war fought between 1941 and 1945 in Pacific skies makes great sense when the voices that expressed themselves here and there—at Pearl Harbor and at Wake, over Guadalcanal, and on missions from Saipan and Tinian—are regarded as parts that finally fit together, as they do in the study that follows.

Pacific Skies follows the same calendar that the American flyers in this theater lived by as war with Japan loomed in the future, became a terrible reality in the present, and eventually sorted itself out in a series of benchmarks by which the victors could pace their way toward the conclusion. Again, every American knows the story. But studying firsthand accounts, whether written at the time or drafted from long memory, adds a particular dimension to experience that gives each phase of the air war a distinct human personality. Readers today may wonder at the heady, almost innocent nature of prewar flying, when the joys of peacetime made military aviation seem almost like sport. Then, when the Japanese attack on Pearl Harbor turned flying for the Army Air Force, Navy, and Marines into a deadly business, another trait takes over: ingenuity. Most obviously at Pearl Harbor, but evident everywhere in the first several months of war, American flyers distinguished themselves with qualities not always ranked as desirable among the enemy's forces: initiative, individual thinking, and an improvisational approach that not so much threw out the book as recognized that there had been no real book available in the first place. Thus the transition from prewar naiveté to combat experience is accomplished with an emphasis on the individual, the kind of person needed to win this unwanted conflict.

Individualism would seem an obsolete factor in modern global warfare, but in air combat it never loses importance. With the great fleet engagements in the Coral Sea and at Midway, naval warfare took on a new dimension, as air elements struck vital blows—and also allowed action descriptions centering on single men in single planes. While often grossly dramatic, these descriptions provided the necessary measure for the public to comprehend the war and for fighting personnel in larger units to remain motivated to win. Humankind is always its own best standard for reckoning the scope of things, and the war's next phase allowed an attractive form for it. Fighter aces of the South Pacific, including Joe Foss, Pappy Boyington, Dick Bong, and many others, put a human face on the war and eminently countable victory markers on the sides of their planes. Often fought one-to-one with the enemy, their encounters let readers personalize Japanese adversaries and their methods as well. Indeed, it is in these ace narratives that the stereotypical opponent of prewar days and of Pearl Harbor treachery becomes knowable, though rarely more likeable. From Guadalcanal onwards, combat is personalized to the extent that Boyington's Black Sheep became as popular as comic strip heroes, while Pappy himself is known almost as well by his enemies as by the American public tracking his exploits from their homes.

In the war's last year, such individualism is put to its greatest test. Each plane still has a single human pilot; and even a B-29, with its larger and more specialized crew, still answers to one person's command and control. But in 1945 a single plane can do what at the war's start was unimaginable. In the endgame strategy playing out at this time, each side made its ultimate move. The Japanese, with their homeland now within range of strategic bombing and their sacred Emperor threatened by enemy air power, turned to a last resort, in both military and cultural terms: the kamikaze. For the first time, a single flyer was empowered to sink a huge capital ship, all by himself; but with it he would also be taking his own life, making it an act of ultimacy on both ends of the transaction. United States forces had their own ultimate, the atomic bomb. Again, it was the expression of an entire culture, in this case combining scientific curiosity, mechanical know-how, and industrial might with a pragmatic sense of getting a job done the most efficient way. But the work of many thousand people came down to the acts of a single pilot, Paul Tibbets, who accepted his role of planning and flying the mission and making the final decision to drop the world's first atomic weapon. Great moral issues were raised by the kamikaze and atomic attacks. More than ever, global warfare became an act of collective responsibility. Once popular styles of improvisation and high-profile personal action quickly became things of the past. But the individual flyer was still at the center of things, now bearing a unique responsibility for a culture's basis of value.

Pacific Skies is about what happened in the Pacific air war from 1941 to 1945, but much more so it is about the very personal act of experiencing and remembering that war. Flying and fighting during these years, American airmen went through changes that in peacetime might have taken a full generation to evolve. Hence what was written in 1941 and 1942 reads quite differently in style, as well as in substance, from something drafted in 1945.

Then there is the sixty-year period during which memories are shaped by time, even as the culture changes still more. Writing as an eighty-year-old, today's veteran will note how the planes have become faster and the bombs larger—but also how different attitudes regarding race, gender, and other peoples have taken hold. Many of these cultural changes were propelled by the events of World War II, and it is interesting to see how memoirs take this into account.

Pacific Skies studies the air combat narratives of a generation now just taking leave of the scene. As World War II was the most significant event of the twentieth century, so too it holds a special significance in their lives. No wonder that it has taken so many writers so many years to get their own special handles on it. Considered all together, their stories of battling the enemy from Pearl Harbor all the way back to Tokyo, Hiroshima, and Nagasaki comprise an epic uniquely knowable in each of its constituent parts.

ACKNOWLEDGMENTS

Pacific Skies is a book not of maps or pictures but of words. My research into the narrative methods by which participants in the air battles of World War II's Pacific theater have told their stories would not have been possible without the help of speciality book dealers around the world, whose stocks have covered the sixty-year history of this literature—a literature still being written today, as veterans who have survived not just the war but the onset of old age present their memoirs of an era more than half a century past. Crawford-Peters Aeronautica in California, Zenith Books in Wisconsin, and Brian Cocks and Ken Owen in England have provided excellent service and advice. Thankfully, many combatants supplemented published sources by offering firsthand accounts. From Hank Potter, navigator for Jimmy Doolittle's B-25 crew that led the first raid on Tokyo, to Jerry Yellin, a P-51 Mustang pilot who escorted B-29s there three years later, these individuals gave me a living sense of what might otherwise seem like misty legend. Neighbors and friends have made contributions, too, including Wendell Lampe (a crew member on the destroyer *Black*, targeted for kamikaze attack) and Kurt Vonnegut (who experienced strategic bombing as a prisoner of war). Neil Isaacs gave my typescript a corrective reading and made many thoughtful suggestions. Finally, the University of Northern Iowa, as ever my sole source of support, provided a Summer Fellowship that got the writing of this book under way.

ABBREVIATIONS

Sources quoted in the text are identified by page numbers preceded by these abbreviations for books fully identified in the bibliography:

A	Porter, *Ace!*
AA	Bong, *Ace of Aces*
AB	Guyton, *Air Base*
AD	Prange, *At Dawn We Slept*
AT	Park, *Angels Twenty*
AY	Glines, *Attack on Yamamoto*
B	Boyington, *Baa Baa Black Sheep*
BA	Spurdle, *The Blue Arena*
BB	Thomas, *Born in Battle*
BC	Eatherly, *Burning Conscience*
BE	Clausen, *Blood for the Emperor*
BO	Gamble, *Black Sheep One*
BP	Cheshire, *Bomber Pilot*
BR	Karig, *Battle Report*
BS	Hoyt, *Blue Skies and Blood*
BW	Mikesh, *Broken Wings of the Samurai*

CC	Mears, *Carrier Combat*
D	Watson, *DeShazer*
DB	Winston, *Dive Bomber*
DBA	Kenney, *Dick Bong*
DH	Buell, *Dauntless Helldivers*
DI	Lord, *Day of Infamy*
DK	Dugger, *Dark Star*
DM	Bong, *Dear Mom*
DR	Glines, *The Doolittle Raid*
DS	Bartsch, *Doomed at the Start*
DSS	Cortesi, *The Deadly Skies*
DT	Millot, *Divine Thunder*
DU	Greene, *Duty*
DW	Inoguchi, *The Divine Wind*
ED	Harwit, *An Exhibit Denied*
EG	Thomas, *Enola Gay*
FA	Hyams, *Flight of the Avenger*
FC	Glines, *Four Came Home*
FF	Finney, *Feet First*
FG	Dickinson, *The Flying Guns*
FH	McWhorter, *The First Hellcat Ace*
FI	Kawato, *Flight Into Conquest*
FO	Hynes, *Flight of Passage*
FP	Gaskill, *Fighter Pilot*
FQ	Winston, *Fighting Squadron*
FS	Bergerud, *Fire in the Sky*
FSG	Brand, *Fighter Squadron at Guadalcanal*
FT	Caron, *Fire of a Thousand Suns*
FV	Cheshire, *The Face of Victory*

G	Stinnett, *George Bush*
GB	Furey, *Going Back*
GD	Tregaskis, *Guadalcanal Diary*
GL	Snyder, *General Leemy's Circus*
GR	Johnston, *The Grim Reapers*
GS	Prange, *God's Samurai*
GY	Davis, *Get Yamamoto*
H	Smith, *Hellcats Over the Philippine Deep*
HD	Forsyth, *Hell Divers*
HI	Hersey, *Hiroshima*
HP	Huie, *The Hiroshima Pilot*
HS	Olds, *Helldiver Squadron*
IA	Sakamaki, *I Attacked Pearl Harbor*
IC	Doolittle, *I Could Never Be So Lucky Again*
IE	Coffey, *Iron Eagle*
IM	Morehead, *In My Sights*
IV	Lord, *Incredible Victory*
IW	Nagatsuka, *I Was a Kamikaze*
J	Blackburn, *The Jolly Rogers*
JF	Foss, *Joe Foss, Flying Marine*
JG	Gurney, *Journey of the Giants*
K	Kuwahara, *Kamikaze*
KJ	Lamont-Brown, *Kamikaze: Japan's Suicide Samurai*
KN	Burt, *Kamikaze Nightmare*
KS	Hoyt, *The Kamikazes*
KT	McGregor, *The Kagu-Tsuchi Bomb Group*
LB	Hall, *Lightning Over Bougainville*

S	Sakai, *Samurai!*
SF	LeMay, *Superfortress*
SK	Winters, *Skipper*
SM	Moore, *The Sky Is My Witness*
SP	Kenney, *The Saga of Pappy Gunn*
SQ	Hardison, *The Suzy-Q*
SS	Gay, *Sole Survivor*
T	Boyington, *Tonya*
TB	Tibbets, *The Tibbets Story*
TBS	Gamble, *The Black Sheep*
TD	Dyess, *The Dyess Story*
TE	Wolfert, *Torpedo 8*
TF	Lundstrom, *The First Team*
TG	Naito, *Thunder Gods*
TK	Cundiff, *Ten Knights in a Bar Room*
TL	Toll, *Tropic Lightning*
TO	Michener, *Tales of the South Pacific*
TP	Slackman, *Target: Pearl Harbor*
TS	Lawson, *Thirty Seconds Over Tokyo*
TT	Burns, *Then There Was One*
TY	Cox, *Too Young to Die*
TZF	Okumiya, *The Zero Fighter*
U	Walker, *Up the Slot*
W	Yellin, *Of War and Weddings*
WB	Blount, *We Band of Brothers*
WD	Markey, *Well Done!*
WP	Kinney, *Wake Island Pilot*
WS	Sakaida, *Winged Samurai*

PACIFIC SKIES

INTRODUCTION
A WORLD AWAY FROM WAR

What American air power would accomplish in the Pacific during World War II was, in the late 1930s, almost completely unimaginable. That the German Luftwaffe and British Royal Air Force would soon be fighting it out in the skies over Europe was no useful measure: that conflict, begun with dogfights and sustained with high-level bombing, used tactics and strategies that would prove worse than useless for conducting an air war in the Pacific. Nor were the achievements of Japanese airmen in China and Southeast Asia a good picture of what was to come. What worked for Japanese flyers in these early stages only led to failures once America was engaged. Not that the American military was interested in getting any previews; when a former Army Air Corps captain named Claire Chennault hired trained American pilots to forfeit their commissions and fly for China, the briefings on Japanese aircraft and methods he volunteered to Washington, D.C., were ignored.

Yet the issue is not how the United States was caught off guard or unprepared. The war did start with a surprise attack by a greatly underestimated enemy, but even with the smoke cleared and bodies buried the progress of a three-and-one-half year air war against Japan could not be predicted—other than that somehow, some way, it had to happen. Dogfights? Not with the Japanese Zero, if American flyers were to survive. High-level bombing? That was fruitless against an enemy's navy, difficult against shore installations on scores of islands reaching halfway across the ocean, and ineffective against the Japanese mainland even once it could be reached—until, after lower-level firebombing crippled his cities, the enemy could be dealt two decisive blows from the air that ended the war in a manner almost incomprehensible at the time, let alone half a decade before.

Memoirs of an air war are always interesting, but especially so for the Pacific theater of operations in World War II. Out here, everyone was undergoing a radical learning experience, and an especially challenging one at that, because no established body of knowledge was available to be acquired; almost from step one, everything had to be figured out from scratch. How does one fight a strong naval power when most of one's battleships have been blasted out of action in the war's first hour? How does one take an air capability designed to defend the shores of the American continent and direct it to a scattering of targets half a world away? And when the air war is finally brought to the enemy, how does an American fighter pilot, in instinct as well as by training disposed to face his enemy directly and stay with him until victory is secured, adapt to the strange necessity of hit-and-run tactics? How does a bomber pilot, trained for strategies at twenty thousand feet above the earth, come down to the deck to skip bomb, strafe, or light afire his suddenly personal targets? And how, having been raised in a country so dedicated to humane values, could one go back to high altitude not just one but two times and drop a fearsome weapon of almost total mass destruction?

In the war to come, Robert A. Winston would fly fighter planes off the carriers *Lexington* and *Enterprise* and eventually lead Navy Fighting Squadron 31 into the Marianas Turkey Shoot in June 1944 from the light carrier *Cabot*. By 1946, when he wrote *Fighting Squadron*, he could answer all of the above questions and more, for ways had been devised to fight and win this new style of war. But a decade earlier, when all he wanted to do was learn how to fly, the nature of this coming conflict was far from his mind. Fortunately, he wrote a book about that stage of his awareness as well: *Dive Bomber*, published in 1939. His reason for joining the Navy and working for commission as an aviator echoes sentiments of many who would fly in World War II: "Eighteen dollars an hour," he exclaims when learning what private lessons would cost. "I had expected flying lessons to be expensive," he notes during the Great Depression when even half the price would be difficult to pay, "but I didn't think they were going to tear such a hole in my pay-check" (*DB*, p. 11). And so he turns from a flying school he can't afford to one that he can: the U.S. Navy, unable to staff its growing aviation program with the limited number of cadets coming out of the U.S. Naval Academy at Annapolis, but willing to consider Reserve commissions for graduates of civilian colleges and universities. With his bachelor's degree from Indiana University in hand, Winston qualified and was on his way to becoming one of the pilots ready when war began.

Elsewhere across the United States, young men with similar hopes found them satisfied with another device for training pilots, this time outside the military: the Civilian Pilot Training Program, established on college campuses in 1939 and giving lessons in planes as light as Piper Cubs to classes of students before they left school. Here, too, the services could draw on a pool of future officers from outside their academy and career ranks, while a generation of eager young men (and three thousand young women as well) could get the instruction and flying hours otherwise beyond their economic means. Joe Foss, who would become the leading Marine ace while flying from Guadalcanal, got his start this way. As he recalls in his autobiography, *A Proud American* (1992), "Flying was not an inexpensive sport, even in the 1930s. It cost six dollars an hour just to rent a plane" (*PA*, p. 38). But to attend college itself was a financial struggle, given his father's death and his mother's need for him to help run the family farm. So government-sponsored flight instruction had to share time with academics, plus allow for Joe's part-time job in the college maintenance department, his weekends with the National Guard, and the effort needed to win some money now and then in the prizefighting ring. One way or another, America would have its flyers.

Being paid for learning how to fly was even better. For another future Marine, the night fighter expert Bruce Porter, picking up a $500 annual bonus for pledging to serve four years in the Reserves was a great inducement; as he admits in his memoir, *Ace!* (1985), "attending college posed a severe financial burden on my family" (*A*, p. 5). Eventually, the requirement that officer candidates have at least two years of college was dropped in favor of an entrance exam, but being paid extra remained an attractive proposition. John Boeman, who'd fly B-24s in the Southwest Pacific, makes the case clearly in *Morotai: A Memoir of War* (1989): draftees for the infantry were paid $21 per month, while aviation cadets earned $75 even while being trained (not to mention the $150 per month a commissioned second lieutenant moved on to, supplemented by $75 flight pay and $21 subsistence). "Seventy-five a month beats detasseling corn at thirty-five cents an hour" (*MO*, p. 4), the young man quickly calculates as he walks the cornrows, the Midwestern sky above him. Getting wings seemed the obvious way to go.

Yet the strongest impulse among these prewar, Depression-era pilots is the chance to have their wildest dreams realized. Consider the case of Frank Kurtz, one of the first B-17 flyers in the Pacific to earn fame as pilot of *The Swoose*, named for the half-swan, half-goose creature in the novelty song recorded by bandleader Kay Kyser—perfect icon for an Army Air Force patching itself together after its pasting in the Philippines and awkward retreat through Indonesia to Australia, where the task of rebuilding an aggressive force could begin. *The Swoose* and its crew were written up early in the war by W. L. White, who had already found heroism-at-odds in the story of Torpedo Squadron 3, *They Were Expendable* (1942). *Queens Die Proudly* (1943) follows Kurtz and his men through their initial wartime sagas, but the personal story waits until 1945, when Frank's wife Margo publishes *My Rival, The Sky*. Here is the full story, still happening in wartime but with ample attention to the life she and her husband shared before—a life that for both of them centered on the idealistic aspects of flight.

They meet in college, in front of the Sigma Chi house at the University of Southern California, as if in a scene from a Mickey Rooney/Deanna Durbin movie that future flyers could enjoy as an escape from the Great Depression's hard times. Their courtship is spent buzzing up and down the coast in a hot little coupe they name *Nippu Ji Ji* and learning about aviation in a trainer Frank flies, which they call *Yankee Boy*. Nothing seems beyond his reach, for the young man is also a champion diver, qualified for the U.S. Olympic team. The situation is not unrealistic; in his own memoir, *Pilots Also Pray* (1944), Tom Harmon, a football star at Michigan and already a famous sports broadcaster before serving in World War II, writes fondly of the joyful college-days world he's fighting to preserve. In contrast to dirt-poor Joe Foss and struggling John Boeman, these were the type of future officers the services were so hopeful of recruiting as supplements to the graduating classes of Annapolis and West Point. As for Frank Kurtz, his heart is certainly in it: he is committed to his diving and applies the same rigorous discipline to aviation. He wants to fly, and he wants to dive. Each demands proficiency, and each depends upon a world that will understand its benefits. And so he is devoted to the Olympic ethos and becomes just as eager to teach the world the benefits of flight. He sets records in both fields, garnering publicity for the endeavors he loves. He writes newspaper articles and magazine essays on both. But World War II causes the 1940 Olympics to be canceled, and economic reality eventually puts limits on his flying. Therefore he joins the U.S. Army Air Corps (not to be called the Army Air Force until halfway through 1941).

It's 1937, two years after Robert Winston reported to Floyd Bennett Field for his first stage of Navy flight training but still four years away from Pearl Harbor. Margo Kurtz absorbs the reasons Frank should pass up job offers as various as performing as a diver in the Billy Rose Aquacade and working for the airlines. As her husband-to-be explains, his seven years in the cockpit have been "just the first chapter, and I can darn near learn the whole book in this one year with the Army." It's like studying to be a doctor, with more crammed into an intern's year of actual practice than in all the coursework before. Figuratively speaking, "that master's degree from the Army Air Corps would mean everything, Margo. And it's right there in the AAC that so much is being done to build this country's aviation" (*MR*, p. 42).

And so the young woman accepts the postponement of marriage, saluting her rival, the sky. "She's a pretty gal dressed in soft blue who wears stars for her jewels at night and the sun as her bonnet by day" (*MR*, p. 43). She knows Frank will come back to her and will in the meantime be more than just happy, for a year's training in the Air Corps will be giving him the best foundation for his professional dreams:

> *He was flying the planes he wanted to fly, learning just what he needed to know, doing the kind of a job he loved, the kind where he could put in something extra for the health of aviation. Always before, when he'd been forming aviation clubs or flying teams, or writing articles to persuade more boys to fly, he hadn't been able to tell them how to go about their airman's education. Now he could write of Randolph Field, where a young flier could get a $50,000 aviation course free, paid for by his Uncle Sam. I don't think any honor ever paid to him till then, and there had been some high ones, meant half so much as a letter he received after the first article. It was datelined Washington, D.C. It said this was the best story of Randolph that had yet appeared, and it would surely bring many boys into the service. The signature—General H. H. Arnold. A commander's word to a would-be air lieutenant that he was already doing a job. (MR, p. 47)*

Although there is a preciousness to Margo's rhetoric, the simple economic facts are there. That the numbers have been inflated—the military equivalent of Robert Winston's $18-an-hour tuition and of Jose Foss's $6-an-hour airplane rental has become an astronomical $50,000—does not change the fact that this is what it really costs to learn the ultimate skills in flying. As the coming war would prove, it was cheaper to build a plane than to train a pilot. To the great benefit of an America that after December 7, 1941, could start turning out airplanes as fast as Fords and toasters, the much longer process of teaching pilots their trade was already under way. And the young men being trained—Robert Winston, Joe Foss, and Frank Kurtz among them—were an uncommonly dedicated group.

What a grand life some of them had: in the 1930s, at least, military life need not be foreboding. Robert Winston's introduction to the actual work of Navy flying comes at an Elimination Base— as the name signifies, an installation where inductees are not only given their first flying instruction but face the first and most drastic of cuts. Even during wartime, washout rates remained high, and when at peace, only the very best would get through. But in 1935 Winston finds the mood to be almost all smiles. "The eleven other students were a likeable bunch, most of them from eastern schools, and we were all enthusiastic about the prospects ahead of us," he writes. "We were prepared for a good deal of military discipline, and were pleasantly surprised to find that the friendly, easy-going manner of the instructors was not merely a front assumed when talking to prospective recruits." Make yourself comfortable, the lieutenant in charge welcomes them, apologizing for the lack of creature comforts and promising improvements soon. In the meantime, they're told, "If you like you can go home on week-ends" (DB, p. 15). Instruction comes easy, with no one getting chewed out; when Winston proves stiff and awkward in the air, his check pilot takes him aside for a friendly smoke and reassurances that the young man should "take it easy and relax. There's nothing difficult about this. Just forget I'm up here, and practice a few landings like you've been doing all week. You won't have any trouble" (*DB*, p. 21).

Winston's next stage of training—at the center of Naval Aviation, Pensacola, Florida—is equally blithesome. "Crack-ups were frequent," he admits, "but cadets seemed to have charmed lives" (*DB*, p. 42). In the program's first year of operation, during which over five hundred students were taught to fly, *not one cadet was injured*, he emphasizes. Planes are wrecked, but somehow the young men always walk away with just bumps and bruises. As war looms closer and the intake of cadets increases, such good luck comes to an end. By late summer of 1941, when John Howard McEniry Jr. reports to Pensacola, the contrast with what he had been experiencing in the Civilian Pilot Training Program at the University of Alabama is startling; as he writes in *A Marine Dive-Bomber Pilot at Guadalcanal* (1987), "the Navy training was so different from civilian flying that I almost washed out before I caught on to the Navy way. In civilian flying, safety was paramount. Not so with the Navy" (*MD*, p. 7). Training fatalities increase, and by 1943 memoirists are recalling almost one per day. But in Robert Winston's distant prewar world of 1935, all is rosy. Skippers of successive training squadrons (one for each type of aircraft the Navy flies, from seaplanes to fighters) go out of their way to make the author "feel at home" (*DB*, p. 74). The planes themselves respond as if they've read his mind, "almost like having a personal set of wings" (*DB*, p. 76). Assigned to the *Saratoga* for his first cruise on a carrier, Winston is pleased to see that the officers' staterooms "were as large and comfortable as any I had seen aboard the average ocean liner" (*DB*, p. 87).

Setting the tone for everything is the introduction Cadet Winston is given on his first day of serious business, the day he reports for primary flight training. Their reception is "cordial," with a car being ordered to take them from the gate to their barracks. "So far, no hazing," Winston reports; he will in fact never see any, as the senior cadets are friendly and polite. The main concern seems to be showing these newcomers to the beach, where they can "take it easy, for there won't be anything to do until Monday" (*DB*, p. 26). The beach itself is postcard perfect, with fine-grain sand as white as drifted snow. The water is crystal clear, the deeper water equipped with diving towers; for any cadets not interested in the water, there are "attractive girls" on hand for socialization. Afterwards, the young men are signed into the Officers' Club, even though they're not yet commissioned; everything they wish to eat and drink is signed for with a chit. To work off any fat from this diet, the cadets are provided with facilities for tennis, handball, and badminton, with dances every weekend. Meals will be "the best steaks and sea-food you ever ate." The list of treats is endless:

> As the day wore on we found even more to interest us. The dances were free, and so were the station movies, in an air-conditioned theater. There were several motor launches available for fishing in the Gulf of Mexico, complete with tackle, ice-box, and crew, and the Gulf of Mexico was alive with game fish. There was a well-equipped gymnasium, a football field, a baseball diamond, and a large basketball court. A stable of well-kept horses was ready for polo or riding over miles of bridle paths. Working hours were from seven to three, with a five-day week that gave plenty of time for us to take advantage of these excellent recreational facilities, which had been provided to keep us in good physical and psychological condition for the serious business of learning to fly the nation's war planes. The Navy had

learned that adequate facilities for relaxation after the strain of military flying paid big dividends. (*DB*, pp. 27–28)

As late as June 16, 1941, when Hamilton McWhorter III reports to his initial elimination base at Atlanta, Georgia, military conduct is still relaxed. "There wasn't yet a high-pressure boot camp mentality," he writes in *The First Hellcat Ace* (2000). Certain chores existed to get recruits accustomed to Navy life, but "there wasn't the rushing around and shouting that characterized the training a couple of years later, when they were putting thousands upon thousands of young men through flight school" (*FH*, pp. 11–12). That the intake of future flyers during these prewar years was an elite of sorts certainly contributed to the nicer atmosphere. As Bruce Porter describes his own elimination base experience at Long Beach, California, in September and October of 1940, it is a geographically diverse but socially narrow group of young men that he joins. "Most of us had Anglo-Saxon surnames, and there was a great sprinkling of Hispanics, mainly from old California families" (*A*, p. 9), and every one of them had been to college (in an era when less than 20% of American high school graduates continued their education and some rural students did not get beyond sixth grade).

In such homogeneous circumstances, military rank is less important than a bond of common purpose. In *Air Base* (1941) Boone T. Guyton describes how a crash at North Island Naval Air Station in San Diego brings out everyone's prewar best. "From the third-class enlisted man in his barracks, to the admiral in his spacious quarters, the aid gathers as a family," Guyton notes. "White dinner jackets mingle with green uniforms, blue denims and half and half pajamas with service blues" (*AB*, pp. 5–6), as everyone rushes to the site offering help. This attitude would prevail into wartime. On the first combat cruise of the carrier *Lexington*, war correspondent Stanley Johnston reports in his *Queen of the Flat-Tops* (1942) that "A stranger looking on could not have identified the officers from the enlisted men" (*QF*, p. 215). About the same time, Jimmy Doolittle is preparing his special force of B-25s to bomb Tokyo from the carrier *Hornet*, taking the same training as pilots. As he insists in his autobiography, *I Could Never Be So Lucky Again* (1991), he does it with humility: "if I couldn't pass the course or wasn't as good as the younger pilots, I was going to go as a copilot" (*IC*, p. 246). Army Air Force, Navy, or Marines, flyers take pride in this attitude. "The bigger a man gets," B-17 pilot Rowan T. Thomas says in *Born in Battle* (1944), "the more unassuming and considerate he becomes. I never saw an exception to this observation during my entire time in the war" (*BB*, p. 160).

Some ideals would survive the onslaught of war. Others would not. Flyers completing their training would be both impressed with and shocked by the size of the aircraft that marked their transition to full-fledged combat aviation. For students who had started in the civilian program's Piper Cubs, this last step made for quite a difference. Even the first two stages of military flying were tame in comparison, stooging about in relatively slow planes, often light, underpowered craft with open cockpits. Imagine Robert Winston's awe when he and his fellow cadets are introduced to the Grumman F3F-2, still a biplane but with its strong, stubby fuselage, retractable landing gear, and closed cockpit anticipating the rugged look of the F4F Wildcat that in just a few years would be taking on Japanese Zeros and managing to hold its own. What takes their breath away, however, is what's up front. "Golly, look at that engine!" a cadet exclaims. "A thousand horses, and all for *one man*!" (*DB*, p. 147).

Commanding one thousand horsepower was indeed the threshold to deadly serious flying. As opposed to the emphases on safety, courtesy, and good living that characterize the training atmosphere of Robert Winston's *Dive Bomber*, the regular service life Boone Guyton experiences in *Air Base* is a more serious affair. Even though peace still prevails, Guyton and his colleagues are flying first-line equipment—powerful machines that leave no room for pilot error. The book opens with the sound of a crash siren, all the more disturbing for the fact that it is happening in peacetime, on a naval air station located in far southern California, to the eyes of flyers from harsher climes one of the nicest places on earth. When he surveys the region's bombing ranges, Guyton finds it hard to think about war, given the spellbinding nature of their locales: "Border Field, down Mexico way; Otay, cut out like a patch from the heart of the sprawling Otay Mesa; Oceanside, on the coast toward Los Angeles; San Marcos, in the green, grassy valley of San Marcos River; Ocatilla, lying in the blistering heat of the Imperial Desert across the high range of Lagunas" (*AB*, pp. 16–17). To a former citizen of North Dakota, Alabama, or Nebraska, these places sound like a travelogue or phrases from an exotic song. But there's a lesson lurking nonetheless: "You can't foresee those days when you will be practicing dive bombing at one of these fields and suddenly have to land to help pull a broken shipmate from the wreckage of his plane because 'something went wrong' and he didn't pull out. It is good that you can't" (*AB*, p. 17).

Out on the *Lexington* for his first cruise, Guyton learns another lesson: when you are flying from a carrier, life is never dull. Takeoffs and landings are life-or-death matters—for both the pilot and the many others on deck. In difficult conditions, such as low haze, the risks are even greater, including those of midair collision. Even the utmost caution isn't perfect insurance, as the author notes when forming up carefully after taking off in such murk. As below him the last four planes of his unit line up in position on the deck, "the heartbreaking sound of 'CRASH, CRASH, CRASH' screeched through the earphones. Almost at the same time, down past the yellow wings of our squadron, I saw a huge ball of black, ugly-looking smoke rising slowly from the water." Guyton knows what this means. "There is something about smoke from a burning plane that you never mistake" (*AB*, p. 159). In coming years, losses could be expected. With war on the horizon, flyers would consider themselves foolish if they didn't plan for the worst. But an accident in peacetime is especially hard to bear:

> *A plane-guard destroyer was nearly at the spot, ploughing the seas like some mad porpoise. There was a spreading oil slick covering half a mile of water where the planes hit. Even from four thousand feet I could make out a crumpled wing and a piece of white cloth that must have been the parachute. What a tough break. Only two weeks out on the cruise and to have such a nasty accident! There were four men in those two Vought scout bombers—two pilots and two mechanics. We couldn't tell until after we had landed who it was, and the suspense was awful. You just sat there, trying to imagine who wasn't alive any more and how the damned thing happened.* (*AB*, pp. 160–61)

The *Lexington*'s cruise continues. Guyton and his fellow flyers follow drills and conduct exercises, executing war games with a smaller carrier, the *Ranger*, as enemy. Until they are nearly halfway across the Pacific, this playing at war continues. Peace is won only when the group reaches Hawaii, a well-known destination but one that looks so different when approached not by ship but in the air. Although the calendar has only freshly turned to 1940, Guyton can note the strong irony. "For the last few days our mock battles had led us around the [Hawaiian] islands, out nearly to Midway and Johnston Islands and across French Frigate Shoals, to end up close to Molokai as maneuvers ended." He has the prescience to know what these locations mean, far beyond the travelogue nature of the California airfields serving as satellites and bombing ranges for the station at North Island. "Naturally, it is around these waters that sooner or later in an actual engagement we may have to meet the enemy," he confides. "It is because of the vital importance of the Hawaiian Islands that we spend so much time practicing how to defend them" (*AB*, p. 175).

Farther on across the Pacific, a war had been waged since 1937. The adversaries were Japan and China, and almost from the start efforts were made to get the United States involved. There was a China lobby in Washington, D.C., that enjoyed some influence with the Roosevelt administration. But more immediately pertinent to American involvement was the experience of U.S. Army Air Corps Captain Claire Chennault, who after a frustrating career of trying to develop the role of fighter aircraft in a service establishment that favored bombers above all, had retired on April 29, 1937, and taken a trip to Japan and China just before hostilities began. Ostensibly employed as a consultant by the Bank of China, Chennault was in fact working for the country's National Secretary of Aviation, Madame Chiang Kai-shek. She had hired him to evaluate her country's air force; on July 7, in the midst of his first inspection tour, a shooting incident at the Marco Polo Bridge ten miles outside Beijing inaugurated outright hostilities between China and Japan, and Chennault's three-month consultantship turned into an eight-year involvement with the air war in the Far East.

First came an international squadron, staffed by an odd collection of European and American adventurers that proved almost totally undisciplined. Chennault disbanded it and in 1939 began pursuing the idea of a volunteer force of British and American professionals. The Royal Air Force, with its own war looming, would hear nothing of it. But by October of 1940 the U.S. government was listening to the former captain, now self-styled as a colonel, as he made his pitch. Let a commercial firm known as the Central Aircraft Manufacturing Company (CAMCO), already active in China as a sales force and repair operation for planes built in America, hire some pilots, too, such as those brilliantly trained young men presently flying with the Air Corps, Navy, and Marines. They would have to resign their commissions, of course, but could earn $750 per month, thrice what they were making in the U.S. military. If in the process of flying for CAMCO they happened to shoot down any Japanese aircraft, the Chinese government would pay them a bonus of $500 per plane. One hundred Curtiss P-40s, inferior to such European theater fighters as the Spitfire and the Messerschmitt 109 but still quite capable, were being added to Chinese inventories and being placed at Chennault's disposal, and during the spring of 1941 CAMCO recruiters signed an equal number of pilots for them, plus 200 ground crew and support staff. The whole assemblage, with no connection to the United States government but as American a group as could be imagined, bore this reality in its name: the American Volunteer Group, or AVG.

Exploits of the AVG quite soon became the stuff of legend, equaling stories of bona fide volunteers from the United States presently flying with the RAF in England and just then being organized into the three Eagle Squadrons. The first AVG recruits landed at Rangoon in July 1941 and spent the next several months training in Burma. Not by definition part of what would become the Pacific theater of operations, they nevertheless set an example (sometimes a rather questionable example) for the colleagues they'd left behind in their old units. By December 7, 1941, the AVG had already fought in Burma, Thailand, French Indo-China, and China itself—intercepting Japanese flights, escorting Chinese bombers, tangling with Japanese fighters, and doing some strafing and improvised bombing of their own. In England, the U.S. declaration of war made it inevitable that American volunteers would be reintegrated with forces from their own country; on September 29, 1942, the long and careful process was completed as the Eagle Squadrons became the nucleus of the Fourth Fighter Group of the U.S. Eighth Air Force, the air armada that with RAF Bomber Command would take the war to Germany. For various reasons, including Chennault's independence and the Army Air Force's worry about the headstrong attitudes developed by his pilots during their year of work as mercenaries, a transfer to U.S. colors such as the Eagles enjoyed didn't happen. On July 4, 1942, the AVG was somewhat ignominiously dissolved, the USAAF's 23rd Fighter Group taking over their positions and appropriating their nickname, the Flying Tigers. The only Tiger remaining in place, however, was their leader: Claire Chennault, recommissioned in the Army Air Force with the rank of general and left in charge of American air power in China until just before the war's end.

While some farsighted aviators could gaze west from Hawaii and anticipate warfare with Japan, Chennault had already experienced it firsthand. In 1937, he could observe the effects of strategic bombing in not just subduing but taking over large parts of a country, as the Chinese government of Chiang Kai-shek was forced to give up coastal areas and retreat ever farther inland, until what remained had to be administered from the mountains of provincial Kunming. Later in the 1930s, Chennault learned the value of early warning, developing a network of spotters that let him have his defensive fighters in the air by the time enemy bombers approached their target, in some cases intercepting them along the way. When in 1940 Japan introduced the new Zero fighter, he could study its tactics, so that as American P-40s became available (with well-trained American pilots to fly them) workable rules of engagement could be devised. Never turn with a Zero, Chennault instructed his men. Don't get into a dogfight. Strike from above with one quick pass and then dive away, building speed so that height could be regained.

All this information was reported loyally to Air Corps offices in Washington, D.C., even though its author was working for the Chinese. Claire Chennault knew war between Japan and the United States was coming. So did many American airmen still wearing their own country's uniform. Chennault's reports were read, but it is doubtful that they were believed, certainly not in their close detail about Japanese fighter capability. Championing the fighter's role in military aviation had made Captain Chennault a pariah in the bomber-happy Air Corps, and the materials he submitted now were never disseminated to those who after December 7, 1941, could have benefited. For half a year afterwards, inexperienced Americans in P-40s and Wildcats would meet Japanese Zeros and learn Chennault's lessons the hard way.

From Japan's perspective, the 1930s were anything but a pre-war decade. By 1935, when Cadet Robert Winston was choosing his afternoon's recreation from the tennis, badminton, or deep-sea fishing facilities at Pensacola, and when Captain Chennault was fussing through his last unhappy years in the hidebound Air Corps, Japanese flyers had been occupying Manchuria for four years; within another two they would be doing battle with the Chinese Air Force over China's major cities on an almost daily basis. But it would be incorrect to assume that these engagements, fought under these conditions, gave Japanese military aviation an unassailable advantage over the Americans who would not begin fighting until several years later. This was no nascent Luftwaffe testing its wings in Spain, no Condor Legion using the Spanish Civil War of 1936–39 to devise the tactics that would give them such an advantage in the first year of World War II. Both German and Japanese flyers were accumulating hours and acquiring combat experience that would make them veterans while their first British and American adversaries were novices at actual warfare. But whereas by 1938 Luftwaffe aces such as Adolf Galland and Werner Molders had written the book on fighter combat that RAF pilots even by war's end could only imitate, bad habits picked up by their Japanese counterparts in China often became their undoing when facing U.S. Navy, Marine, and Army Air Force flyers at Midway and over Guadalcanal.

Untested as they were, American forces were nevertheless far superior to anything Japanese flyers had seen in the skies over China. Chinese pilots were poorly trained. In addition to weak resources, the country's system suffered from a military tradition of favoring young men from prominent families; one of Colonel Chennault's greatest challenges was to get these favorite sons out of the cockpits of planes they simply couldn't fly.

Equipment was laughable, consisting at best of obsolete planes discarded by other countries' air forces. The first raiding force of Japanese bombers to be turned back in four years of warfare was the one that encountered P-40s, flown by the AVG, introduced over Kunming on December 20, 1941. The AVG went on to astronomical success over the Japanese, but their planes soon wore out; for lack of parts, the Flying Tigers were soon fighting with one hand tied behind the back—and by the end fewer than two dozen of the group's one hundred planes were even able to get off the ground.

More critically, Japanese pilots enjoying such great successes against their inferior adversaries of 1937 and 1938 fell in love with the concept of dogfighting. They could fly circles around the pathetic Curtiss and Seversky fighters of the Chinese Air Force and dart in to pick off lumbering bombers at will. As Japanese aviation geared up for the global conflict of World War II, the desire of these pilots blooded in China influenced the design of next-generation fighters—particularly that of the Zero, the aircraft that would serve in greatest numbers right to the war's end.

Jiro Horikoshi designed the Zero. His story parallels that of Reginald Mitchell, who about the same time was developing the RAF's breakthrough fighter, the Spitfire, from his Supermarine Schneider Trophy racer. Each man made quantum leaps in design theory and practice, to the point that their planes not only redefined notions of air combat but became the key aircraft in their respective theaters, one of the very few to be first-line equipment on both the war's first and last days. Both men struggled with limitations of their industries and demands from their military; each paid for it with his health. But unlike Mitchell, who died before his creation could fire its guns in anger, Horikoshi survived the war and the hard peace that followed.

With Masatake Okumiya and Martin Caidin he wrote two memoirs, *Zero!* (1956, for American readers) and *The Zero Fighter* (1958, a parallel but more technically inclined version published in England); his own countrymen read of his exploits in *Eagles of Mitsubishi: The Story of the Zero Fighter*, published in Japanese in 1970 and given an English translation by the University of Washington Press in 1981. In *The Zero Fighter*, he recounts how many of his design's key features were virtual mandates from the pilots flying in the earlier, Chinese phase of Japan's war:

> *The lack of pilot armour plating and self-sealing fuel tanks simplified our task in striving to achieve high flight performance. Although there later appeared good cause to regret this omission, at the time our pilots preferred not to sacrifice maneuverability through increased weight of armour plate and self-sealing fuel tanks. Agility in aerial combat in China more than justified this view, our Navy fighters enjoyed overwhelming superiority over the enemy's planes. (TZF, p. 103)*

The first Zero squadrons arrived in China on July 21, 1940, and by the end of the year this new fighter was clearing its Chinese adversaries from the air. "As a result of its unquestioned superiority over enemy fighters in China—the *Zeke*'s performance enabled its pilots to repel an enemy challenge—it was impossible for us to foretell that the good features which the *Zeke* exhibited in the China war might also be its undoing under different circumstances" (*TZF*, p. 172), something Horikoshi admits:

> *In retrospect, it seems regrettable that we could not disabuse the fighter pilots of their belief that the dogfighting ability of*

a fighter was entitled to precedence over all other qualities. Even the designers were prone to sacrifice performance to dogfighting ability; in all our tests we made every effort not to lose out to the agile A4N1 Type 95 biplane fighter in maneuverability. (TZF, p. 61)

The fighter that would lead Japan into the global conflict of World War II was designed to outturn a biplane! The startling nature of this revelation gives one pause when comparing relative air power assets in the late 1930s. Whether it be the RAF's Spitfire, the Navy's F4F Wildcat, or the Army Air Corps's P-40 Tomahawk, a fighter taking to the skies for the Allies looked to the future. Biplanes in the American inventory were relegated to the early stages of training. Among Allied forces, only the RAF's Gloster Gladiator carried on the double-winged tradition of nimble agility—and when the last three in front-line service went down in the valiant defense of Malta, its age was over. In his own more recent account of the plane's history, *Zero Fighter* (1996), Akira Yoshimura gives readers a surprising picture of two Japans coming face to face (*ZF*, pp. 1–5). The date is March 23, 1939, and this most modern of technological achievements is being pushed through the gates of the Nagoya Aircraft Works, on its way to a first test flight at the Kagamigahara Airfield forty-eight kilometers away. That the Mitsubishi Company does not have a field at its chief aircraft works is one surprise, but only a minor one. Downright astonishing is the fact that this first Zero will be hauled through the streets by oxcart, so narrow and bumpy is the way. The relatively short trip would take twenty-four hours. Remarkable enough for the prototype. But six years later, production Zeros would still be transported the same way.

Did what flyers were doing in the late 1930s and first year of the new decade foretell the course of a world war to come? The picture of Cadet Winston pondering the delights of recreation at Pensacola Naval Air Station appears in soft focus when contrasted with the view of Jiro Horikoshi working long nights and weekends to design the Zero that would flabbergast the first American pilots who had to face it. But the image of Horikoshi loading his first plane onto an oxcart for a creaking, plodding, two-mile-per-hour journey to the airfield is surprising, considering that the same American industry that had produced such a world of playtime activities for its aviation cadets could, when need arose, retool and gear up to provide the materials of war. Plants turning out the snappy little roadsters such as Frank Kurtz and his girlfriend loved to drive up and down the coastal highways of southern California could be converted very quickly to the production of bombers his squadrons would fly around the world. True, Japan had been militarized all these years; its aviation cadets were not piling up the miles in sports cars or sampling the resortlike facilities of Pensacola, but neither was there an immense peacetime industry waiting for conversion to war. For transportation, the designer of what would be one of the war's best aircraft could only turn to oxcarts, with no prospect of improvement in the many years to come.

Not that American flyers of the immediate prewar years can imagine the massive nature of such a conversion to war. There is a certain naiveté to Boone Guyton's memoir regarding such necessities-to-come as foul weather flying and the merits of camouflage. "Don't fly in a solid overcast!" This is the warning he's given when learning the ropes of Navy practice, just as firm a rule as "Don't work when you're sick." How such protocols would look from malaria-infested Guadalcanal and various socked-in islands across the Pacific just a few years later is amusing, but for peacetime aviation Guyton can understand the motive. "Uncle Sam would just as soon let the instrument flying, unless absolutely necessary, be done by the air lines in their scheduled work," Guyton writes. "He is not interested in pushing you out of the field in foul weather with a fast, valuable fighting plane, touchy to handle on instruments, in order to put over a flight." As for the expertise involved, "most service pilots are far too busy to go through the process of practicing for hours, flying a beam, making procedure turns and letdowns to the field" (*AB*, pp. 56–57). It's far nicer to get one's work done in the clear, as when, preparatory to their war games cruise, Guyton and his colleagues line up their planes, "the yellow wings and silver fuselages shining in the noonday sun" (*AB*, p. 126).

Prewar livery was easily changed, but weak experience on instruments, as well as precious few hours of live ammunition firing, would take its toll once war began. Listen to James B. Morehead in the early pages of his memoir, *In My Sights* (1998), quoting a squadron-mate's diary about arriving in Australia just five weeks after the declaration of war, with no experience in aerobatics and hardly any time at all firing his guns:

Some of the boys from Manila are down here. 1st Lt. Buzz Wagner, America's first Ace of World War No. 2, and some more of the boys are down here trying to get planes to take back. They've been giving us some instructions on combat flying. From their stories they let us gather that the Jap Zero is no toy, but they try to make us believe that American planes with experienced pilots are a match for them, but where are the experienced pilots? The ones we have here are kids just out of flying school . . . kids just like me. Speaking for myself it sort of gives us an empty feeling in our guts. (*IM*, p. 40)

A year into the war, preparation for actual operations was not much better. When John McEniry flies his Dauntless dive-bomber to Guadalcanal, the simple act of getting there adds up to his most time yet in a combat-ready SBD. "Some of the pilots had only a checkout flight in the aircraft," he notes. "None of us had ever fired the machine guns on the SBD. None of us had ever dropped a live bomb. None of us had ever flown the plane at night." And, as if to reference Guyton's prewar advice on service policy, "None of us had ever flown the plane on instruments" (*MD*, p. 18).

To fight World War II from the air, Americans would have much to learn. The peacetime years had been used to the best effect they could, but looking back on them today gives an impression of almost charming innocence. Jimmy Doolittle describes the situation well, recalling how the military saw its interwar mission as arousing interest in aviation. "The official policy was that the Air Service should accept invitations to put on exhibitions and demonstration," he writes, noting that any and all reasonable requests to field commanders were approved. "We found that county fairs, patriotic parades, and other large public gatherings were excellent events to show off what our planes could do." Today, memoirs by many of the younger men who fought from the air in World War II begin with just such scenes, witnessed in childhood and giving inspiration for a flyer's career. But little did these children know that this was how the mighty airmen of the time were getting in their own hours, accruing experience as they could. Displays were one way. Competitions were another, as Doolittle continues: "The word came down from Washington that we could attempt to set or break records and make cross-country flights that were considered newsworthy and would project a favorable image of the Army Air Service" (*IC*, p. 48). This is the method Frank Kurtz uses in his own one-man campaign to dignify modern aviation; in *My Rival, The Sky*, his wife Margo recounts the first year of her courtship as a series of flights Frank makes to set new marks for speed and distance. He loves every minute of it, and Margo admires his devotion.

As late as 1940, Boone Guyton, on active duty and as ready for combat as any flyer can be, still takes time to marvel at the opportunity he's been given for a one-day coast-to-coast trip. "It is still the honest desire of just about every flier in the country who hasn't had the chance to take his plane, alone, across the mountains, rivers, plains, and deserts that go to make up our broad country" (*AB*, pp. 232–33). The flight he makes from Washington, D.C., to North Island is still, in these prewar days, a considerable achievement. That he pulls it off successfully seems quaint, given what similar planes and pilots would be asked to do in combat less than two years later. But even then there would be moments that recall such innocence, as W. L. White notes in *Queens Die Proudly*, a book about Frank Kurtz and his B-17 crew. On December 28, 1941, the man who would become Kurtz's bombardier is out in the South Atlantic, concerned because the navigator cannot find Brazil. The day is saved when he tells the pilot that "in my old geography book, it said you could see the line where the yellow Amazon mixed into the blue Atlantic as far as four hundred miles out to sea—maybe he could pick this up and follow it in" (*Q*, p. 147). The pilot does, just like Boone Guyton hopscotching the Santa Fe Trail:

I rested my chin on the side of the cowl and, gazing down at the snaking highway, tried to visualize the old wagon train, oxen and all, plodding along over all that land I had crossed today. With a look at the instruments and their flickering needles again, the future replaced the past. How far will we go in flying? War was already spurting airplane performance and speeds to dizzy numbers, even in "fast" talk. What would we see forty years from now? (AB, p. 247)

Had Guyton known that at this very time oxcarts were carrying the newest Japanese fighter from factory to airfield, he might have felt even more confident. As it is, the F4F Wildcat, one of the first new Grumman fighters and the Navy's best weapon against the Zero until the Hellcat and Corsair could come online after the first year of fighting, is all the pilot needs to be in total command of all this geography. Taking off from Anacostia Naval Air Station, he looks back to see the ranks and ranks of experimental aircraft awaiting their first military testing, the future of Naval aviation fading into the physical distance as he notes his first landmark, the Washington Monument. The legs of his trip stretch out before him: "Washington to Columbus to Kansas City. Kansas City to Wichita, Wichita to Amarillo, out over the flat Texas land to Albuquerque." To Winslow, Arizona, "for a last tank of gas, and then out across the desert and high Lagunas to the sloping terrain that angles down to the sea at San Diego" (AB, p. 233). All of it is seen, because the entire flight would be accomplished in the light of a single day, the full manifest destiny of the American continent spanned in just fourteen hours. Needless to say, such capabilities, modest as they seem now, make a flyer such as Boone Guyton feel empowered.

As Jiro Horikoshi designs his brilliant fighter in Japan, Americans who would be facing it in the Pacific skies can be found at work on their own aircraft. In Seattle, Greg Boyington, not yet "Pappy" and still years away from flying with the AVG and then leading the Black Sheep Squadron, works as a draftsman for Boeing, drawing plans for the XB-15 bomber. In Los Angeles, Ted Lawson, who would become one of Jimmy Doolittle's Raiders and write about it in *Thirty Seconds Over Tokyo* (1943), is doing even more serious aeronautical work, designing the landing flaps, and appropriate hydraulics for these systems on another mighty bomber, the Douglas XB-19. Although neither was developed beyond the prototype stage, each made an important contribution, the XB-15 testing designs that would see use in the B-17 Flying Fortress and the XB-19 establishing the stress margins and weight loads that would make feasible the B-29 Superfortress—two of the war's three heavy bombers. Working on the third, the B-24 Liberator, is John F. Kinney, who through his mechanical experience with the seaplanes of Pan American Airways contributed to the revolution in wing-load design that helped Consolidated Aircraft build this new style of plane. The seaplanes Kinney works on lay over at an island in the Pacific where as a Marine flyer he would find himself stationed December 7, 1941, ready for the experiences to be written about in *Wake Island Pilot* (1995). These, among others, are the experimental planes Boone Guyton sees at Anacostia, some of them to be flown in combat by the same young men who in civilian life had helped draft and develop their designs.

Infinite as the Pacific skies of World War II would seem, the flyers poised to take off into them beginning on December 7, 1941, make for a rather finite group. In the late 1930s, the Americans among them can be seen at interesting air-minded tasks:

patching together self-educations in the Civilian Pilot Training Program, working to publicize aviation in ways that only indirectly lead to military flying, training in cadet programs where among all the sweet distractions of recreation air combat seems an abstract technicality, and working on prototype designs that seem as much fantasy as fact. On the first page of his memoir, *Carrier Combat* (1944), Frederick Mears takes a moment to recall the morning of December 7, 1941—not just the "Orson Wellesian announcement" that breaks the Sunday peace of the junior officers' lounge at San Diego Naval Air Station, but the time he and his fellow ensigns had enjoyed in the hours after breakfast that day, "stretched out on the carpet reading the funny papers and listening to the radio or sitting smoking and basking in the sunlight or just asleep together in leather chairs" (*CC*, p. 1). Mears identifies his comrades by their lives as established to date: college track star, professional football player, this fellow famous for his way with the girls, that one known for his strong opinions. In a flash all these lives are changed, as whatever existed beforehand is now eclipsed by what's to come:

> *Among us that morning were Harry March, college track star and fighter pilot, who had two Jap planes to his credit the last time I saw him; Jim Shelton, of Great Falls, Montana, a dive bomber pilot last seen after attacking a Jap ship at Midway; Bill Pittman, a Florida boy who, week after week on the carrier, talked only of his girl, "Little Natalie"; Jamie Dexter, of Seattle, lost from the carrier two degrees from the equator and never found; Jerry Stablein, a big football player who delighted in making bucktooth faces and talking like a Jap; Hank Schneider, of Texas, who spun in off Diamond Head; Tom Durkin, survivor of fourteen days in a rubber boat in the*

Coral Sea; Bill Wileman, killed at Guadalcanal; Dick Jaccard, from Manhattan, Kansas, ace dive bomber, the gayest of us all, who planted a 1,000-pound bomb in the center of the flight deck of the Jap carrier Akagi and later died on the Wasp; Jerry Richey, of Denver, veteran pilot who always seemed to feel so strongly on every subject and everybody we discussed; and Harry Frederickson, from Spokane, who kept the girls in Coronado running around in circles and who probably is in action right now somewhere in the Pacific. (CC, pp. 1–2)

All these individuals, from so many different states, with such diverse personalities and experiences, brought together now in a litany focused on what after December 7 became the greatest event in their lives: World War II. A universe of knowledge surely existed in that junior officers' lounge, but much of it was unimportant now. "Suddenly we realized that nobody knew anything about the Japs" (CC, p. 3), Mears admits. In the hours that follow, the learning curve would begin, with new identities to match.

★ ★ ★

GOING TO WAR IN PEACETIME

It seems incomprehensible that World War II could have started any other way. Certainly from America's standpoint, the war already under way in Europe had all the hallmarks of a distinctly European affair. Take the belligerents: England, France, Germany, and Italy had been at each other's throats for over six hundred years. This present conflict had grown from troubles left unsolved in World War I and exacerbated by certain terms of the peace. Various diplomatic crises of the 1930s had forecast the eventual confrontation, crises in which the United States played no part. German aims were continental, but that continent was half a world away. With England the United States shared a common language, but by 1940 there were more German-Americans in the United States than direct, pure-blooded descendants of the English subjects who had colonized this land. By 1940 American culture was certainly distinct, with its own language, literature, and art. Pitching in to help England was by no means an automatic assumption, and many Americans, from Ambassador Joseph P. Kennedy to aviation celebrity Charles Lindbergh, argued for neutrality.

But the Japanese attack on Pearl Harbor changed everything. Here concerns of another half-world away, those of a hypothetical East Asian Co-Prosperity Sphere, were quite literally dropped on America's doorstep, from an air armada of bombers and escorting fighters that in less than two hours on the morning of December 7, 1941, brought the last two international powers into the war.

And what a confrontation it was. First of all, hostilities began with a sneak attack. Almost as importantly for the nature of the war that followed, the adversary was considered radically alien. Here were no European contributors to the great melting pot, much less makers of a western humanistic culture the various threads of which were woven distinctively yet compatibly within the whole cloth of what in the past three centuries had become America. What influence Japanese immigrants had on the nature of life in the United States was limited by circumstance and by decree. It is no less surprising than it is regrettable that people of Japanese origin were at once considered a hostile presence, an alien threat. That the sneak attack had taken place simultaneously with a style of diplomacy that could only look duplicitous made the aggression seem all the more outrageous.

On December 7, a sleeping giant was awakened; what might otherwise be dismissible as mythology here tested out as truth. But the effect of Pearl Harbor on the flyers who went on to fight the war is measured in something far greater than a same-day or day-after response. One of the noteworthy groups to carry the air war across the Pacific was the Black Sheep Squadron, captained most famously by Pappy Boyington but active as a unit from its commissioning on July 1, 1942, to the end of the war—and even afterwards as Boyington, freed from a Japanese prison camp, began a celebrity's postwar career that would make his squadron an icon for waging war against those who had attacked a peaceful United States. The Squadron intelligence officer, Frank Walton, would write a book about the Black Sheep, *Once They Were Eagles* (1986), supplementing his history with interviews of surviving pilots forty years later. One of them, Bruce Matheson, speaks for the whole group's motivation:

> *I don't think I've ever seen people as motivated to go again and again without question and hang it out as much as the Black Sheep and some in the other Solomons' squadrons. I think the shock of Pearl Harbor literally carried me to and through V-J Day, through years of effort to try not only to survive but to right the wrong that was done there. There was no such impetus for Korea, and you might say there was negative impulse for Vietnam.* (*OT*, p. 163)

A stab in the back, a blindside hit, a sucker punch—whatever metaphor American flyers would use to characterize the event, Japan's attack on Pearl Harbor was seen as a violation of the rules. "Fair play," that trait by which Americans liked to characterize themselves, had been disgraced; being hit certainly was devastating, but it hurt all the more because of the presumed unfairness of the blow. It would take decades of historical perspective before historians could even start explaining how this new adversary had never considered surprise attack to be a dishonorable tactic. For them, no declaration of war was more practical and authentic than the first bomb that brought the news; this was how the Russo-Japanese War had begun half a century before, with European and American opinion in Japanese favor.

From a Japanese perspective, the events of December 7 (December 8 on calendars west of the International Dateline) appear differently: not a sneak attack but a boldly aggressive move. And not just a single act but a painstaking coordination of effort spanning much of a hemisphere. Masatake Okumiya, serving at this time as an air staff officer for the 11th Combined Air Flotilla that trained many of these forces, speaks proudly of the achievement:

> *In all military history I do not know of any country which simultaneously launched so many battles of such magnitude and, in addition, so completely defeated its opponents on that fateful morning of December 8, 1941. We coordinated our combat operations across a distance of six thousand nautical miles, spanning the ocean between Hawaii and Singapore.* (Z, p. 65)

Looking at the larger picture, Okumiya's air war is quite different from Matheson's. In it, Pearl Harbor is not a sucker punch but rather one strike of several, all carefully arranged in the manner of Japan's opening of its war with Russia in 1904. Nor is it a lucky punch; that U.S. forces had adequate warning in the Philippines, for example, did not make the outcome for them any better. Nor are the issues motivating this war alien. Most Japanese air combat memoirs, even those written specifically for American readers, take pains to enumerate Japan's very real concerns for raw materials and opportunities for trade, matters quite literally on their own doorstep. Bringing them to America's threshold simply constituted a harsh awakening to the international scope of these concerns. Not that any of these matters make it easier for flyers like Matheson (or any American, for that matter) to absorb the shock, or even such aftershocks felt half a century later when reading Okumiya's account of a young Japanese pilot refueling that day at a base in Indo-China and being congratulated by a French army officer "for our navy's successful attack on Pearl Harbor" (*Z*, p. 98).

For long afterward, "Pearl Harbor" would resonate in American culture, inspiring James Jones's novel *From Here to Eternity* (1951) and the memorable Burt Lancaster/Frank Sinatra movie derived from it that reinforced attitudes for a generation to follow. The classic account not just of the attack but of the immediate effect it had on American consciousness is Walter Lord's *Day of Infamy* (1957). Written when memories of the war were scarcely more than a decade old, its attitudes have prevailed through the years and remained unaltered by the various debates over whether certain doings of the Roosevelt administration may have invited the attack, if warning was unaccountably delayed by officials in Washington, or if the military commanders on Oahu simply should have known better. Towering over these concerns are the facts of life Lord notes at Pearl Harbor, all of them so indicative of a peacetime world that could scarcely believe the peace was being shattered. Here can be found the motivations that kept Bruce Matheson, the other Black Sheep pilots, and so many American flyers fighting against initially long odds and continuing through many hard years of a very long war.

"Hypnotized by peace" (*DI*, p. 42)—this phrase, used in an offhand manner to describe an establishment at Pearl Harbor resistant to the new reality of war even as the December 7 wake-up call rang all around it, characterizes the state of military affairs. The U.S. Navy itself, here at its Pacific Fleet headquarters, is less of a mean fighting machine than a happy family—and a small one, at that, years of exercises in scaled-down peacetime form having let almost everyone become acquainted with everyone else. Hence the famous announcement, hedged as a necessary qualification: This is no drill! Drills were as close anyone had come to combat in a full generation. If the action taking place was not a drill, then it had to be a mistake. "Some damn Army pilot has gone buster—he's diving on BOQ [Bachelor Officers quarters] and shooting!" (*DI*, p. 84). This report, from a Navy ensign holding a warm bullet as evidence, is a typical first response. "They must be drunk, practicing with live ammunition!" (*DI*, p. 87) an amateur pilot believes. A seaman aboard the destroyer *Bagley* sees a Japanese torpedo bomber hit by antiaircraft fire, its rear gunner slumping in the cockpit, and registers that it is "just like in the movies" (*DI*, p. 88). Bombs themselves come floating in like fly balls, seemingly catchable as an easy out. To another observer, "Caught in the bright morning sun, the falling bombs looked for a fleeting second like snowflakes" (*DI*, p. 92). Except in the movies, by definition so removed from reality, there are no references to war. And why should there be, Lord asks, noting that the same scramble for terms took place back on the mainland when news of the attack was first received. "Like the men at Pearl, who kept linking their experiences to football and the movies, the people had nothing better to go by. A nation brought up on peace was going to war and didn't know how" (*DI*, p. 215).

In the innocence of this response, however, lies a strategy for striking back. "Not knowing how" translates at once into an improvised "know-how," and what soldiers, sailors, and airmen do in the first minutes of the Pearl Harbor attack becomes a model for the style of action that would carry through to victory during the nearly four years to follow.

Take Lieutenants Ken Welch and George Taylor. With their planes at Wheeler Field destroyed on the ground, the two drive ten miles across the island to Haleiwa, where some of their squadron's fighters have been moved temporarily for training. Without bothering to inform their commanding officer, much less ask permission, they take a pair of P-40s aloft and shoot down a Val dive-bomber each on their first pass. Other kills follow, with the P-40s landing to refuel and rearm back at Wheeler. No war-games exercises or rules of engagement apply; spur-of-the-moment action is what, under these new conditions, gets results. At Pearl Harbor itself, ships swing into action without their captains; in many cases destroyers go to work under the command of ensigns, as on this sleepy Sunday morning these are the only officers available. In all cases they do well. Shipfitters become gunners; a crane operator in drydock devises a way to have his machinery spot incoming targets. Civilians throw down their tools and become combatants, fighting side by side with the military, which has itself thrown most considerations of rank aside. On their own initiative, sailors commandeer garbage scows and rescue others who have jumped or been blown overboard.

The new style of tactics works. Pearl Harbor holds together and, although suffering massive damage during the two air assaults, immediately starts reorganizing for war. Part of this effort involves recognizing the spirit that had characterized American response. No one was court-martialed for initiative or even for disobeying orders when the brute force of circumstance had dictated other, better action. In one of the first official histories, *Battle Report: Pearl Harbor to Coral Sea* (1944), Commander Walter Karig and Lieutenant Welbourn Kelley go out of their way to describe the special mentions made and even Navy Crosses awarded for doing just this (*BR*, pp. 330–34).

More than tactics and spirit would change. That the event could happen speaks for two fundamental misunderstandings about the new worlds being born, new worlds of both military planning and cross-cultural appreciation. There was almost none of the latter operative in the events preceding the Japanese-American conflict. Despite Admiral Yamamoto's warning to his superiors, based on the years he spent in the United States, that Japan was drastically underestimating the American people's power and their willingness to apply it in a long, protracted war, the attack was launched. On the American side, the blow was able to be landed because of what historian Gordon W. Prange highlights from a subsequent analysis by Navy Secretary James V. Forrestal, that no matter how much responsible Americans knew of Japanese intents, none of it could "reach the state of conviction" necessary for proper realization. As Prange states in *At Dawn We Slept*, "This fundamental disbelief is at the root of the whole tragedy" (*AD*, p. 736). Part of this disbelief hinged on a dismissal of Japanese capability; how could this stereotypically inferior race from so far across the earth's largest ocean pose a threat to the strongest and most modern of western nations? Images of Japanese pilots as myopic, buck-toothed imbeciles trying to fly airplanes fashioned from bamboo permeate American narratives of the time— and as usually happens, the perpetrator of such stereotypes suffers along with the object. But beyond the all-too-common prejudices is an even more dangerous attitude, the cultural misunderstanding that reasons if Americans would consider the only possible way of attacking Pearl Harbor to be, as Prange puts it, "fantastic, an inadmissible risk, almost suicidal" (*AD*, p. 188), then so would the Japanese think this way. That they didn't—that Americans had to learn this cultural fact the hard way—is the first clarification made by the events of December 7.

The second involves more specifically military thinking. Pearl Harbor would be the first engagement among several that redefined the nature of war in this theater. For decades, the notion of this major naval base needing a system of defense seemed tautological, because the better part of the Pacific Fleet, in all its might and majesty, was right there. What enemy would ever take on the United States Navy in its stronghold? Such thinking, of course, envisions a naval war fought by previous generations, with the image of Japan's Combined Fleet steaming along the horizon and threatening American ships to come within battleship range and start slugging it out. That by 9:30 A.M. the bulk of America's battleship assets would be sitting on the bottom of Pearl Harbor never figured in the thinking, much less that Japan could position an air armada to be able to accomplish this. That a carrier force did attack this way is the true nature of December 7's surprise.

Japanese memoirs, particularly those addressing the preparations for war and the early battles, make reference to Admiral Isoroku Yamamoto, with equal emphases on his air-mindedness and his experience of living in America, where he observed its industrial strength and strong national culture. But for the specific nature of Japan's initial air war itself, the stories of two younger men stand out: those of Minoru Genda and Mitsuo Fuchida. As air officer for the force that attacked Pearl Harbor, Genda was central to all aspects of the operations' inception, planning, and execution. Fuchida, his classmate at the Eta Jima Naval Academy and close friend throughout their service careers, was the lead pilot at Pearl Harbor, overseeing the event and directing tactical actions as specific needs evolved. The stories of these two airmen set the style for what America would be facing in the long war ahead.

As early as 1934, a style of air combat had been developed known as Gendaism. To this young innovator, fighters were not merely defensive weapons but should accompany bombers to the target—and not just as escorts. Command of the air was his doctrine, and in effecting it he demanded fighters with maneuverability and speed; the Zero was designed with his needs in mind. For his part, Fuchida was working out new formations that took a smaller number of aircraft and concentrated them for heavier attack. Without such innovations, the operation against Pearl Harbor may well have failed, as American planners believed any such attempt was destined to. Combining Genda's and Fuchida's innovations gave the attack just the shape it needed to succeed. When torpedo bombers of the British Royal Navy's Fleet Air Arm were dispatched to attack the Italian fleet at Taranto and managed to sink it on November 12, 1940, the belief that ships at anchorage were safe was proved untrue. Americans thinking of the U.S. Pacific Fleet at Pearl Harbor didn't give this event a second thought; for Genda and Fuchida, it was the final proof they needed for advancing their ideas to the highest level of Japanese planning, where Admiral Yamamoto asked for a full report on the Taranto operation with a mind to making plans for a crippling strike against American naval forces.

In the way that Japanese naval aviation paralleled the development of the Royal Air Force and Fleet Air Arm, mythologies were turned inside out. From the American point of view, the RAF stood for everything that was noble, and Japan for all that was not. But the architects of each country's air power went about developing it the same way. Before taking command, Isoroku Yamamoto in Japan and Hugh Dowding in England were chiefs of the technical divisions of their respective countries' air arms;

they were men who, in the early 1930s, set the standards for planes that would fight the air war of 1939–45. Without Yamamoto and without Dowding, there would be no Zero and no Spitfire. Nor would there have been younger men like Genda and Fuchida in Japan, and Keith Park and Douglas Bader in Britain, ready to rule the skies in their respective theaters. It is no accident that the United States had to draw on the private sector for its early successes—whether the raid on Tokyo led by Jimmy Doolittle (who'd spent the interwar years as an air racer and as a technical innovator trained at the Massachusetts Institute of Technology) or the new generation of aircraft rushed into production at factories that just months before had been building Studebakers and Fords. At the time, Americans marveled at the RAF's achievement in the Battle of Britain, when a similar example was available where it was least expected.

Without Minoru Genda's influence, the force that sailed against Pearl Harbor would have been radically different. As Gordon Prange illustrates, he was the architect of the modern carrier group, in which as many as six flattops were "concentrated as a unit to achieve maximum offensive power, with other vessels acting as defensive escorts" (*AD*, p. 101). As air officer for the First Air Fleet, Genda assumed monumental importance. According to Prange, "Although strength is not necessarily identical with numbers, with the formation of the First Air Fleet the Japanese Navy took on greater strategic potential than the U.S. Pacific Fleet" (*AD*, p. 106). One strike from this new kind of enemy force put the United States in the condition of having to fight a carrier war, too, for its battleship force had been knocked out of the equation. But one reason Japan maintained an edge was that it was a planned choice, not one thrust upon it; it would take a little bit of time before an American generation capable of such innovative planning could come into its own. As more than one memoirist has said, a large number of prewar admirals had to be swept away before.

With Genda and Fuchida working together, images of the air war being fought in Europe began coloring their thoughts— again with the irony that these men were emulating those whom Americans considered the good guys, rather than their own Axis partners. Yes, Germany's lightning advances in the war's first year had been aided by the brute air power. But the fact that Stukas could range freely over Poland, yet were turned back from England, made for an important lesson, one that Minoru Genda explained to his friend. In *God's Samurai* (1990), a biography of Mitsuo Fuchida that draws heavily on the flyer's own autobiographical materials, Gordon Prange recounts a conversation between the two in which Fuchida notes that Germany's previously unchecked progress has stopped at the English Channel:

> *"There is one important reason Hitler did not invade England," answered Genda in his direct fashion. "He doesn't have control of the air over England. And the only reason he doesn't have it is the superiority of the RAF fighters."*
>
> *Genda being an expert on fighter aircraft and their tactics, his opinion carried weight. Furthermore, he spoke with admiration of the dogged British resistance and will to fight. For the first time, a cloud of doubt about final German victory scudded across Fuchida's mind. (GS, p. 22)*

In seeing the larger picture, Genda plays his typical role, offering the "originality and bold intelligence" that complements Fuchida's "practical industry and contagious enthusiasm," a combination that in the conclusion of *At Dawn We Slept*

Prange characterizes as "the brain and heart behind the tactical plan" of Pearl Harbor (*AD*, p. 737). The very atmospherics accompanying their attack contributes to the almost mythological role these two flyers play. Through the days of bad weather that precede December 7, Genda worries that the omen may be bad. But then, minutes after his planes are launched, Fuchida notes the particular nature of the day's sunrise. In the darkness before his takeoff, a crew chief gives him a *hachimaki* scarf as a symbol of all the hopes accompanying him in spirit; touched by the emotion, the pilot ties it around his helmet in the manner of a samurai. Now at altitude for the trip to Oahu, dawn breaks over the horizon, rays shooting out from the red ball of the rising sun. "A chill of awe ran through Fuchida," his biography notes. "He pushed back his canopy. The wind beat against his face and sent his *hachamaki* streaming out behind him like a banner. Behind him thundered the first attack wave, the rising sun glittering on its wings." It is the spearhead of 353 planes, the largest naval air force launched so far. In the sunrise, it is an awe-inspiring sight. "He was proud to be a man living at that time. The destiny of his country rested on his shoulders. O glorious dawn for Japan! he thought. Raising both arms, he waves exultantly to his air fleet. Some of the men saw the gesture and waved back" (*GS*, p. 34).

A short time later, Japanese and American forces will be in touch. Despite the sometimes abstract nature of aerial bombing, contact will be felt. In the introductory material to his study of the other great attack in which he'd participate, *Midway* (1955), Fuchida recalls how his own level bombing attack on Pearl Harbor from ten thousand feet proceeds. Antiaircraft fire is thick, coming from both ships' and shore batteries. Dark gray puffs surround his plane, and before long one of these exploding shells finds its target. "Suddenly my plane bounded as if struck by a club," the Japanese attack leader notes:

> When I looked back to see what had happened, the radioman said: "The fuselage is holed and the rudder wire damaged." We were fortunate that the plane was still under control, for it was imperative to fly a steady course as we approached the target. Now it was nearly time for "Ready to release," and I concentrated my attention on the lead plane to note the instant his bomb was dropped. Suddenly a cloud came between the bomb sight and the target, and just as I was thinking that we had already overshot, the lead plane banked slightly and turned right toward Honolulu. We had missed the release point because of the cloud and would have to try again. While my group circled for another attempt, others made their runs, some trying as many as three before succeeding. We were about to begin our second bombing run when there was a colossal explosion in battleship row. A huge column of dark red smoke rose to 1,000 meters. It must have been the explosion of a ship's powder magazine. The shock wave was felt even in my plane, several miles away from the harbor. (M, p. 29)

The explosion is in fact the *Arizona* being transformed into the image that for Americans would characterize not just the attack but the entire war to follow. Half an ocean away, U.S. forces in the Philippines would also be attacked—not as dramatically, and not with such stunningly immediate results, but with consequences much more in tune with the nature of what was to come. Although Genda and Fuchida argued for a follow-up raid on Pearl Harbor, larger strategies dictated caution, and so Hawaii was left damaged but still in American hands. The Philippines were a different story. Almost from the start, it was assumed the territory would fall, something that became a certainty once early promises of relief turned into admissions from Washington that assets had to be saved for elsewhere. Because a ground fog at Japan's staging bases delayed the attack by almost half a day, there was no element of surprise. Hearing the news from Pearl Harbor, American forces knew what was coming and had time to prepare. But prepare with what? The interval provided only revealed how weak defensive assets were. For a time, there was discussion about sending out a preemptive bombing raid of B-17s—discussion that was quashed by the unwillingness to act as an aggressor. The Philippines did fall, but only after several months of resistance. In terms of air combat narratives, the story is one of attrition but also of great ingenuity as resources were used the best way possible. Whereas the first engagements in the skies over Pearl Harbor took place within ninety minutes of a single Sunday morning, defending the Philippines allowed American pilots to show what they could do for well over ninety days, almost every one of which presented a unique challenge. At home, a worried public yearned for good news, even news of valor in defeat. This the air war soon provided.

Air assets at this most distant (and most exposed) of American bases were either laughable or pitiful, depending on point of view. At Clark Field near Manila, one could still find P-26A's, the venerable "Pea-shooters" that with their fixed gear and open cockpits looked more like 1933 vintage air racers than modern fighters—1933 was indeed the year they had been ordered for service. The U.S. Army Air Force knew they were obsolete, but this just meant that in late 1941 they were being flown by Philippine Department forces. What replaced them with the two

American pursuit squadrons brought in late in 1940 were fifty-seven planes taken over from an export order to Sweden, obsolescent Seversky P-35s that vexed American pilots with their instruments scaled in metrics and service instructions in the Swedish language. Only in 1941 would current fighters arrive: thirty-one P-40Bs in March (the same basic model being sold to the American Volunteer Group in China) and fifty new P-40Es in August. With this latter delivery the War Department asked General Douglas MacArthur how many pursuit squadrons he'd need to defend the Philippines. Twenty-seven, he answered. On December 7, 1941, he had five.

The men who'd fly these planes against the Japanese that day were, on their arrival in Manila, just out of flying school, coming from classes 41-C and 41-D at Stockton Field, California. Other pilots arrived later, fresher and with even less training. Indicative of the state of preparations is the experience of Randy Keator, who in shooting down a Zero on December 7 was firing his P-40B's guns for the first time. Less than a week later, these flyers are veterans, with the first fighter pilot hero among them already emerging. December 12 is the day Buzz Wagner becomes one of the new household names in air exploits, turning a routine reconnaissance flight into a newsworthy combat story. Letting down from the overcast that has screened his flight for two hundred miles, Wagner discovers two Japanese destroyers off the coast at Aparri. Their antiaircraft barrage drives him inland. His combat report, detailed in William H. Bartsch's *Doomed at the Start: American Pursuit Pilots in the Philippines, 1941–1942* (1992), forms a story people on the homefront were eager to read. "Suddenly tracer fire tore by me from overhead," Wagner reports, and his flyer's instinct leads him to turn into the sun, where his plane becomes a much tougher target for anyone on his tail. Indeed, there are "two Nippos" behind him, but not for long—a full-throttle climb directly into the blazing light causes them to lose their aim. At this point he swings into a half barrel roll and comes out on their tails, in perfect position to flame them. The two enemy flyers go down with their planes. The "steep chandelle" with which he answered their attack has paid off. But that is not why he's here:

> *Then for the first time I realized that I was right over their airport. Almost directly below me was a runway and on it twelve enemy pursuit planes. I made two passes at the field, strafing the grounded planes as I swept over. I saw five of them burst into flames.*
>
> *Just as I was pulling up from my second pass, I saw that three pursuits above had seen me and were pouring down on me. I dropped an empty belly tank for greater speed and dived close to the ground, making it difficult for them to see me, then gave it the needle and easily outdistanced them.*
>
> *I had filled my assignment, and as gas was getting low, headed for home. The last I saw of the field was two long columns of black smoke. (DS, pp. 157–58)*

Just five days into the war, Wagner's narration sets the style for air combat action. *Chandelle* is a term from a fighter pilot's vernacular, signifying a climbing turn at high speed, during which the plane is suddenly turned to head in the opposite direction. The name sounds flashy and so is the maneuver, the stuff of air shows that folks back home had admired during the barnstorming 1920s and the air-racing 1930s. *Barrel roll*: easy to picture, and dramatic to imagine as the daring pilot stunts himself into position behind his adversaries. There go the enemies, both of them, down in flames. But this first frame of action only brings our hero from the frying pan into the fire, right over the adversary's field. On the ground and in the air, he shoots them up again. And then the use of more hot flying and technical tricks to make a quick escape. But not before a laconic "mission accomplished," which in this case refers to the rules of engagement under which he'd been operating: strict orders to avoid combat, preserving assets for reconnaissance. With a smile, readers could surmise that the pilot was only defending himself, and just coincidentally decimating Japanese forces in the process.

Along with Buzz Wagner's, another name from the Philippines known across America within a few days would be Colin Kelly. Because he died heroically, his story became the stuff of legend, memorialized on magazine covers and bubble gum trading cards. "Captain Colin P. Kelly—Sir; Reporting, Sir, for Duty" reads the caption on the Memorial Day issue of *Liberty* magazine dated June 6, 1942, as the young aviator is pictured saluting at the pearly gates. An oil painting hung at West Point, commemorating Kelly's cadet days at the Academy, is done in the style appropriate for a warrior prince: not just dress blues to mark the occasion, but sword, scabbard, and cloak. As a B-17 pilot, Kelly is sent out on December 9 to seek an aircraft carrier off the north coast of Luzon—near Aparri, where Buzz Wagner's success would take place three days later. No aircraft carrier is found; Japanese attacks had come from land bases on Formosa, the Zeros' fuel mixtures leaned out for greater range. Finding no carrier, Kelly chooses a target of opportunity and believes he sinks it, reporting the kill as a battleship. On its return to base, however, his plane is attacked by Zeros; by keeping it under control so that his crew can bail out, Kelly himself forfeits his life. A hero is born.

Throughout the war years, Kelly's exploit would be reported this way, often embellished with the false but irresistibly appealing climax of the brave pilot, mortally wounded by enemy fire, deliberately crashing his plane into the battleship as a way of confirming his victory. Not until 1994, with the publication of *The Legend of Colin Kelly* by Dennis E. McClendon and Wallace F. Richards, would fact and fiction be sorted out. Not that for the purposes of understanding mythic narratives they need to be; for while military history is one way of accounting for the deeds of warfare, legend is certainly another, and it was a legend that America needed in these first dark days of World War II. The legend would live well into the future. One highly publicized part of it is President Roosevelt's letter "To The President in 1956," futuristically nominating Kelly's infant son for an appointment to West Point—an appointment that was made, with Lieutenant Colin P. Kelly III graduating to serve in the Army armored corps before becoming a priest and Army chaplain, a religious calling several notable veterans of the Pacific air war would follow.

More vibrantly corrective are the emendations made by other legends. Flying the Zero that brings Kelly down is not just any skillful Japanese pilot but Saburo Sakai, his country's most famous ace to survive the war. Sakai would live to age eighty-four, and by the time of his death on September 22, 2000, he had made friends with many Americans he'd flown against and become as well known in the United States as at home. His memoir *Samurai!* (1957) recounts many of his sixty-four aerial victories, but as he states in an early chapter, "The third day of the war is one I will long remember, for on December 10 [as Japan counted from the international dateline] I shot down my first Boeing B-17; it was also the first of the Flying Fortresses to be lost by the Americans in combat. After the war I found that this particular bomber was piloted by Captain Colin P. Kelly, Jr., the American air hero" (S, p. 76). And so two legends meet. From Sakai's perspective, the details are easily confirmed. No battleship is present; what American reports identify as the *Naruna* is in fact a lighter cruiser of the *Nagara* class, and it is no hit at all—from 18,000 feet Sakai can see Kelly's bombs form explosive spouts and large water rings near the ship but not on it. Sakai is disturbed because the American bomber has penetrated the screen of Zero fighters but sets aside his annoyance when he sees that Kelly's B-17 has no fighter escort of its own. "We had never heard of unescorted bombers in battle, especially a single bomber in an area known to be patrolled by dozens of enemy fighters," he observes. "Unbelievable as it seemed, that B-17 had made a lone attack in the very teeth of all our planes. The pilot certainly did not lack courage" (S, p. 77).

From Sakai's view, Kelly's greatest asset is speed. It takes the Zeros' full throttle to overtake the B-17, the great plane flying on as if bothered by nothing worse than gnats—at 22,000 feet the Flying Fortress has the advantage over the more nimble fighters, whose performance suffers in the higher, thinner air. But this early model Boeing lacks a tail turret, and so Sakai is able to make a closing attack from behind:

> *The Fortress' guns flashed brightly as the pilot fishtailed from side to side, trying to give the side gunners the opportunity to catch us in their sights. But despite the frantic defensive flying the enemy tracers missed our planes. I moved in ahead of the other two fighters and opened fire. Pieces of metal flew off in chunks from the bomber's right wing, and then a thin white film sprayed back. It looked like jettisoned gasoline, but*

it might have been smoke. I kept up my fire against the dam-
aged area, hoping to hit either the fuel tanks or oxygen system
with my cannon shells. Abruptly the film turned into a geyser.
The bomber's guns ceased firing; the plane seemed to be afire
within the fuselage. I was unable to continue the attack; my
ammunition was exhausted. (*S*, p. 78)

Inside the B-17, of course, conditions look even worse. Describing the scene in *The Legend of Colin Kelly*, radio operator Bob Altman recalls that "The first heavy burst from the fighters went right through the middle of our ship and burst the pilots' instrument panel and absolutely sliced off the top of [flight engineer] Sergeant Delehanty's head. That's how the bullets went, right through the ship." Confirming how Sakai is on target, Altman adds that "they also set us on fire in the middle of the ship. We had all those gasoline lines and oxygen lines right in there. We were on fire like an acetylene torch" (*LK*, p. 23). Gunner Jim Halkyard barely escapes Sakai's bullets, having just returned to his right waist gunner's position after handing the crew chief a cigarette. "If I had still been on Delehanty's side," he notes, "it would have gotten both of us" (*LK*, p. 23).

Meanwhile Sakai has pulled back to let another Zero get into position:

The pilot hung grimly to the B-17's tail, pouring in a stream
of bullets and cannon shells. The damage was already done,
however, and even as the other fighter closed in the bomber
nosed down and was speeding toward the ground. Miracu-
lously, its wings were on an even keel and the bomber's pilot
might have been trying to crash land on Clark Field. I dove
after the crippled Fortress and, maintaining several hundred

yards' distance, took pictures with my Leica. I managed to get in three or four shots. At 7,000 feet three men bailed out. Their chutes opened and the next moment the B-17 disappeared into an overcast. (S, p. 79)

Colin Kelly's plane emerges from the clouds within sight of Clark Field, from where Frank Kurtz, his own B-17 having been destroyed in the first raid of December 7, is observing in the tower. "A little after noon I happened to be looking up at the overcast toward the roar made by one of our planes which I thought maybe would be trying to come in," he reports in W. L. White's *Queens Die Proudly*, "when suddenly I saw a parachute blossom." Others follow, but not enough for the full crew. That evening Kurtz learns whose plane it was and how the Zeros brought it down. "They put a lucky incendiary into his oxygen system, and of course it started to burn like cotton soaked in gasoline. But Colin wasn't rattled. He gave the regular orders over the interphone system for the other eight boys of his crew to climb into their chutes and abandon ship, which they did," (Q, p. 45).

Queens Die Proudly was published in 1943, and in characterizing the event, Frank Kurtz addresses a wartime readership. He describes how in the standard bail-out procedure, the pilot is the last to leave—not a sometimes gallant gesture, as in the Navy tradition of a captain going down with his ship, but for a very sound reason. "In the Air Force it's the real McCoy," he explains. "Because if a Fortress is on fire, somebody has to stay on the stick to keep her level and right side up while the other eight make their jumps. That somebody is the pilot, and that's one of the things you must be ready to do in order to wear those pretty silver wings on your chest that the better-upholstered girls stare at in the better-upholstered bars" (Q, p. 46).

On board Kelly's plane, there is no mention of heroism, much less sexual conquest. Everyone but the navigator has his headset on, and the order to bail out is heard clearly. "Just seconds after we got out," the navigator states, "the ship exploded." The copilot adds that "the last thing he remembered before the explosion was that Captain Kelly was still sitting in the pilot's seat, flying the airplane" (*LK*, p. 24). For the Kelly book, published thirty-seven years after his own memoir, Sakai depicts his own actions at this point: "I had expended all my ammunition, and I flew up the left side of the B-17. I looked right down into the cockpit and saw the pilot, apparently not mortally wounded, in control of the aircraft and descending into the clouds, with fire coming from the fuselage behind the pilot's compartment" (*LK*, pp. 24–25). In both his 1957 and 1994 accounts, Sakai emphasizes his reaction. "At this time," he recalls for the Kelly book, "I remember having a feeling of tremendous respect (I still do) for the pilot, who had ordered his crew to escape while he was apparently attempting to save his aircraft" (*LK*, p. 25). Back at his base, Sakai describes how "the bomber pilot's courage in attempting his solo bombing run was the subject of much discussion that night in our billets. We had never heard of anything like that before, a single plane risking almost certain destruction from so many enemy fighters in order to press home his attack" (*S*, p. 79). To Frank Kurtz, the feat to be praised is the fact that "Colin stayed on the stick as his plane dropped with its oxygen flaming" (*Q*, p. 46), so that his men could escape; if he had other thoughts at all, this colleague insists, "he wasn't thinking about how many gross tons that Japanese ship displaced, but about his parents and [wife] Marian and [son] little Corkie" (*Q*, p. 47). But as Sakai sums it up, "The discrepancies of the surviving crew's reports in no way detracted from the act of heroism. Later that afternoon, back in Formosa, we found the wings of two Zeros riddled with machine-gun bullets which had been fired by the bomber's gunners" (*S*, p. 79).

Going down in flames might well be the only way America's first narratives from the new air war can find heroism. In Frank Kurtz's case, his B-17 never gets off the ground, but the nature of its destruction is reported in the same respectful tones used for Colin Kelly. Rowan Thomas mentions the event early in his own memoir, *Born in Battle*, as part of a checklist of friends who died in the first attacks on the Philippines. "Arthur Gary was killed during a raid on Clark Field," Thomas reports. "He was standing by his plane waiting for the first pilot, Frank Kurtz, who was being briefed, when the Japs came over. He and Burgess, the engineer, were killed manning guns positions and firing on the Jap planes" (*BB*, p. 30). Published in 1944, this account finds heroism and defiance even in the B-17's hopeless position. But Frank Kurtz's own stories, presented by W. L. White in *Queens Die Proudly* and expanded by his wife Margo in *My Rival, The Sky*, do not hesitate to let their wartime readers see the emotion involved. American flyers stationed at Clark have witnessed the scene, with dramatic results such as reported by P-40E pilot Sam Grashio in William Bartsch's *Doomed at the Start*: climbing from his plane, Grashio "was struck with how deserted everything appeared to be at the base," here in the first minutes after the Japanese attack. "Near a pile of smoking debris, he saw something that made him feel sick—a helmet with a hole in it and a piece of bone in the hole." Wrecks are everywhere, including planes, trucks, and even automobiles. But most disturbing is the sight Frank Kurtz will soon be facing himself: "Some of the dead were still lying where they had fallen, including a whole B-17 crew next to its burning plane" (*DS*, p. 117).

It is this scene that begins *Queens Die Proudly*, and Kurtz's reaction to it fills the first chapter, which is titled "Eight in a Line." That there weren't nine, with Kurtz at its head, is simply due to a circumstance that makes his own experience an ironic reversal of Kelly's (the second story he tells), where the crew survive but its captain dies. The plane is crewed up, preflighted, and ready for a photo reconnaissance mission to Formosa; all that's waiting is the wind-up of the squadron pilots' meeting, but that's the delay that makes Frank Kurtz one of the war's first tragic survivors, the sole survivor whose fate will soon become legend.

Standing alive at the head of this line, Kurtz experiences the defining moment of his war. But at the same time he worries that readers won't fully comprehend. The scene is indeed a riveting one, yet "only if I begin here, maybe nobody would understand what his plane and his crew means to a pilot; that it's like his home and his family. Boys you've lived with and worked with for months. Your life has depended on them and their lives on you." Beyond duty, there have been the pictures of loved ones carried in places you know about, just as they know your own treasured memories and where they are stored. "And they know what you hope for in the future, and what you haven't told them they've guessed, and the same with you about them" (*Q*, p. 6). His greatest treasure is Margo, who runs the same scene through her own sensibility in *My Rival, The Sky*, picturing how her husband runs across the battered airfield to see the "twisted, crumpled, blackened skeleton of our plane." From Frank's written account and the confidences he's shared with her, she reconstructs the moment:

Four men, burned, under the plane. The crew lying on the other side of her, eight of them, sprawled in a crooked line,

one by one where each was struck as they ran toward shelter:
boys Frank had worked with and lived with and depended on
for his life; our boys whom he had kidded and cussed and
bucked up—lying dead by their twisted ship.

And they were still so much themselves, and after the first
moments, Frank walked to the farthest one, Tex [Arthur
Gary], his copilot, and lifted him in his arms and talked to
him. He talked to each one, somehow, slowly, puzzling with
them how this terrible thing could have happened, talking it
to them over and over, reaching to pillow them with some-
thing, some kind of sense in this utterly senseless horror, and
telling them this couldn't be the end—whatever it took we'd
fight on and win, and Ole 99 [their plane] somehow would
be making the long flight, too, with all of us. (MR, p. 11)

Recalling the experience, Frank admits that he "could see it
but not realize it even though I knew it—knew which ones
would have their wives' and girls' crumpled pictures in their
pockets." Because "very suddenly it began to get to me," he does
as Margo has described: "going along the line, talking to each the
way I always would, and patting him on the shoulder like he
were alive, because for me they weren't dead yet. And crying.
And crying. And I'm not ashamed of that" (Q, p. 9). The sentiments Margo remembers are the ones Frank shares with copilot
Arthur "Tex" Gary—a true conversation, not something told to
a dead body, because "it wasn't a body yet," it is still someone
with whom Kurtz can "sit down and talk it over, lifting his curly
head with one hand and patting his hairy back with the other"
(Q, p. 10). These descriptions appear in a book published early
in 1943, when American successes are still of the bloody, Guadalcanal variety. But they are as well received as the heroic accounts

of Buzz Wagner and Colin Kelly. Deep emotion will be an important asset in this new war.

With a new crew and new plane, Kurtz would be sent south, helping with the rearguard action attempted in Java and ending up in Australia to regroup. Meanwhile, fighter pilots and their dwindling numbers of P-40s fight on. Here the story becomes one of attrition, defeat held off only by acts of courage and improvisation. Captains and majors act with the initiative of colonels and generals, getting the job done even if it means using sidearms to threaten recalcitrant supply officers. Planes patched together from several wrecks are kept in the air. As Private First Class Jim Brown says in *Doomed at the Start*, "the jury-rigged repair work would have resulted in a court-martial of every mechanic in the squadron if it had been done in peacetime" (*DS*, p. 162). Sometimes jury-rigging is too kind a term, as in the case of a P-35A that gets one pilot back to base with "a bent propellor and one landing gear strut replaced by a 2 X 4" (*DS*, p. 179). For long-range transportation, a Beech 18, essentially a civilian light plane, is set up with an auxiliary fuel system as homemade as a hillbilly's still. Another light aircraft, a Bellanca Skyrocket, is bartered from the Philippine Aerial Taxi Company and put into Army Air Force service. A hybrid patched together from crashed P-40Es and a P-40B engine found in the supply depot is termed a "P-40 Something" (*DS*, p. 338). By the time American forces are withdrawn to Bataan, more basic skills are needed. One pilot raised on a ranch in Oklahoma knows how to butcher steers, and so after each Japanese bombing raid he collects injured carabao, putting them out of their misery and putting meat in the flyers' mess. As supplies dwindle, meals become smaller and farther between; toward the end, a "training table" (*DS*, p. 349) is set up to keep the few pilots on duty better fed, while the others make do with even less, uncomplainingly. Because there are more flyers than planes, groups of pursuit pilots are formed into makeshift infantry units, as old sergeants with World War I experience give them crash courses in infantry tactics.

Many men in these pursuit squadrons get evacuated from Bataan before its fall on April 9, 1942. Others do not and are forced to endure the terrible Death March and spend the war, if they survive, in prison camps. Because one flyer escaped imprisonment, the whole story would become known to American readers through newspaper reports and *The Dyess Story* (1944) by William E. Dyess. Ed Dyess had commanded the 21st Pursuit Squadron, and although his memoir would be marketed primarily for its account of the Death March horrors—his account of an American soldier being immediately beheaded when found to have some Japanese currency became one of the best known atrocity stories during the war—its first three chapters detail the air action he experienced from the first attack on Clark Field to the final defense of Bataan.

From Ed Dyess, Americans learn just how unprepared the flyers were on December 7—it was only that day that the 21st Pursuit got its P-40Es, and as the first alert came there was heavy grease to be cleaned from the planes' gun barrels. When shortly after New Year's Day the squadron withdraws to Bataan, its commander reports that "our equipment looked as though it might have been picked up at an ordnance rummage sale" (*TD*, p. 38). On Bataan, there is infantry duty for some of the pilots, hunting parties for others, where the Luzon jungle yields up its desperate fare of monkeys, lizards, and occasional fowl. By mid-February his assets are down to ten aircraft, but only five of them are P-40s: "The other planes, some of them flown in from the southern islands, included an o-1 army biplane, a ram-shackle Bellanca, a dilapidated Beechcraft, and a couple of other jobs. These boneyard jobs were called the Bamboo Fleet" (*TD*, p. 46), and soon an old Grumman Duck is raised from the seabed and put on the flight line. Occasionally the "P-40 Something" is rigged with a bomb and sent off on a mission. Mostly the flyers just try to keep alive. What keeps them going is the fatherly care of the remaining forces' commanding officer, General Harold H. George. Some of Dyess's warmest feelings are reserved for this "grandest" of all the leaders he has served, but his highest accolades are for the squadron's enlisted men, who, when asked if they'd agree to the duty pilots getting a better ration, answer in all sincerity that "if the new stuff isn't enough they'll give you theirs!" As Dyess reports, "I've never felt prouder to be an American" (*TD*, p. 62).

On April 9, Bataan is surrendered and Dyess begins his life as a prisoner of war, a period lasting almost a year until on April 3, 1943, his work detail of ten men trick their way out of the camp. Via an underground network still secret at the time of publication, he makes his way through the Philippine jungle and escapes to Australia. After hospitalization and recovery in the United States, Dyess tells his story and returns to duty, only to crash when testing a P-38 Lightning at the Lockheed plant in Burbank, California, the same field where Richard Bong, a Lightning pilot and America's leading ace, would die test-flying a P-80 jet. His narrative is more famous for its revelation of the Death March horrors and terrible conditions of POW life in Japanese hands, but his reports on the long fight at odds before-hand would add to the growing reputation of America's flyers, especially their abilities to improvise with anything at hand and carry on well beyond the limits of conventional stamina.

Throughout this experience, ironies would abound: how American reinforcements were available but considered better invested in Australia; how a domino effect was taking place from Singapore to Sumatra and Java, with one poorly equipped colonial air force after another falling before the Japanese onslaught, as planes even weaker than the "P-40 Something" and the obsolete P-35s flew briefly, if bravely, against hordes of Zeros; and how even as men on Bataan lived in near starvation conditions with only ramshackle equipment to defend themselves, flyers sent down to Del Monte just a few hundred miles south to pick up vitally needed spares would find themselves entertained by planters' families at lavish dinners in a civilian world still enjoying peace.

To the fighting at Pearl Harbor and the Philippines can be added the holdout on Wake Island. One of the reasons a carrier fleet wasn't waiting to be targeted at Pearl was that the *Enterprise* had not yet returned from taking twelve Marine fighter pilots and their planes to Wake as reinforcements; the *Lexington* was en route on a similar mission, while the *Saratoga* awaited repairs on the U.S. West Coast. The Japanese had been successful in the Philippines thanks to the absence of an early warning system that could have had Ed Dyess and the other P-40s pilots in the air to intercept incoming raids. Although Wake would fall much more quickly, the heroic stand effected there would allow America to claim it as a moral victory. Even the Japanese agreed. The early chapters of *Zero!* are filled with tales of technological and military success, but as Masatake Okumiya explains at the start of chapter 10, Wake would be another story. Japanese air power had just sunk the British Royal Navy battleship *Prince of Wales* and battle cruiser *Repulse* one hundred miles from Singapore. As Okumiya notes, "The dramatic victory of air power over sea power as demonstrated in the Malaya sea battle was still being jubilantly received in Japan when the invasion force which had attacked tiny Wake Island was soundly thrashed by small defending American forces and forced to flee for safety." The author's measure of this situation makes the judgment clear, for "considering the power accumulated for the invasion of Wake Island, and the meager forces of the defenders, it was one of the most humiliating defeats our Navy had ever suffered" (Z, p. 122).

One of the Marine pilots there is John F. Kinney, and at the start of his *Wake Island Pilot* he has historian Donald M. Goldstein give a concise summary of the event:

> *The Japanese began air raids against Wake within hours of the attack on Pearl Harbor, and on December 11, 1941, they attempted an invasion. They were repulsed, with heavy losses, by four hundred U.S. servicemen and a thousand civilians. Ironically, during all of World War II, this was the only Japanese amphibious operation in the Pacific that was a failure. Stunned, the Japanese detached two of Vice Admiral Chuichi Nagumo's Pearl Harbor attack carriers to a new task force, and on December 23 they tried again. Although they again received heavy losses, this time they were successful. The Americans surrendered on December 23, one day before reinforcements from Pearl Harbor were scheduled to arrive.* (WP, p. ix)

Looking back on the invasion, Masatake Okumiya credits distinct parts of the American resistance for particular successes. It's the American guns that damage the cruiser *Yubari* and sink the destroyer *Hayate*, "compelling the attack force to withdraw beyond the range of the enemy defenses." Here air power takes over:

> *Also opposing the invasion force were about four Grumman F4F Wildcat fighters of the United States Marine Corps. Our fleet was at the mercy of these few fighter airplanes, which made consistent machine-gun and bombing attacks upon our ships. The persistent strafing and bombing caused consider-able damage to the light cruisers* Tenryu *and* Tatsuta, *and sank our destroyer* Kisaragi. *The destroyer sinking resulted indirectly from bombing by the little American fighters, a bomb from which exploded amidst depth charges stored on deck, causing a greater explosion which tore the ship apart. The Wildcats were among the few American fighters active in the early days of the war. Their pilots were indeed gallant men.* (Z, p. 123)

Resistance, then, is not the entire point of Wake Island's story. Located halfway between Hawaii and the Philippines, the trio of tiny atolls were of strategic importance to neither the United States nor Japan; Americans were only there because it had been developed as a refueling base for the flying boats of Pan American World Airways, which through the 1930s had operated a pas-senger service between the West Coast and the Orient. For that matter, Japan's success in the days before the *Repulse* and *Prince of Wales* was scarcely strategic; Singapore would fall to a land army, and there were no Allied naval operations underway in the area. These two great ships were there to show the flag, and down they went—by aerial attack, which is just as much the point as the success of those few Grumman Wildcats holding off an entire invasion fleet. Historians look forward to the Battle of the Coral

Sea in May and the Battle of Midway in June as examples of the first naval battles carried out entirely by aircraft, and so defining how World War II in the Pacific would be fought. But from the very start, Pearl Harbor had demonstrated the effectiveness of air attack, while the Wake experience made clear that even much smaller air assets could mount a successful defense.

John Kinney joined the Wake contingent in late November 1941, part of the reinforcements brought by the *Enterprise*; he left the island as a prisoner of war of the Japanese. Another Marine, Walter L. J. Bayler, arrived about the same time, aboard a ship bringing the unit that would establish air-ground radio communications at the flying field. As the title of his own memoir, *Last Man Off Wake Island* (1953), indicates, he barely escaped the fate Kinney and the other defenders suffered. His talents were needed elsewhere, at places soon to mark America's progress on the long march to victory: Midway and Guadalcanal. His memoir also would serve as an early firsthand account of the fighting going on out in the Pacific, raising spirits with its tale of Wake's heroic defense and setting the terms by which combat—particularly air combat against the Japanese—could be understood.

For a wartime memoir to do its job, there must be a certain amount of rallying to the cause, and in this theater such rallying involved deprecating the enemy. Walt Bayler's book reflects the tone of other books to come, most of them far more outspoken than his in characterizing the Japanese as a particularly alien foe. He begins astutely by pegging America's lack of preparation to cross-cultural incomprehension, although his very expression of this fact shows evidence of this limiting prejudice: "We said, truthfully enough, that for Japan to pick a scrap with us would be equivalent to committing national suicide, forgetting that hara-kiri, or as they more correctly call it, *seppuku,* is a favorite indoor sport of the little saffron-colored so-and-sos" (*LM,* p. 12). As the action heats up, so do Bayler's invectives, until by page 92 his adversaries are being called "little bucktoothed monkey people" and by page 102 "slant-eyed cannon fodder." The danger of such rhetoric is pointed out half a century later by Bayler's comrade in the air, John Kinney, who ascribes the crippling underestimation of the enemy's air power to "the stereotype most Americans held of the Japanese people as short, bandy-legged men with prominent front teeth and very thick eyeglasses. We were convinced that even if the Japanese planes were mechanically adequate it would be all the pilots could do to fly them in straight lines" (*WP,* p. 49). But the better part of Bayler's narrative is positively inclined toward praising his flyers' morale, as demonstrated from this radio exchange he monitors from the island base:

> *"Cripes! Are we sitting on top of the whole Jap Navy?"*
> *"Jeez!" No suggestion of profanity in that; just pure ecstasy.*
> *"Wouldn't that be wunnerful?"*
> *Four little fighters on top of the whole Jap Navy. Yes, wunnerful was the word, I reflected. And wunnerful was the word for the high spirits, the devil-may-care courage and the fine morale of those swashbuckling youngsters. I loved them. (LM, p. 82)*

When the flyers themselves adopt anti-Japanese attitudes, it seems purely for revenge against a foe, with the personal elements crowding out any racially based animosities:

> *"I got 'em, Walt! I got 'em! I told you I would! Two of the dirty murderers! Just like I said—one for Holden and one for Strawberry!"*

Yes, Davidson had kept the promise he made for his two dead friends. He had come down on the tail of the Jap formation and sent the two rearmost planes plunging to the sea in flames. No wonder he was doing a war dance of triumph. (*LM*, p. 97)

Writing about the same events more than a half-century apart, Walt Bayler and John Kinney disagree on more than the appropriateness of cultural defamation. Take the famous radio message sent off by Major James Devereux, commander of the First Defense Battalion, when the Wake defenders, like their counterparts in the Philippines, were praying for any kind of help. "Send us more Japs," the major had requested. Bayler and the officer responsible for sending out Devereux's transmission see the grim joke involved, but "agreed it was a snappy come-back and in keeping with the best traditions of the Service" (*LM*, p. 101). The two men study the statement, evaluating it word by word, and decide it is destined to assume its place in history with other such challenges from earlier wars—and indeed it has. Kinney, however, takes a different view. Sitting on Wake with death looking him in the face, he listens to radio broadcasts coming from the U.S. mainland. "One commentator went to great lengths to praise our small garrison in the face of erroneous Japanese reports that Wake was the most strongly held American post in the Pacific. But that wasn't enough." With utter dismay, Kinney listens to the broadcaster saying that given such a small garrison on Wake, the Japanese must surely be massing heavier forces against it. "Nothing like letting the enemy know our status," the beleaguered flyer complains. "But this was not the worst of it," he adds. "At about the same time we heard another radio report full of praise and bravado. That part we didn't mind, but the report continued by saying, 'When asked if they needed anything the Marines had said, *Send us more Japs!*'" Kinney sees no humor in the statement: "This, of course, was ridiculous—we had more than enough already. More Japanese were absolutely the *last* thing we needed" (*WP*, p. 69). Again, like the cultural cat-calling that only served to weaken U.S. preparation, this penchant for heroic phrase-making—Remember the Alamo, We Have Not Yet Begun to Fight—makes Kinney feel the enemy is being sent precisely the wrong message.

A better and certainly truer picture of what life was like on Wake comes from other parts of Bayler's narrative. When not scrambling against Japanese raiders, the flyers sit around talking—about the Pearl Harbor attack, their families in Honolulu—"when would we hear news of them? And *when* would relief units turn up at Wake, now that it was common knowledge at home how few planes we had left?" (*LM*, p. 124). Meanwhile, civilians and military personnel work alongside, just as at Pearl Harbor; the Pan American clipper station makes as big a contribution as any military service facility in keeping the island going under the relentless Japanese assaults. Other aspects correspond to conditions in Manila. There, P-40E pilots at Clark Field had never fired their guns at all until the first Zeros appeared in their sights; here John Kinney can only hope "that the war would wait a little longer before it got to Wake. None of us in VMF-211 had ever fired the machine guns in the Wildcats yet" (*WP*, p. 54). Nor have these pilots had a chance to practice bombing runs; their first target is not a bull's-eye back on a California training range but the Japanese destroyer *Kisaragi*, which Kinney attacks just as the fires lit from a previous bomb reach an ordnance storage area: "a huge explosion engulfed the ship and she rapidly began to sink" (*WP*, p. 66). And again as in the Philippines, the lack of early warning makes the island's airfield a sitting duck:

> *The destruction that greeted me when I landed was more than I was prepared for. The enemy bombers had come in low, the constant roar of the surf masking the noise of their engines, and caught most of the men on the atoll by surprise. Our total lack of radar further prevented their detection until they were already over the island and beginning to release their bombs. None of our aircraft revetments were complete. Our planes on the ground were like targets in a carnival shooting gallery, stationary targets that could not shoot back. The Japanese pilots began that day to disprove the stereotypes we had of them of being only mediocre aviators and so near-sighted that they could not hit their targets. Japanese machine-gun fire and bomb fragments hit every one of our planes still on the ground.* (*WP*, p. 57)

But unlike the P-40 squadrons in the Philippines, the Wake Island Wildcat pilots are luckier the next day, when December 9 finds them already airborne with their four remaining planes to intercept the raid coming in. Two bombers are shot down in aerial engagements, while antiaircraft guns damage several others; together, the Wildcats and AA emplacements scatter the Japanese formation so that most of its bombs fall off target and the strip escapes further damage. A few days later, a new adversary appears: Zeros, flying from the two carriers detached from Nagumo's Pearl Harbor force now on its way back to Japan. By now mechanics are lucky to have even two Wildcats flying at one time, but this pair takes on the Japanese fighters and sends two of them down, "ironically exacting a little Pearl Harbor revenge in the process," as Kinney puts it, for "the pilot of one of these planes was Petty Officer Noboru Kanai, whose bomb release over the *Arizona* two weeks earlier had sealed the fate of that ship" (*WP*, p. 74). But attrition mounts. "The Japanese would continue to inflict half a dozen casualties per day on the military personnel at Wake, and we would very quickly become too weak to repel an actual invasion" (*WP*, p. 63).

On December 20, 1941, the last Navy patrol boat to visit Wake leaves with Walt Bayler. As with the Philippines, a few men are needed elsewhere for their special expertise, and so they are the ones who benefit from the extremely limited evacuation space. With him Bayler carries messages to be transmitted to the Wake defenders' families—he does this, and also reproduced them in his memoir as a tribute to the men he'd had to leave. Early on the morning of December 23, the garrison learns that the last U.S. Navy subs in the area have departed, and that there are no friendly ships within a day's sailing time; the relief force has been recalled. With the Japanese invaders in sight, there is no alternative but surrender. For a time, Kinney finds himself on his captors' list of "war criminals," to be executed for flying against Imperial forces. This edict dissolves into simple curiosity; as Kinney says, "I think they found it hard to accept that a force as small as ours has been able to inflict so much damage on theirs" (*WP*, p. 84).

Bayler has left for Midway, where another radio installation needs his service. Kinney departs for forty months of imprisonment, most of it spent in China. Meanwhile, the B-17 bombers have left the Philippines. Their ragged numbers and the nature of the war make it clear that what remains on Bataan are even less than the makings of a defensive war—the last few P-40s will be supporting General Wainwright's holdout and little else.

Heading south, the Flying Fortresses can bomb Japanese shipping from a base in Java. For a time, Frank Kurtz is stationed there, with his new plane, *The Swoose*, having replaced the Fortress alongside which his first crew died. From Surabaya he pleads with his commander to stay a day longer—so that he can help evacuate the fighter pilots still there and so that he can continue trying to place a long-distance telephone call to his wife, Margo, back in the States. After hours of trying, the international operator puts him through, and from the exotic colonial Dutch hotel that shortly will be occupied by the enemy he talks for hours. At six dollars and fifty cents per minute, a fortune at the time and inconceivable on a flyer's pay? Well, as he tells Margo, don't worry, the government will pick up the bill. "I didn't tell her what government it was on," Frank recalls. "She didn't know that the Japanese were taking over tomorrow, and that they would get the bill" (*Q*, p. 225). This is not the first time the Imperial government is involved with a Kurtz communication; his last letter to Margo from the Philippines was carried on the same Pan American clipper that flew Ambassador Saburo Kurasu to his final meeting in Washington.

Getting to Australia means getting out of the war. The immediate impression is a shock, for on touching down Kurtz is met by Commonwealth flyers who "greeted us almost as casually as though we'd just stopped in from a routine cross-country hop" (*Q*, p. 76). Christmas Day is a time of contrasts; while Kurtz's Australian hosts expect him to share in their Christmas festivities, his mind is on the news just come in that a squadron mate's B-17 has been shot up at high altitude, a burst of fire from the attacking Zeros killing the radio operator who was helping the gunners rearm. Even Christmas via shortwave is a disappointment, for instead of getting nostalgic holiday news from home and some carols, Kurtz and his fellow listeners pull in "a lot of politicians doing their stuff on war aims ... sounding off all over the dial," a gang of babblers "all stuffed full of roast goose, optimism, plum pudding, hard sauce, and production figures" (Q, p. 82). But a Christmas layover is of use for making key adjustments to *The Swoose* and the other early D-model B-17s that only combat conditions had brought to light, such as the need to extend the hose tubes on oxygen masks so that crew members have the mobility to help the wounded and getting pressure right in the oxygen tanks—points learned the hard way as Frank's colleagues are shot up in the Fortress trying to make its way in. The day ends with one last radio message, cutting through the commercial broadcasts:

> *It was from Schaetzel. He'd waited until he flew out of the danger zone before breaking radio silence. He said he'd be in after dark with one body aboard and to have the ambulance on the stand-by at the field. That meant there were more wounded. It finished Christmas for us. We didn't say much, and neither did the Australians. But pretty soon one by one we got up and wandered out of the hut.* (Q, p. 83)

One of the first fighter pilots sent to this new theater being created from the safe haven of Australia is James Morehead. His *In My Sights* has much to say about the forethought for such action. It bothers him that pilots have never fired the guns nor dropped bombs from the planes they are flying into combat—or, even worse, that they've had no training on the particular type of aircraft at all. His own Seventeenth Provisional Pursuit Squadron, thrown into the fray on Java, has fortunes that are soon fading. "We were all aware that we were being thrown into the path of the onrushing military juggernaut of Japan to honor a commitment to our Allies, and I suppose it had to be done," he allows, "although just a few weeks of training together would have helped make us a military unit instead of the conglomerate that we were. Like the title of Bill Bartsch's book about the struggle in the Philippines, *Doomed at the Start*, our meager effort was, indeed, doomed from the start" (*IM*, p. 71). The fact that Claire Chennault's intelligence report on the Japanese Zero fighter was never passed on is another failure Morehead rues. "This oversight cost the lives of many of our fliers, for we desperately needed this knowledge," he attests. "The fighters in the Philippines had few victorious experiences, and were essentially decimated, both on the ground and in the air." Morehead finds his own Army Air Force going the way of colonial air arms, applying the famous book title by Christopher Shores about their condition to his own: "All the British, Dutch, and Australian contacts in India, Burma, Malaya, and Sumatra had been, in terms of one British author, a 'bloody shambles'" (*IM*, p. 72).

"Civilians in military clothing"—that's how a disgusted Jim Morehead describes 89 of the 102 American pilots arriving in Australia in February 1942. He cites Admiral H. F. Leary's report from the Battle of the Coral Sea that too many of these flyers had just "three months training at an airport, and are then sent out here to be entrusted with important missions, [for] which they are in no sense qualified, but it is all they have" (*IM*, p. 87). Morehead's task with these men is a tough one. "So the flying school graduates were to receive two weeks' training in P-40s and then rush north to try to discourage the Japanese conqueror," he writes. "My job was to try to keep these young folks from getting killed and still pose as a force to threaten a Japanese invasion" (*IM*, p. 89). From veterans of the Philippines attacks he knows a few things that will be of use: don't try to outmaneuver a Zero (the P-40 is far less agile), don't stay in a hot combat area without a specific target (the P-40's cockpit has poor visibility), and watch at all times for a Zero getting on your tail or coming at you out of the sun. But younger, inexperienced flyers are just half of his problem. At times just as bad are the irresponsible practices ordered by senior officers, such as four-ship takeoffs in heavy dust, flights led into the face of typhoons, and attempts to maintain close formation in dark clouds, while at the same time damaging morale by avoiding combat, not just in the air but even on the ground, where shooting small arms at low flying Zeros is discouraged lest the enemies return and strafe. But as Frank Kurtz observes from his own job as a B-17 pilot helping Morehead's fighter squadrons, "It was our duty not to dissipate ourselves in lost causes, but to do what damage we could, and conserve our strength to strike again" (Q, p. 222).

Another refrain repeats itself from the Philippines and Wake: "My God, Margo, where are the planes and the men," Kurtz writes his wife from Java. "It will be too late if they don't get here soon." As Margo adds, "It takes a lot to make Frank Kurtz frantic, and this is why I worried so" (MR, p. 150). Jim Morehead, whose assets Kurtz would help conserve, knows the answer: trained reinforcements just aren't there, and won't be for another six to nine months—pilots only half-trained have been rushed to the front, making for an even greater gap behind them. As the Japanese advance, all efforts are spent not to lose American forces in their path. When manned bases are lost, the emotional effect is a terrible one, as Kurtz describes:

It isn't pretty to fly over and watch the end of a war. There is no noisy death rattle; it's just very still down there. Nobody lights a flare path. The green tower lights don't come on. You *know the enemy in his gray uniform is maybe training your own antiaircraft guns on you in the dark, or herding around with bayonets our own disarmed boys in khaki who are listening to your motors, bitter because you couldn't have held them back a few hours more, so they could have been taken out.* (Q, p. 247)

When the Japanese advance falls short of Australia, where Allied air forces are eventually conserved, Frank gets his first leave of the war. He's debriefed at the Pentagon and given a hotel suite for a reunion with Margo. What he tells her, and what she reports in *My Rival, The Sky*, shows the heartbreaking nature of this stage of the air war:

"Their faces, I can't forget them, Margo." This is real war that came into our bedroom last night.

"I stayed behind because there wasn't anyone to get the pursuit pilots out of Java. They were the last to go because they were still fighting even as the Japs landed. So I stayed, and Headquarters said they'd try to send a bomber in for us.

"I'd been to the hospital so many times, and I went again. This time to see if some could be moved, flown out. I walked up and down the lines of beds and those American boys just looked at me. They were too sick, too injured to talk, most of them, but their faces—they asked me to take them with us. And that's what I can't forget. Those faces.

"The nurse would just shake her head at each bed and this meant no, this boy couldn't be moved either.

"And the boy knew what it meant. He must have, the way he looked up at me."

So here is the real war. (MR, pp. 180–81)

That Frank has managed to get seventy-five fighter pilots and several bomber crew out of Java and back to Australia can't stop his tears.

Safe in Australia with no further relief missions to Java because Java has fallen, Frank Kurtz's rank and experience land him a special job: using his B-17 to ferry U.S. brass and Australian officials around the northern reaches of the country to scout out future air bases for the American rebuilding. As many as sixteen important passengers crowd into *The Swoose*, making weight distribution a problem. One dignitary carries more than average weight, and throws it around somewhat: a young, second-term congressman from a rural Texas district, here to make headlines in his county newspapers on a fact-finding tour. Even this early in the war, fame does not turn heads. Charles Lindbergh will soon be visiting the theater, flying missions in a P-38 to experiment with fuel mixtures (while unofficially shooting down enemy planes in the process); cadets will find Boston Red Sox slugger Ted Williams taking fighter pilot training alongside them; Henry Fonda, already famous as the star of *The Grapes of Wrath*, will draft combat reports as an air intelligence officer, while actor Tyrone Power, at the peak of his career, draws crowds as he lands his Navy R5C transport plane—not because he's a Hollywood personality, but because he has so much trouble with crosswinds. And so some junior politician from the Texas outback is not about to turn heads, especially in a crowd of generals and air marshals and other brass hats, even though he's taken Navy rank as a lieutenant commander.

Flying far out into the Australian bush, Kurtz's navigator loses his way. This causes the congressman much worry. Between frequent trips to the cockpit for information and his pacing back and forth through the fuselage, the worried man is throwing the plane out of balance, something that becomes critical as Kurtz calls for an emergency landing. Here the crew chief steps in, telling the congressman that he respects his rank and office, but that in this situation he's "just two hundred pounds of ballast"—and promptly pushes him down on a plane's lavatory seat and holds him there through the rough landing.

The landing is a safe one, but that's just the beginning of the congressman's story. The event has attracted a number of local ranchers, enough to form a crowd—and any politician knows what to do now. The congressman "gets busy," as the crew chief recounts. "He begins to get acquainted. They tell him where we are" and so forth, arranging for help. But the politician won't leave them alone. He's out there all the time shaking hands, "and he comes back and tells us these are real folks—the best damn folks in the world, except maybe the folks in his own Texas. Pretty soon he knows all their first names, and they're telling him why there ought to be a high tariff on wool, and there's no question he swung that county for Johnson before we left" (Q, p. 266).

Johnson? Yes, the man's been identified as Lyndon Baines Johnson, half a lifetime before becoming thirty-sixth president of the United States and commander-in-chief of the armed forces that will fight another war in this corner of the world.

★ ★ ★

AN AIR WAR
AT SEA AND
ON LAND

The Doolittle Raid on Tokyo, flown on April 18, 1942, stands as America's first offensive action of World War II. The Battle of Midway, fought between June 4 and June 6 of the same year, is considered the first major victory by U.S. forces in the war, the Coral Sea Battle of a month before coming out a draw. Although the attack on Tokyo would prove most of all a morale lifter, the insignificant damage it inflicted on the Japanese was enough to revise enemy thinking and direct it toward Midway, where matters of immense substance were to be decided. In between, Japanese and American naval forces engaged each other in the Coral Sea, where on May 7–8 a major battle was conducted with the two sides out of sight and out of range of one another— except for their air elements, which inflicted all the damage and determined the outcome. When American air power foiled the enemy's plan for taking Midway Island and wrought havoc on its carrier fleet in the process, the new character of this war in the Central Pacific was determined: air action would play a big part.

Japan, of course, had set that plan in action by virtue of its carrier-based attack on Pearl Harbor. But its land-based strategy was equally important for the war's conduct and even more crucial for the economic matters that had prompted military force in the first place. World powers need raw resources for their industries, and in the 1930s Japan had none: from petroleum to cotton, the colonial interests of Britain, France, and Holland had Southeast Asia sewn up. And so in terms of geographic conquest, it was in this direction that Japan proceeded. By May of 1942 Japanese forces were ready to invade and occupy Tugali in the Solomon Islands and Port Moresby on the south coast of Papua New Guinea, each of which was presently occupied by Australian forces as defenses for their own homeland. The thought of Japan taking over Australia was too hideous to imagine; but an enemy foothold in the southern Solomons and on New Guinea was a possibility whose effect could be easily measured, for such a presence would disrupt the U.S. to Australia supply line that was building up Allied forces for an offensive role. Therefore, with the Battle of the Coral Sea putting a temporary halt to Japanese advances, American attention turned to inaugurating an air-supported land war of its own, beginning with the landings on Guadalcanal commencing August 18, 1942. From that day onwards American efforts headed "up the slot" through the Solomons toward the Philippines, a two-year campaign that wouldn't end until the South Pacific was retaken and a strategic bombing assault on Japan from the Marianas could begin.

How does the Doolittle Raid figure at the start of this complex progression? As a symbol of American ingenuity and resolve, for its meager bomb tonnage and total loss of its attacking aircraft hardly qualify as conventional success. In their 1944 narrative, *Battle Report*, written well before victory was assured,

Navy publicists Walter Karig and Welbourn Kelley find the perfect phrase for describing Doolittle's action: on April 18, 1942, just nine days after the sickening fall of Bataan with Americans knowing full well that they were losing the war, Doolittle's flyers "had come out of nowhere and laid a trail of bombs across the main island of Honshu from Tokyo to Kobe" (*BR*, p. 293). The raid may not have had the material effect of Pearl Harbor, but the surprise was more insinuating. It was not just that the planes had come, but from where? That the sixteen B-25 medium bombers had lifted off the deck of the carrier *Hornet* was kept secret for a full year. President Roosevelt took special delight in saying how the planes had come from "Shangri-La," the fantasy land of James Hilton's novel (and popular Frank Capra movie starring Ronald Coleman) *Lost Horizon*. All the better for confounding the Japanese. In terms of strategy, they would for a time think the bombers had somehow extended their range so as to fly from Midway Island, presenting Japan with a reason to capture that base, or at the very least extend its Central Pacific power to a much wider range. For the raid's great impact had been psychological. Even more than the typical Japanese fighting man, Admiral Yamamoto was obsessed with the military's avowed role of protecting the Emperor. Doolittle's bombers had flown right over the Imperial Palace; though ordered strictly not to attack this site, for fear of rallying the Japanese people to even greater effort, they had dropped bombs on the homeland's soil, at once changing the character of Japan's war. From now on many fleet elements were recalled for close defense, while others prepared to extend homeland security as far out as Midway Island. As Jimmy Doolittle writes in the first page of his autobiography, "the primary purpose of the raid we were about to launch against the main island of Japan was psychological" (*IC*,

p. 1), but not even this great flyer could know how great the mental effect would be, or what consequence such thinking might have on the conduct of more than three further years of air war.

The raid itself proved something to Americans: that in planning beyond the ordinary, even attempting what is supposedly impossible and taking on what can't be done, the greatest leap is the imaginative one. Having the idea and deciding to follow it through are the major accomplishments; once the mind has traveled this distance, the technology quickly follows. As it happened, precious little technology was involved, and much of it was of a hardware store/carpenter shop variety. For range, extra fuel tanks were added, with weight saved by eliminating the B-25's bottom turret. But to prevent intercepting fighters from thinking the Doolittle planes were weakly defended, broomsticks were sawn in half, painted black, and mounted in the same position as standard twin-fifties would occupy in the tails of B-17s. Because the top-secret Norden bombsight dare not be risked on this mission over Japan, something simpler had to be rigged, consisting of two pieces of aluminum costing twenty cents. At the lower levels from which the Raiders would be bombing, this improvised device actually worked better than the complex Norden. And so for the price of a broom and two scraps of metal, plus a 60-gallon fuel tank replenished in flight from 5-gallon gasoline cans, a regular B-25 could be made mission-ready to take off from an aircraft carrier and bomb Tokyo.

No B-25 or any other twin-engine medium bomber had ever become airborne in so short a distance, let alone from a carrier pitching at sea. Nor did Army Air Force pilots have any training in these respects. But as happened with the technology, training proved clear and simple. Within two weeks of the Pearl Harbor attack, President Roosevelt began telling his top advisors that he wanted to mount a morale-building raid against the Japanese home islands. Chief of Naval Operations Admiral Ernest J. King, already at work on the North Africa invasion (to happen in November 1942) was arguing for a carrier force that would launch not just fighters but cargo planes and bombers; in working out such possibilities, General Henry H. Arnold, chief of staff of the Army Air Forces, prepared the ground for a fortuitous seed of thought dropped by a Navy man at Norfolk, who in seeing Army twin-engine planes making simulated bombing passes at an outlined carrier deck wondered if these same planes could fly from a real carrier and bomb Japan. The plan needed a leader to make it work, someone the general had in mind: Jimmy Doolittle, Air Corps veteran, champion air racer, aviation expert for Shell Oil, and world famous as a "master of calculated risk." Could Doolittle prepare two dozen planes and crews (including backups) for such a raid? If a B-25 could be lifted off in such a distance, yes. On February 3, 1942, two Mitchell bombers were loaded aboard the carrier *Hornet* for a test in the waters off Norfolk. Two veteran pilots took off in turn, launching into flight with deckspace still before them. On March 3, Doolittle met with the men chosen and commenced their three weeks of training in the carrier takeoff manner of quarter flaps down. The biggest worry would be keeping the project secret.

The plan was for the *Hornet,* accompanied by the carrier *Enterprise* for defense, to sail within 450 miles of Tokyo. From here the sixteen planes and crews transported for the raid would take to the air for a night bombing of targets on the home islands, including factories in Tokyo, then fly on to China for safe landings in the light of dawn. Their planes would be assigned to Far East service, while the flyers would be returned for service in their own Army Air Force. Right here were the makings of future problems. Chiang's politics and the presence of General Claire Chennault, still commanding the independent American Volunteer Group of Flying Tigers, made it too risky for them to be made partners in the operation. Not told of the mission, they were unable to make preparations for helping the Doolittle Raiders, should they arrive in need. And arrive in need they did. On April 18, a day before scheduled, naval forces observed a Japanese picket boat and sank it, unsure if it had been able to send a report to Japan. Unwilling to risk his carriers, their commander, Vice Admiral William F. Halsey Jr., decided that the Doolittle planes should fly at once: at greater range and at the wrong time of day, meaning they would arrive over Japan in broad daylight and be seeking out their Chinese airfields in the dark. Not a single B-25 would land safely.

How the Raid succeeded under these last-minute trying circumstances and how Doolittle and his men struggled to survive afterwards make for the first grandly heroic air narrative from the Pacific in World War II. Published in 1943 only shortly after the mission's secrets were declassified, Ted Lawson's *Thirty Seconds Over Tokyo* became an instant best-seller, an air narrative serving as the war's first combat classic. "Bombs over Tokyo!" schoolchildren would call out on playgrounds across America, creating a new generation of fame for the Jimmy Doolittle known to their parents as a 1930s air racer. Of the surviving crews, many Doolittle flyers wound up in North Africa a year later. There, replete with Air Force publicity photos, a reunion was held, the first of well over half a century's worth. Carroll V. Glines describes the reunions in his history, *The Doolittle Raid* (1988), with a photograph of seventy goblets, some inverted, sharing a cabinet with a bottle of fine brandy:

Each year, Doolittle's raiders hold a reunion. These silver goblets are taken to the reunion and used for toasts to the crew members who are no longer living. These men are represented by the cups that have been turned down. The last two surviving members will open the bottle of brandy and drink a final toast. Between reunions the goblets, presented by the city of Tucson, are on display at the Air Force Academy Museum, Colorado Springs, Colorado. (DR, photo insert, p. [xiv])

The reunion plan, first announced as a promise by Doolittle to inspire his men when even survival was a poor bet, thus not only works out but in a way that carries the Raiders' fame through the postwar decades until a "greatest generation" legend can be nurtured for all such wartime achievements. But other legends are born from the experience as well. One crew lands in Russian territory and is interned in the Soviet Union, beginning a virtual captivity that provides an early lesson in how tense relations with this ally will be. Of the eight flyers from the two crews captured by the Japanese, three were put on trial and then executed, stirring American anger and emotion equal to that provoked by the Pearl Harbor attack. The others became prisoners of war, one of them, Jacob DeShazer, dedicating his postwar life to missionary work in Japan and receiving worldwide attention for it. Doolittle himself would go on to command air forces in North Africa and England, and become even more famous as a postwar hero than he'd been as a popular aviation figure beforehand; his autobiography, *I Could Never Be So Lucky Again*, ranks with Chuck Yeager's life story as one of the narratives able to teach a new generation about what constitutes "the right stuff."

From the shelf of narratives generated by the Doolittle Raid, several themes emerge. One of the most important is the leader's own: that his "daredevil" reputation was not only based on false assessments but caused him unfair and unmerited trouble during his whole career. Daring, he counsels, goes with skill, and each is based on experience. "Constant practice had simply expanded my limitations," he writes. "The trick was to learn your limitations, gradually expand them, but never go beyond them" (*IC*, p. 144). Yet from his early career in the service to its peak, certain superiors did not understand the difference between foolish risks and calculated ones. Such skepticism accompanied his planning for the Tokyo Raid; and two years after its success, his commander in Europe, General Dwight D. Eisenhower, still suspected the man for presumed recklessness. It's true that Doolittle's actions sometimes gave the impression of a show-off, but such demonstrations were for a purpose. His own Tokyo-bound B-25 was the first to take off not because the glory of leadership was to be up front but because leadership's real purpose is to show that the job can be done: being first meant Doolittle's planes had the least amount of deck space before it on the carrier, making its take-off the hardest. In similar manner, when medium bomber pilots were threatening to mutiny over the allegedly underpowered B-26, Doolittle assembled them on the airfield to watch him put the notorious Martin Marauder through its paces—on one engine! When Eisenhower faulted him for apparently hotdogging it by flying top fighters when he should have been planning bombing missions from his desk, Doolittle insisted he could lead an air force only by being able to pilot every aircraft in his command. The lesson was twofold. In facing tests, if Jimmy Doolittle could do it, so could anyone; but if anyone could do it, why not then Doolittle too?

Another important theme from the Tokyo Raid experience is the humility of such success. On landing in China, Doolittle's first thoughts are not to the carrier launch he's accomplished or the bombs he's dropped on Tokyo, both of which have been great successes. Instead, he judges himself a failure, expecting nothing less than a court martial at home. Why so? Because he feels he has failed his own crew, crash landing and losing their plane, and failed the force behind him, which is now scattered across China and points north. It is a scene he makes part of his autobiography's first chapter, a poignant moment when he and the crew's engineer-gunner, Sergeant Paul Leonard, survey the crash site.

"There is no worse sight to an aviator than to see his plane smashed to bits," Doolittle recalls. He feels awful as he sits near the wreckage and surveys "the shattered metal that had once been a beautiful airplane." What's gone into the log as his first combat mission, one he planned and led, looks to him like it might be his last. Judging himself a failure, he presumes the military will have no further use for him. Bad off as he is, Doolittle has dire fears for his men, many of whom may have died in crashes such as his own. Soon his crew chief, Paul Leonard, joins him, and has to allay his commander's fears of court-martial and military prison. "No, sir," Leonard protests. "I'll tell you what will happen. They're going to make you a general." And more: "they're going to give you the Congressional Medal of Honor." Doolittle comes up with a weak smile that speaks the worst for his prospects, which prompts Leonard to try one more suggestion:

> *"Colonel, I know they're going to give you another airplane and when they do, I'd like to fly with you as your crew chief."*
> *It was then that tears came to my eyes. It was the supreme compliment that a mechanic could give a pilot. It means he was so sure of the skills of the pilot that he would fly anywhere*

with him under any circumstances. I thanked him and said
that if I ever had another airplane and he wanted to be my
crew chief, he surely could. (IC, pp. 12–13)

Although Jimmy Doolittle's suppositions turn out to be wrong, he is accurate in his weighting of the raid's importance for the American spirit. Dropping an extremely light bomb load on Tokyo may have been instrumental in influencing Japanese attitudes, but for Americans the true heroism comes with the flyers' fates afterwards. The carrier launch had been the easy part, the technology for it even simpler. And as far as the bombs placed on target were concerned, the effect was not intended to be strategic or even tactical. *Getting back safely* was the area of greatest risk, one that proved literally impossible. Sixteen crash landings are hardly a secure finish to the operation. Here is where the Doolittle narratives take life. In any of them, the offensive part—from inception through training to execution—occupies relatively small space. The real stories begin when the flyers have to search for their landing fields in China and, not finding them, face the terrors of crash landings on land or at sea. Ted Lawson's landing is one of the worst; he and his bombardier are frightfully injured, and though they are helped from the start by friendly Chinese forces, repatriation is a long and difficult process. For the two captured crews, whose fate is either execution or imprisonment, the stories are even more compelling, especially since the Japanese made their show trial an international propaganda event. Yet in terms of psychology, the Doolittle Raid would work both ways to American benefit: the bombs over Tokyo raised U.S. spirits and severely disconcerted the Japanese, while stories of the captured and executed crew members galvanized stateside opinion all the more.

The greatest military result of the raid would be the Battle of Midway just two months later. In his autobiography, Jimmy Doolittle takes pleasure in counting up the Japanese losses from that engagement: "Four of their carriers and a heavy cruiser were sunk, 5 other large ships badly damaged, 322 aircraft destroyed, and 2,500 men killed, including many of their most experienced pilots." He also emphasizes the cause-and-effect relationship, reminding readers how "Historians now agree that the battle took place because our raid induced the Japanese to extend their forces beyond their capability" (*IC*, p. 293). Consequences also involved contraction, equally harmful to Japanese planning because air assets needed for the Solomons were withdrawn for homeland defense, allowing U.S. forces to begin an offensive operation on Guadalcanal in a more favorable position. This push from Guadalcanal up the slot would be the Pacific war's major action for the next eighteen months, after the Battles of the Coral Sea and Midway ended major carrier action for two years.

The Coral Sea and Midway engagements are best seen as Japanese initiatives met head-on by U.S. responses, taking enemy power in the air and destroying it on its own terms. Strategists of the highest order have marveled at the achievement in these battles, where surface fleets remained out of mutual sight and range while planes inflicted the damage and decided the issues of victory and defeat. But it is a Navy lieutenant, Clarence E. Dickinson, who draws the broadest conclusions based on his firsthand participation. *The Flying Guns: Cockpit Record of a Naval Pilot from Pearl Harbor through Midway* (1942) presents a narrative he feels "is evidence bearing on the greatest change in the art of naval warfare since the advent of the *Monitor* and the *Merrimac*." His evidence is specific, that "the coming of the divebomber and the torpedo plane and their use at sea has completely changed the capabilities of the old style naval vessel. Thus far in the war our victories have been caused in a large measure by the presence of such planes; our defeats, by their absence" (*FG*, pp. v–vi). In the Coral Sea, where Japanese forces seeking to extend their hegemony even closer to Australia are fought to a draw by carrier-born air elements, terms for such engagements are first determined; and at Midway, where efforts to protect the Emperor push Japanese offensive capabilities past their limits, the reality of just how much can be lost is shown.

What is the principle involved? Once again, Jimmy Doolittle says it clearly: "fleet actions were determined on the issue of control of the air over the fleets. Without that control no fleet could survive" (*IC*, p. 479). In the Coral Sea, the Japanese fleet might have started with that advantage, had its planes not mistaken the large oiler *Neosho* and its escorting destroyer, the *Sims*, for the main U.S. task force and attacked it, sinking the *Sims* and forcing an abandonment of the *Neosho*, but tipping its hand for the greater battle to come. As Mitsuo Fuchida and Masatake Okumiya observe in the Coral Sea chapter for their larger study, *Midway: The Battle That Doomed Japan*, "a precious opportunity to strike the first blow at the enemy carriers was lost" (*M*, p. 102). For a style of warfare that has never before existed, lessons must be learned in practice, and here is one of the major ones: even before any fighting begins, the outcome may be determined by who sees whom first. Aircraft not only have guns and bombs but provide eyes as well; and just as a fighter pilot's greatest asset is his quick vision, so too does a carrier fleet depend on a reconnaissance—a small mistake for the Japanese in the Coral Sea, and a disastrous one at Midway.

Not that U.S. forces are perfect. In the first battle, search elements sent out from the *Yorktown* miss Admiral Takeo Takagi's fleet carriers altogether, mistaking two old light cruisers, a sea-plane carrier, and three gunboats for the main force. When the *Yorktown* and the *Lexington* launch their planes against this target, they leave themselves a weaker defense against the real enemy, planes from the Japanese carriers *Zuikaku* and *Shokaku*. A major battle develops. War correspondent Stanley Johnston on board the *Lexington* quotes the carrier's captain to the effect that "at the present time an air attack group cannot be stopped. It's likely that the position will be similar to that of two boxers, both swinging a knockout punch at the same time, and both connecting" (*QF*, p. 214). The thought of strike forces from both sides being in the air at the same time, heading toward each other's carriers, is a daunting one, and Captain Frederick Sherman's analogy is especially apt. Up to this point in naval history, such major engagements had been decided by battleships—and especially by those mighty ships' hitting power. Boxing could be a metaphor there, too, but with a different style of fighting, as heavyweights pound each other against the ropes. Now the form of combat is different: a slugging match decided not by stamina and final points but by the knockout punch, the stuff of a prizefight that can end the match as little as a few seconds into the first round. And the contest would be not just among contenders but between the acknowledged champions. As Edwin P. Hoyt puts it in his *Blue Skies and Blood: The Battle of the Coral Sea* (1985), "The cream of the American crop was meeting the cream of the Japanese crop, for these pilots of *Shokaku* and *Zuikaku* were among the most experienced of the war. They had fought at the very beginning in the Pearl Harbor raid" (*BS*, p. 85), while on the *Lexington* and *Yorktown* were concentrated the best trained elements of U.S. Naval aviation.

Among the finest is Lieutenant Commander Robert E. Dixon, second in command of the *Lexington*'s dive-bombers. From the carrier itself, correspondent Johnston listens to the radio transmissions, anxious about Dixon's mission as it constitutes "the first such attack ever made on a carrier by American crews." Everyone strains to hear through the static, but "all the tension on the carrier exploded the moment we heard Commander Dixon's voice come through strong and clear: 'Scratch one flat-top! Dixon to carrier. Scratch one flat-top!'" (*QF*, 181); the Japanese carrier *Shoho* is no more, and another famous line is added to the phraseology of World War II.

In his second book, *The Grim Reapers* (1943), written aboard another carrier, the *Enterprise*, Stanley Johnston looks back to tell another Coral Sea story, that of Lieutenant Commander James Flatley. As executive officer of the *Yorktown*'s fighter squadron, Flatley has discovered and shot down the Kawanishi flying boat that has provided evidence of the Japanese carrier force. After scout planes find the target, out go the dive-bombers and torpedo bombers, with Flatley's fighters protecting the latter squadron of slower, low-flying planes. When Japanese Zeros attack this force, the commander swings into action, getting an enemy in his sights and sending tracer bullets into its fuselage. His report to Johnston sets the terms for what will become a typical combat report of American firepower against the maneuverable but unarmored fighter:

I was astonished at the way the stream of .50-caliber slugs from my four guns chopped the Jap 'plane into shreds. But even more awe-inspiring was the manner in which the heavy bullets threw up a great shower of water as they splashed into the sea below and in front of me. Never before had I fired all four guns at once into the water. Before the war, while training, we economized and never fired more than two at a time. As I recovered and made ready to take a shot at another Zero, I had the feeling of having an instrument of tremendous destructive ability in my hands. From that moment, the Wildcat meant a good deal to me, because I'd seen what it could accomplish. (GR, p. 28)

Other things are learned about the aircraft that will fight this new style of war. Present at the Battle of the Coral Sea (and at the four other carrier-versus-carrier engagements of the war: Midway, Eastern Solomons, Santa Cruz, and First Philippine Sea) is Harold L. Buell. His *Dauntless Helldivers: A Dive-Bomber Pilot's Epic Story of the Carrier Battles* (1991) tells how the prewar theory that Douglas SBD Dauntless dive-bombers could be used as interceptors of incoming enemy torpedo planes is shot down in flames just as thoroughly as are the nine Dauntlesses (of twenty-three) sacrificed to stop just four of the enemy. The greatest loss, however, is of a carrier. With Stanley Johnston on board until almost the last moment, the *Lexington*'s fate is the best described for any American flattop that would go down in battle.

From the bridge, Johnston starts his reporter's clock ticking at 10:50 A.M., May 8, 1942, as the second and most serious warning comes in from the *Lexington*'s scout planes: a large force of enemy aircraft are closing in from just sixty miles away. At 11:06 a column of smoke far off the port beam signals the interception and crash of the Kawanishi flying boat preceding the enemy onslaught as its eyes and ears. Then at thirty seconds past 11:16 the first torpedo bombers are sighted, and the carrier takes its first evasive move, turning hard to the starboard. "Even as the Captain speaks," Johnston reports, the attackers "are getting larger, and fanning out to cover a wide front as they approach. They are coming in at a scorching pace—I judge that with their dive and wide open throttles they are probably doing almost 300 miles an hour." Two of them fly right across an American cruiser and "as they do one disintegrates in the air, simply disappears as if snatched away by some giant magician. Evidently it has been struck by one of the cruiser's heavier shells which also explodes the torpedo" (*QF*, p. 221). By thirty seconds past 11:18 the first torpedo hits; a minute and a half later the carrier shakes from a second strike—two of the eight attackers have been successful. Now come the dive-bombers and a second wave of torpedo planes, each force scoring hits. "In the midst of all this," Johnston notes, "I'm attempting to dictate into the mike in my left hand and with the other hand make a few scribbles in my notebook while trying to see everything that happens, when a quite illogical thought passes through my mind: 'There's so damned much noise here I can't hear any single explosion—it's almost like a complete silence'" (*QF*, p. 225). For Americans reading this account in book form just months after the event, the effect is compelling, as Johnston's words so vividly recreate the scene:

> *Suddenly I see a Grumman following a Jap as he dives down toward Carrier II [Yorktown]. They disappear into the smoke of the umbrella of bursting, heavy anti-aircraft shells and emerge into a literal hail of the machine-gun fire thrown up from her decks. The Jap releases his bomb and begins to flatten out—he bursts into flame as the bullets from our fighters rip into his gas tanks. The Jap flames into the sea and the Grumman zooms back into the fight.*

Dive bombers are still coming down, only a second or so apart. Most of the missiles are falling toward the after end of the ship, close, but not quite hitting. Above we see the Jap machines diving in a chain. Watching closely I see the bombs leave each plane. The aircraft follow, gradually flattening out. Their machine guns and wing cannon wink momentarily. Each plane sweeps over the Lexington's deck and then becomes a tiny shape, swiftly diminishing in size as it speeds away. (QF, p. 227)

The entire assault takes just sixteen minutes. Johnston counts more than one hundred planes, nineteen of which are shot down within sight of the carrier. He makes errors of observation—understandable ones, such as mistaking the new Kawasaki Ki-61 Tonys for "Japanese Messerschmitts" (QF, p. 231), conveying the misidentification from a Wildcat pilot who has engaged one. Many early narratives from this stage of the war refer to phantom German aircraft and even speculate that Luftwaffe pilots on loan are flying them, part of the reluctance to believe that an Oriental enemy denigrated before fighting broke out can be flying so brilliantly. But for everything else his account is accurate, stunningly so, especially when fires started by the five torpedoes that have struck the Lexington initiate a series of underdeck explosions that force the great carrier to be abandoned.

Writing over thirty years later, Edwin P. Hoyt can detail just how the *Lexington* is destroyed. One of the five torpedoes has ruptured some freshwater tanks and the vertical gasoline tanks located next to them. "The torpedo had created a mining effect—it had bulged the plates of the ship inward, and damaged the inboard bulkhead," Hoyt writes. Behind this bulkhead is the motor-generator room, into which the gasoline fumes seep: "So, in essence, the generator room was a huge bomb, just waiting for the proper concentration and a spark. The spark came at 1247" (*BS*, p. 142).

Johnston's account of the *Lexington*'s demise centers on the technology of it, Hoyt's on the human casualties a wartime account could not detail. In fact, Hoyt describes the correspondent's experience, sitting in the navigator's compartment and writing up his first report for the *Chicago Tribune* as the massive explosion from the generator room rocks the ship: hurrying below, he confronts the raging fire and learns that "now, nearly four hours after the battle, more men were dying than had been killed by the Japanese attack" (*BS*, p. 144). Hoyt also reproduces another testimony to loss, the communications record between Bill Ault, Commander of the Lexington Air Group (CLAG), and the surviving *Yorktown*, too far away from the airborne flyer to give him anything but the most general guidance:

> *CLAG to* Yorktown: *Shall I circle? Do you want me to gain or lose altitude? I have gas left for about 20 minutes.*
> Yorktown: *You are not on the screen. Try to make the nearest land.* (*BS*, p. 150)

In Edwin P. Hoyt's words, this communication from the ship is "a death sentence." Neither the *Yorktown* nor Ault knows where the other is. There's little chance of finding land—both parties know that. Nothing can be argued, nor can anything be done. Therefore the last messages they exchange are poignant with the flyer's understated sense of heroism:

> *CLAG to* Yorktown: *Nearest land is over 200 miles away. We would never make it.*

Yorktown *to CLAG: You are on your own. Good luck.*

CLAG to Yorktown: *Please relay to* Lexington. *We got one 1000-pound bomb hit on a flattop. We have both reported 2 or 3 times. Enemy fighters. Am changing course to North. Let me know if you pick me up.*

Yorktown *to CLAG: Roger, you are on your own. I will relay your message. Good luck.*

CLAG to Yorktown: *OK. So long, people. We got a 1000-pound hit on the flattop.* (BS, pp. 150–51)

As Bill Ault, shadowed by enemy fighters and almost out of fuel, disappears, his own carrier *Lexington* sits abandoned, dead in the water. Ninety-two percent of her crew has been taken off successfully, but the ship makes for a sorry sight. Stanley Johnston, aboard a rescuing cruiser, looks on past nightfall. "It might have been a starry night—but none of us could tell," he reports, because "the leaping, towering flames from the *Lexington* hid all the feebler light from the skies" (*QF*, p. 268). The fleet moves off, and a lone remaining destroyer carries out Admiral Frank Jack Fletcher's order to sink the burning hulk.

Histories of the war list Coral Sea as only a tactical victory for the Japanese. Their loss of the converted 12,000-ton *Shoho* was less serious than the *Lexington* going to the bottom, all 33,000 tons of her. Yet in terms of strategy, the United States comes out ahead, because the Japanese objective of capturing Port Moresby had been denied. The *Yorktown* was damaged, leaving a trail of oil that might well have been spotted by reconnaissance flights or submarines and led to another Japanese attack. But no such follow-up happened, leaving this great carrier to fight and die at Midway, doing immense damage to the Japanese before coming to her end. There was yet another benefit for the Midway operation coming just a month later: the men commanding American carriers had learned several vital lessons. Better planes were needed; that would take time, but for now what they had could be used more effectively if fighter patrols were sent out at 20,000 feet instead of at 10,000, giving them a better chance for early spotting of the enemy. At Coral Sea, the first wave of attacking planes had been missed entirely, for this simple reason. And never again would dive-bombers such as the Dauntless be wasted against torpedo planes.

Thanks to Doolittle's Raid and the Japanese failure to strike a decisive blow against both American carriers in the Coral Sea, Admiral Yamamoto was moved to take his air war farther east than first planned. Such American activity had not been expected; Pearl Harbor was supposed to have given Yamamoto's forces a free hand for at least a year, and here it was, less than six months later, that the United States was threatening the Japanese homeland and cutting off the southwestern expansion needed for Japan to secure its basic war aims. Yet if the U.S. Navy could be defeated in a major engagement (a variation of the "big battle" scenario Japanese planning had entertained for more than a decade), then Roosevelt's government might be willing to sue for peace, on Japanese terms. And so the Midway operation was conceived.

Keys to it were secrecy (so that Midway Island itself could be taken with the advantage of surprise), diversion (accomplished by a movement against the Aleutian Islands far to the north), and awareness of American fleet locations. In all three aspects the Japanese failed. U.S. code breakers learned of the attack in advance, letting American forces make ready for the Midway assault and recognize the Aleutians move for what it was. Yet even more critical was the failure to know the size of the American force preparing for this meeting, and its location even as the initial engagement began. As Masatake Okumiya states in his preface to the book he coauthored with Mitsuo Fuchida, *Midway*: "The Pacific War saw air power finally come of age" and "In this new type of warfare the Battle of Midway was the outstanding defeat suffered by Japan" (*M*, p. xv). In this particular battle, he believes, are the grounds for a thesis: "that the Pacific War was started by men who did not understand the sea, and fought by men who did not understand the air." Knowing how the Japanese Army controlled its country's politics in the 1930s, one can agree with the first part of Okumiya's statement. But what of the Imperial Navy, surely one of the world's best? Here is where Okumiya's insight is confirmed by the nature of what transpired at Midway. "Because she judged the sea by land standards and applied to air warfare the concepts of sea fighting," he avers, "Japan's tragic fate was foreordained" (*M*, p. xvi).

The Midway part of Admiral Yamamoto's plan was clear and simple: occupy the island, and by doing so lure the U.S. Pacific Fleet out beyond it where destruction by Admiral Nagumo's force would be waiting. Japan's First Air Fleet would operate in advance, covering the landings and screening the main force of battleships, cruisers, and light carriers holding off at three hundred miles, waiting for a weaker U.S. surface fleet to engage it and be drawn into a trap. Yet the two men who had translated Yamamoto's Pearl Harbor plan into action withheld their enthusiasm here. Minoru Genda thought it was too early. Following the Doolittle Raid, many of the best Navy pilots had been restationed at land bases; replacements would have to be trained, and an operation in early June would not allow sufficient time. He also disliked splitting his force—an Aleutians diversion simply wasn't worth the cost. As for Mitsuo Fuchida, this otherwise aggressive officer spoke up vehemently against the whole plan.

His flyers were exhausted from half a year of constant warfare, not to mention the beating their equipment had absorbed. Midway itself, even if captured, would prove untenable because of its distance from other Japanese operations. Yes, there should be a big battle. But why not have it in the Southwest Pacific, where his country's true interests lay?

As for American interests, they are best expressed by one of the men who'd do the fighting. In 1942 Lieutenant Clarence E. Dickinson's *The Flying Guns* would provide an early look at the inside of naval operations, but even at this point the author can discern a shift in the Pacific war's momentum. Years later, American historians could articulate the change in Japanese military terms; Gordon Prange's biography of Fuchida, *God's Samurai*, contrasts the aggressive operations of Japan's first seven months in the war, *shinko sakusen*, with the defensive nature of warfare it was forced to adopt and maintain after Midway, *yogeki sakusen* (*GS*, pp. 80–81). Lieutenant Dickinson speaks no Japanese, and in 1942 the ways of his foe are still new to him. But when on the morning of June 3 the first reports from the scouting PBYs (patrol bombers) come in, he is electrified by the notion that a great enemy force has been sighted. "Our feeling was: At last!" he exclaims. "The long sought contact" (*FG*, p. 138). Going on the offensive against Japan was something he could almost taste: "If only we could sink her carriers we would take from her the one great factor that had been keeping her invasions going, all over the East" (*FG*, p. 139). There, in a nutshell, is the coming battle's importance, one that not only stands the test of history but that provides motivation to American flyers at the time. "All of us fully realized that we were getting a chance to change the whole character of the war in the Pacific," Dickinson writes. "Those who prayed that night certainly prayed, 'God, send the Japanese carriers'" (*FG*, pp. 139–40).

Again, there is familiar misinformation. "After the battle of the Coral Sea," Dickinson insists, "we found out the Japs were using German Messerschmitt 109-F's off their carriers" (*FG*, p. 14)—so preposterous to consider now, but just as convincing at the time as correspondent Stanley Johnston reported, and so flight leaders modify their instructions from dealing with Zeros to these phantom fighters (which are, of course, Kawasaki Tonys). Yet whatever the descriptions, Dickinson is motivated; he is a scout pilot and will play a vital role by insuring the enemy force is known in full detail.

In terms of larger strategy, neither force was actually doing what the other expected of it. In their study from the Japanese point of view, Fuchida and Okumiya spell out the designs. "The first and most limited objective was the seizure of Midway itself as an advance air base to facilitate the early detection of enemy forces operating westward from the Hawaiian Islands," they state, reflecting fears engendered by the Doolittle Raid on Tokyo. "The second, much broader objective was to draw out the United States Pacific Fleet's remaining strength so that it could be engaged and destroyed in decisive battle" (*M*, p. 78), a hypothetical huge surface engagement of battleship against battleship that would end the war in Japan's favor. American readings of the events to come are different. Yes, U.S. flyers are eager to engage the enemy. But as described by George Gay, author of *Sole Survivor* (1986) and the single living member of the *Hornet*'s Torpedo Squadron Eight whose lumbering TBD Devastators were cut to ribbons in their first attack, the situation appears differently:

The Japs were expected to hit Midway on or about June 4. We also expected a diversionary action in the Aleutian Islands preceding this, but Midway was our concern. There were some hitches, however. We were not big enough to meet the Japs head on, so the idea was to find them, wait until they had made an attack, and then try to hit them when their aircraft were out of gas and ammunition and before they could land and reprovision.

Another problem was being sure of where they were actually going to strike before we made our move. We had three prospects: if they hit Midway on or about June 4, that was it; if not, we were to pull back and wait for them to hit Pearl again. If they had not hit Pearl Harbor by the 15th or so, we would race the Japs to our West Coast and try our best there. They were capable of coming to the Coast if they brought a large enough fleet, and it sure as hell looked like they had enough. (SS, p. 19)

Hence the big battle happens, but not the one Japan envisions. Instead, it is big for the United States, given its flyers' understanding that they were defending not just a tiny atoll halfway across the Pacific but the beaches of Los Angeles and San Francisco Bay. Consider Walt Bayler's assessment, published in 1943, from the perspective of the officer in charge of radio traffic between air and shore. "We all know now," he writes confidently. "The terrific four-day air and sea Battle of Midway itself has passed into history, even if its effects still endure." And what are those effects, from the point of view of a Marine now off to direct similar communications from Guadalcanal? "The most vicious thrust of the war, aimed at Hawaii and the Pacific Coast, was turned back by brilliant teamwork on the part of our Army, Navy, and Marine arms. By that, and by individual acts of gallantry which have never been surpassed in any war" (LM, pp. 216–17).

Midway does produce an unusually widespread range of heroes, each of them famous for an individual act that makes a major contribution to the overall success. Ensign George Gay takes his torpedo bomber into the midst of enemy fire coming both from ships and from pursuing Zeros. His torpedo hangs up and he's shot down, left floating in the midst of a fleet still under attack. From here he can bring home something even more valuable than a hit on an enemy ship—he's able to give a stirring, firsthand account of "the whole Jap Navy steaming right down on me" (*SS*, p. 125) as American dive-bombers come rocketing down:

> *There is no way I can describe what a beautiful sight that was! I could see that the Zeros that had come down after us were not up there bothering them and I knew that some of those fellows were not only pushing over in their first dive, but it was also their first time they had ever flown that type of plane. They were magnificent and I did not see a single splash indicating a miss! They laid those bombs right where they belonged and caused the most devastating damage possible. Some pilots would see their target explode, and pull off to pick another one and then come on down. It was almost unbelievable, but I was seeing it. Almost simultaneously, three Jap carriers were wiped out. I knew what that meant. By golly, we did it! We caught them just as we had hoped to while they were retrieving aircraft that were low on fuel and out of bombs and ammunition. (SS, pp. 125–26)*

Hence Midway is not an abstract ocean battle, half a world away from home, but something personally depicted by George

Gay on the cover of *Life* magazine just a few months later. This August 31, 1942, issue would become an icon of the war, the first to start replacing the image so prominent up to this time, that of the *Arizona* in flames, sinking to the bottom of Pearl Harbor. Henderson Field on Guadalcanal would be another; everyone knew its name, given in honor of Marine dive-bomber pilot Major Lofton R. "Joe" Henderson—who, in Walt Bayler's words, "took himself, his blazing plane and a thousand-pound bomb down the funnel of a Japanese carrier" (*LM*, p. 217), one of the four to be sunk at Midway. The heavy cruiser *Mikuma* is taken out in an equally dramatic fashion, as Captain Richard E. Fleming steers his heavily damaged Dauntless into one of the enemy ship's turrets, causing a great explosion and fire that's fed by his load of aviation fuel. Long before Americans would struggle to understand the premeditation of Japanese kamikazes, these examples of selfless sacrifice in the heat of battle, when a crash and death were likely anyway, speak for a determination to push on for victory—a characteristic more of the football field than of a Shinto shrine. But fame and success come from the steadfast performance of simple duties as well, yielding up another name for war correspondents and flyers alike to make famous. Lieutenant Commander C. Wade McClusky, commander of the *Enterprise* Air Group, leads a thirty-three-plane sweep in search of the Japanese fleet a patrol plane has spotted early on June 4. Not where it's supposed to be, because its own observation plane has seen the *Enterprise-Yorktown* task force, the enemy proves elusive. As correspondent Eugene Burns reports in *Then There Was One* (1944), McClusky runs low on fuel but knows that to turn back now will prompt the Japanese to follow him, finding his task force before he has found theirs:

McClusky looked at his gasoline gauge again. He knew that in another half-hour, in this 20,000 foot altitude, the planes could not make it back.

He looked back. Yes, the pilot with the smoking engine was still with him. "He'll never get back," the leader decided. "If he's willing to gamble, so'm I." His mind was made up. He had made what was later officially termed "the most important decision of the entire action."

As the planes swung to the northwest with their commander, the pilots must have thought of their own safety. And like McClusky they must have seen the smoking engine and thought: "If Tony's willing to risk his neck and not turn back, so'm I." (TT, p. 53)

So'm I—the vernacular drawl, reminiscent of legendary American heroes the likes of Daniel Boone and Davy Crockett, completes the picture: McClusky says it, and so do his men. Half a century later fellow pilot Harold Buell will recall "the famous turn that CAG McClusky made to the heading of an enemy destroyer that was observed racing northeast on the ocean below" and add that "following this hunch . . . is considered to be one of the luckiest breaks ever to occur in a major carrier-versus-carrier battle" (*DH*, p. 86). But the rest of the story shows how good luck is turned into great success:

He quickly led an attack that sank three of the carriers in six minutes, losing many of the dive-bombers in his group. Wounded in the arm and shoulder by Japanese Zero fighters, he survived to fly his badly damaged SBD back to Enterprise. *A fourth Japanese carrier was sunk later in the day. In leading this strike, McClusky earned the distinction of conducting the single most successful dive-bombing mission against Japanese naval carrier ever made.* (*DH*, p. 183)

And so McClusky's achievement stands. What if he had turned back and left the Japanese force unsighted? "Almost certainly there would have been no Battle of Midway," correspondent Stanley Johnston reports in 1943, when stateside opinions are being formed, "and possibly all of our carriers would have gone to the bottom with the *Yorktown*" (*GR*, p. 62). Hence an individual name is associated with another success: McClusky, to join Gay, Henderson, and Fleming.

Early warning, effective reconnaissance of fleet locations, and a spirited tenacity for the ensuing fight: these are the hallmarks of victory at Midway, and all three contribute to the narrative of this war taking shape in the American consciousness. Instead of damages from surprise attacks and tales of long but ultimately hopeless holdouts, readers could now digest accounts such as those supplied by Clarence Dickinson, whose flight of dive bombers sink the carrier *Kaga*. "She was on fire from end to end and I saw her blow up at the middle," Dickinson writes in *The Flying Guns*, published in 1942, just months after the event. "From right abreast the island a ball of solid fire shot straight up. It passed through the fleecy lower clouds which we estimated to be 1200 feet above the water." It is a picture he's eager to share with his countrymen back home: "Some of our flyers who were up higher saw this solid mass of fire as it burst up through the clouds, and they said the fire rose three or four hundred feet still higher" (*FG*, p. 160). Such is the pyrotechnic spectacle, worthy of the finest Fourth of July celebration, that Navy dive-bombers can produce when they find an enemy carrier refueling and rearming its own planes, with every combustible element vulnerable to attack with no aerial defense possible. No time in these narratives is wasted on false heroics; in *Carrier Combat*, a contemporaneous work available to American readers early in 1944, Navy Lieutenant Frederick Mears (a torpedo bomber pilot himself) clarifies that the great success of the *Hornet*'s Torpedo Squadron Eight is not that it mounted such an admittedly "do-or-die attack, glorious as that was" (*CC*, p.69), but that the fast-moving enemy fleet was sighted and stopped in time for the dive-bombers to come in and do their job. Caution would have been useless: "If he went in close enough to make a complete estimate of the size, the make-up, and the disposition of the enemy fleet it was more than likely enemy fighters would discover and jump him anyway" (*CC*, p. 71). Thus Lieutenant Commander John Waldron does the right thing with Torpedo Squadron Eight—and is appreciated for the right reason.

The obsolescent Douglas Devastators of George Gay's squadron are by no means the only American losses at Midway. After sinking the carriers *Kaga*, *Akagi*, and *Soryu*, American planes return to their own flattops, including a group from the *Yorktown* that is followed home by forty-six torpedo and dive-bombers from the *Hiryu*. Defensive fighter interceptions cannot prevent three of the attackers from scoring hits, bringing the great American ship to a dead halt, at which point two torpedo bombers place their weapons into the carrier's port side. Listing badly, the *Yorktown* is abandoned. That afternoon the *Hiryu* herself would be hit so badly that she'd have to be sunk by her own escorting destroyers. With a total of five carriers now gone, the devastation is catastrophic. Fifty-six years later, oceanographer Dr. Robert Ballard of the National Geographic Society, already famous for his discovery of the *Titanic*, will lead an underwater expedition to find and photograph the relics of this battle. His *Return to Midway* (1999) is an important last chapter to the narrative of this great engagement, providing a look at how the *Yorktown* has rested for this past half century while the men who served at her stations and flew from her flight deck—those who survived the Battle of Midway and the rest of World War II—lived their lives that eventually won them the title of America's greatest generation. The stunning photographs of the carrier itself, sitting virtually intact in crystal clear water at the sea's bottom, with just clean, empty rectangles marking the locations of its flight deck elevators, make it seem like a model. But close-ups of battle stations where men worked and died—the searchlight platform, machine gun positions, even window-like ports along the bridge and pilothouse—confront the viewer with a stark reality. "Here lies my home for ten months, in peace and war" (*RM*, p. 157); the words are spoken on Memorial Day of 1998 by Bill Surgi, an aviation mechanic with the *Yorktown*'s fighter squadron and a guest of Dr. Ballard during the search, discovery, and last ceremony before departing the scene. The *National Geographic*'s television presentation of this event shows Surgi doing final duty for his lost comrades. Harold Buell compares these men to the soldiers from both sides who fought the Civil War Battle of Shiloh, where the high number of casualties made everyone realize how real the war was and how costly it would be. "Midway was the Shiloh of the Pacific War," Buell concludes; "never again would naval aviators and their gunners consider the war a big adventure—a game to be played for the sport of it—but rather a serious business that, even when you were winning, could exact a terrible toll" (*DH*, p. 84).

The third great narrative event in America's Pacific air war of 1942 takes place over Guadalcanal. This island, the first to be burned into popular consciousness in the next three years of point-by-point advances toward Japan itself, sits near the southern tip of the Solomons, a chain running from the southwest to the northeast. In two ranks, its islands form a long "slot" (as flyers at once began calling it) that indicates the route from Australia to Japan, and vice versa. Beyond its northern reaches lay Rabaul, the center of enemy air power in the region. To the south, Tulagi beckoned as an extension of Japanese range. Because activities there would threaten U.S.-Australian trade routes and eventually Australia itself, American reaction became a necessity. When stepping in to halt any Japanese advance, Guadalcanal would be the place to start. In literary terms, the operation produced an immediate bestseller, *Guadalcanal Diary* (1943) by war correspondent Richard Tregaskis, and at the start of his work the author quotes a Marine officer's pep talk to his troops about to land. "It's the first time in history we've ever had a huge expedition of this kind accompanied by transports. It's of world-wide importance," he emphasizes. "You'd be surprised if you knew how many people all over the world are following this. You cannot fail them" (*GD*, p. 21).

As happens so often, the Marines would do the dirty work on the ground. But getting a foothold on Guadalcanal makes possible a slow but steady air advance up the slot that would eventually open a door to the Philippines and the Central Pacific islands so crucial to the strategic bombing of Japan. During this period, both Japanese and American aircraft carriers—the few that are left—seem to retire from the scene. Land-based planes now dominate the theater, from airfields on island after island through the Southwest Pacific. The motley assemblage of types flown by all the services from Henderson Field on Guadalcanal "proved the superiority of land-based aircraft," historian Eric M. Bergerud believes. His *Fire in the Sky: The Air War in the South*

Pacific (2000) argues that range is the only limiting factor—and that by island hopping up the slot, Japanese strengths were always reachable and ultimately defeatable. "Guadalcanal would show that allowing an enemy land-based air force within one's strategic perimeter," as the Japanese did, "was remarkably similar to allowing an enemy to cross a river and establish a bridgehead." Note how the discussion of air power resembles what the Marines do on the ground, as Bergerud makes his point. "Once a bridgehead is established on land, it will either be destroyed or the attackers will ultimately break out," he observes. "In aerial warfare the problem was exactly the same. If an air base became established there were only two ways to knock it out: a sustained and brutal air offensive, or a naval blockade and bombardment" (*FS*, p. 75). Rabaul, where Japanese air strength was located, remained too far away for the former method; as for the latter, the Combined Fleet was unwilling to take another major risk so soon after the debacle of Midway. Hence American success at starting an aggressive air campaign from this southern point in the Solomons would begin the slow but steady final victory. At each stage the taking of another air base would move the strategy along.

The reliability of this air strategy is best described by Merrill B. Twining, later a four-star general in the Marine Corps, and at Guadalcanal in the heart of the battle as operations officer for the First Marine Division. His *No Bended Knee: The Battle for Guadalcanal* (1996) celebrates what he calls "one of the great turning points of the Solomons campaign—the arrival of thirty-one friendly aircraft" (*NB*, p. 84). These elements of Marine Bombing Squadron 232 (under the command of Major Richard C. Mangrum) and Marine Fighter Squadron 223 (led by Captain John L. Smith) are the start of the "Cactus Air Force" soon to make Henderson Field a household name in news reports. Twining appreciates just how these planes have arrived—catapulted off the deck of the escort carrier *Long Island* from two hundred miles away (as close as the Navy wants a capital ship to the dangerous action around the battle front)— and how one man's foresight contributed to the campaign effort. Rear Admiral John S. McCain would distinguish himself as particularly air-minded, later in the war devising the first workable defense against kamikaze attacks scourging the American fleet in the Philippines. Here, with hostilities still in their early phase of Japanese dominance, he views Guadalcanal, as Twining puts it, "as an unsinkable aircraft carrier that, used in conjunction with carrier forces, could destroy the Japanese naval air force." The product of this vision "turned Guadalcanal from a haunting liability into an operation of such exponential success that the name itself became a synonym for death and disaster in the language of the enemy" (*NB*, p. 84).

On August 7, 1942 (August 6 in the United States), the Marines land on Guadalcanal. For Merrill Twining, the supporting naval barrage is "announcing that the way back had begun. It was an unforgettable moment of history" (*NB*, p. 51). Yet by the next night, with the First Marine Division just getting its foothold established, Vice Admiral Frank Jack Fletcher announces the withdrawal of his force, taking Rear Admiral Kelly Turner's ships with him. The threat of an approaching enemy task force is too ominous, they believe, an assessment drawn more from capabilities than intentions. More than a week later, Richard Tregaskis can note in his *Guadalcanal Diary* that "we are hoping very hard that our planes will arrive before the Japs do" (*GD*, p. 126). The planes do, and on August 20 the correspondent celebrates the "beautiful sight" of their arrival and the new circumstance of not having to dive for cover at the sound of a motor's roar (*GD*, p. 126). Next morning, as the Marines prepare for the enemy's usual dawn raid, one of their lieutenants voices the new level of morale. "Wait until our planes get up and hit those babies," he enthuses. "Won't they be surprised?" (*GD*, p. 128).

Nineteen Wildcat fighters and a dozen Dauntless dive bombers get the Cactus Air Force established. The code name for Guadalcanal fits its rough-and-ready, Wild West image. For the next eighty-eight days it would fight the Japanese Eleventh Air Fleet, which was based at Rabaul, Japan's strongest air installation. Supplied from Japan with the best of its pilots, Rabaul was a fortress. Henderson Field, at the end of America's supply line half a world away, would have to make do with what was available. That meant Navy planes from sunk or damaged carriers, Marine aircraft from distant land bases brought here for temporary service, and Army Air Force P-39 Airacobras taken away from ground support duties to do what they could. In the period from August 20 to November 15, Henderson Field would host a total of eight fighter, twelve dive-bomber, and two torpedo squadrons. Famous names would emerge from among these flyers. Joe Bauer, under direct orders from Admiral McCain, beefed up the Cactus Air Force in October, when assignment there was considered a fatal duty. Joe Foss would pave his way to leading ace status with kills made from Henderson. George Gay, the sole survivor of Torpedo Squadron Eight at Midway, would fly from Henderson as well. In his unit were men noteworthy for past or future achievements. One of them, Ben Finney, had served in World War I, stayed in France to help develop the Riviera and form close friendships with everyone from F. Scott Fitzgerald and Ernest Hemingway to Harpo Marx and Cole Porter, and would write about his adventures as Henderson Field's supply officer in *Feet First* (1971)—a colorful story, to say the least, involving celebrity talents for obtaining the best in liquid refreshments. The other would wait several decades to become famous, or rather infamous. A close friend of George Gay's, he used literary talents developed in Brown University's pre-law program to write a fact-based novel about flying from Henderson Field, *Limit of Darkness* (1944). After the war he'd write more novels, these of the thriller variety, and work for the CIA. In 1963 there was unfounded talk that he was one of the four vagrants spotted in suspicious circumstances on the grassy knoll overlooking the site of President John F. Kennedy's assassination, and during the Watergate Scandal of the 1970s he was given jail time for being one of President Richard Nixon's "plumbers," convicted of breaking into Democratic campaign headquarters and planting listening devices. His name: E. Howard Hunt.

The story that evolves from Henderson Field is an eminently reportable one. As Joe Foss notes in his autobiography, *A Proud American*, "a high percentage of the action was within sight of the field. Time after time, spectators on the ground with field glasses and telescopes kept the score. It was great for the morale of all the troops" (*PA*, pp. 84–85). Navy Lieutenant Frederick Mears describes a scene from mid-October in *Carrier Combat*:

We spent our time during the next few days watching our fighters mix with the Zeros and try to tag the bombers. I saw many thrilling dogfights, one so low directly overhead that I jumped into a foxhole to avoid fire. Jap bombers and Zeros continually were visible—falling, smoking, in flames, and out of control. They disintegrated on the way down and if they were high enough seemed to be in twenty pieces before they were out of sight." (CC, p. 146)

Similar scenes impress war correspondent Stanley Johnston, who describes the ground troops watching from their foxholes as the "magnificent performance" takes place. "They followed the bout blow by blow," he notes, "and as the fight progressed, with Japs crumbling left and right, the men's emotions burst out in cheers and whistles, stamping and shouts" (*GR*, p. 188). On landing, the flyers are taken up on shoulders and carried back to their quarters in a victory parade. Bauer's men are then presented with a Japanese battle flag, one of the ground unit's most prized trophies. Returning the favor, Bauer shoots down four enemy dive-bombers the next day, all within sight of the troops. "So into the night one tale followed another," Johnston concludes. "The story of Joe Bauer was inexhaustible" (*GR*, p. 189).

This imagery is made to order for an eager public at home. Whether it comes from a Navy pilot or an accredited correspondent, language rises to the occasion, painting word pictures to efface the terrible visual details from Pearl Harbor less than a year before. A fight is not only taking place but is being observed—making it qualify as a boxing match of sorts, a decidedly one-sided one in which the adversary is metaphorically shredded. Mears has the combatants "mixing it," Johnston has them in a "bout" that proceeds "blow by blow," all for the spectators' boisterous approval. Afterwards, new metaphors take over: that of a sports team hailed in victory, carried off the field by delirious fans who present a goalpost-type trophy in appreciation. Had this engagement taken place at twenty-five thousand feet, two hundred miles away from the nearest observation site, the effect would be much different—swirling dogfights, yes, but so eminently a flyer's game. Here the action is something in which the spectators can participate, and do so more than just vicariously, for their own fate as ground troops hangs in the balance of this aerial defense. Yet for the air combat taking place, they are observers, a position shared by Mears's and Johnston's readers back in the U.S.A.

Combats like this, especially in front of a grateful audience, are the pilots' great rewards. Less beneficial are the conditions under which they work. Displaced carrier pilots from the *Hornet, Lexington,* and *Saratoga* feel it the worst. In *A Marine Dive-Bomber Pilot at Guadalcanal,* John McEniry describes the fatigue of flying so many different types of missions from a base that didn't provide even a minimum of comforts, in addition to being under attack itself almost every day. He quotes a report to the Bureau of Aeronautics in Washington, D.C., from Lieutenant Commander LeRoy C. Simpler, who'd brought his fighter squadron to the island from the *Saratoga.* "I'd rather operate off a carrier for *two months* than from a good *stiff* land base for one week," Simpler attests, "because on a carrier you're either resting or you are not as far as a pilot is concerned." Carrier life is good: the pilots get every break and aren't called to general quarters all the time. On land, after flying and fighting all day, one's sleep gets interrupted nightly by nuisance bombers; even a single one, the notorious "Washing Machine Charlie" whose unsynchronized engine and occasional bomb infuriate everyone in this theater, makes life hell. "I think that about *5 days of intensive action* is about all a man can stand; with interims I think he can last three weeks" (*MD*, p. 87), Simpler concludes, knowing all too well that such scheduling had been impossible in the many months, from August 1942 to February 1943, it took to get Guadalcanal safely established. One of the best descriptions of

pilot life aboard a carrier comes from Corsair flyer Tom Blackburn, at the point in his memoir, *The Jolly Rogers* (1989), when
his squadron gets some temporary relief from land-based duty
with a welcome to the carrier *Bunker Hill*. Every detail is
savored, because these are the qualities that have been missing
from his life since it became dedicated to flying and fighting up
the slot:

> We used the interval to lay below for dreamy hot showers, I in
> the skipper's in-port cabin, which came complete with a stew-
> ard serving delicious, well-made coffee. Once clean, all hands
> were ushered to the wardroom for a deftly served repast of
> fresh grapefruit, steak, eggs (the real thing!) cooked to order,
> hot toast, and good coffee. All this and sparkling white table-
> cloths and linen napkins; courteous, smiling stewards; and
> seconds and thirds of everything. As we stuffed ourselves,
> ship's officers swarmed in to hear our best sea stories—some
> of which were even true. As I felt more and more like the
> country bumpkin just come from out of the hills to visit rich
> relatives, I found it increasingly hard to believe that I had
> been part of this friendly, well-off tribe until only two months
> earlier. Fantasy briefly suggested that some—maybe all—of
> our pilots would find reasons to stay aboard, and I briefly
> regretted that only twenty-three of us out of forty had been
> awarded this delightful respite. (J, p. 136)

Respite indeed: although some of the Southwestern Pacific
islands had decent climates, most did not. High humidity put
mold on one's clothing overnight, and within a week leather
straps would begin rotting away. Fresh water was a nonentity;
one drank and washed from a Lister bag of chemically treated

liquid. Nutrition was drawn from an unvarying diet of powdered eggs and Spam. All this had to be endured as a base line of existence, while days were filled with combat flying or long patrols, and nights were given over to what sleep could be snatched between mosquito attacks and harassments by enemy night bombers.

How did American flyers endure these conditions, which would prevail throughout the long, hard Solomons campaign until a way was opened to the Philippines? Morale. The worldwide focus on Guadalcanal was heartening, and the lack of strong naval support at the start was soon remedied in a way that transformed the war's entire nature. "Something significant happened within the American forces on October 18," writes Sam Walker in *Up the Slot* (1984), the memoir of a B-24 radio operator and veteran of the Southwest Pacific. Although the development he describes was prompted by concerns at the highest levels in Washington, D.C., it is good to hear it from a flyer in the theater, for it was here that the effect was most deeply felt. "Admiral Chester Nimitz reluctantly concluded that Admiral Robert Ghormley simply wasn't aggressive enough for the job and replaced him with Admiral William F. (Bull) Halsey." What did this mean locally? "This couldn't materially affect conditions on Guadalcanal immediately," Walker admits, "but when word circulated on Guadalcanal, morale shot up like the mercury in a thermometer on a hot day. At last they had a fire-eating, aggressive boss who was willing to throw everything at his command into the fray" (*U*, p. 33). Dive-bomber pilot John McEniry supports this sentiment with further specifics. "Reaction among the aviators was enthusiastic," he reports. "It was said that they now had one of their own in charge. The prior commanders were not naval aviators as was Admiral Halsey.

One of the common sayings among the pilots was that Halsey would turn a task force around to find a lost pilot." Like Walker, McEniry notes that the new leader "certainly had the reputation for carrying the attack to the enemy." Viewing this change from the bottom up, as the flyers do, lends added importance to the work they are doing. For as McEniry notices, it is just six days after Halsey's assumption of command that "President Roosevelt sent a message to each of the Joint Chiefs of Staff in which he insisted that reinforcements be provided quickly" (*MD*, p. 43).

From Guadalcanal, air defense grows into a validly aggressive force that soon begins carrying the war up the slot toward Rabaul. By the time Marine fighter pilot Joe Foss is racking up his record number of victories, the early efforts of a supply officer such as Ben Finney appear quaint, as Finney explains in his memoir, *Feet First*:

> *The night of the day I arrived on "The Canal" all hell broke loose. A Jap battlewagon, two or three cruisers, and a flock of destroyers lay offshore and shelled us all night. From overhead sticks of bombs rained down. Our ammunition dump was completely demolished. The Japs didn't know it, but the next day we had hardly enough ammo left to arm the planes that hadn't been hit. We propped the damaged planes up in line to look operational to Jap observers in the hills and when the "Tokyo Express" came down the slot they were met by our five planes just as though there were plenty more where they came from. (FF, p. 214)*

That dummy planes can have an effect is important. As Walter B. Clausen explains in his early analysis, *Blood for the Emperor: A Narrative History of the Human Side of the War in the*

Pacific (1943), the Japanese perspective makes Guadalcanal a key turning point. As the enemy's "first major effort to crush American strength in the South Pacific," it employed a force "about two and a half times the size" of what the United States could mount in defense—and it failed. "From a naval point of view," Clausen figures, "it turned out to be an action of attrition, costly to both sides." Yet especially when air power is considered—so much of it at Japanese Rabaul, so little of it on Guadalcanal's Henderson Field—"it proved that the most powerful mobilization that Japan ever placed in action was insufficient to achieve its objectives" (*BE*, p. 272). For an American readership early in 1943, this was very good news indeed.

More than half a century later, this interpretation still prevails. "Although the physical point of defeat for Japan was in the upper Solomons and New Guinea in 1943," Eric Bergerud writes in *Fire in the Sky*, "the psychological dagger of the air war was at Guadalcanal. Sometime in early or mid-1943, depending on the local situation, Japanese morale began to waver and Allied spirits rose" (*FS*, p. 343). From the enemy's perspective, errors in strategy, logistics, and overall philosophy conspire toward this defeat. Masatake Okumiya spells it out in *Zero!*, finding that his country's special strengths—the exceptionally long range of the Zero and the numbers of these planes massed at Rabaul—actually worked to its undoing in the Solomons campaign. "The primary failure on our part lay in the utter lack of a fixed policy for the construction of air bases," he attests. For six hundred miles between Rabaul and Guadalcanal, Japanese planes had no place to land, let alone refuel and rearm. "This was perhaps the most serious error committed by our Navy in the south-west Pacific, and stemmed directly from the unjustified optimism created by our initial victories" (*Z*, p. 232). Once the American push began, Japan would have to build such bases, but again "we never studied properly the problems of air-base construction, maintenance, and supply" (*Z*, p. 233); here the American advantage in technology, supplies, and know-how would tip the balance much farther in their own favor. Yet even the main base at Rabaul, where pilots such as Saburo Sakai should have lived in comfort, seems to this Japanese flyer's eyes as unpleasant as the field on Guadalcanal from which his adversaries rise to meet him:

> *I could not believe what I saw. If Bali [his previous station] had been a paradise, then Rabaul was plucked from the very depths of hell itself. There was a narrow and dusty airstrip which was to serve our group. It was the worst airfield I had ever seen anywhere. Immediately behind this wretched runway a ghastly volcano loomed 700 feet into the air. Every few minutes the ground trembled and the volcano groaned deeply, then hurled out stones and thick, choking smoke. Behind the volcano stood pallid mountains stripped of all their trees and foliage. (S, p. 106)*

In the Solomons campaign, American and Japanese flyers face each other on a regular basis; for the first time in this war, a continuous, ongoing aerial engagement defines their lives. In his Dauntless SBD dive-bomber, Harold Buell is returning from an air support mission when something catches his eye: a single enemy fighter approaching his eight-plane formation from below, its extremely high speed making the American pilot think, "My God, he's going to ram the formation!" But something even more remarkable follows:

> *At that instant the Zero's 7.7 guns began twinkling, followed by the slower puffs of a twenty-millimeter cannon, and shells came flying into the formation in lazy arcs. As one man, our*

eight gunners returned the fire, and the power of sixteen .30-caliber guns struck the incoming Zero at point-blank range. The aircraft shuddered as if it had flown into a stall, pieces flew from the wings and fuselage, and it dove under the formation in a roll. Completing the roll, it emerged on the other side, rose slightly, then fell off into a slow left spiral toward the sea below. There was no fire, but it had been badly hit and appeared to be done for. As no one saw the damaged Zero strike the water, or explode, only a probable kill was credited to the gunners when they were debriefed back at the ship. (DH, p. 99)

Buell, composing his memoirs so many decades later, takes advantage of the literature from this field and guesses that his opponent was Saburo Sakai, whose description in *Samurai!* of an almost fatal attack on Guadalcanal matches with time and place details in the American flyer's logbook.

Sakai's memory of the event is a bit different. He thinks the planes he's attacking are Wildcat fighters, and he intends to approach those on the right while three Zeros behind him take the other side. As he closes, Sakai realizes he has flown into a trap, for the planes are not single-seat fighters but rather bombers with a gunner at the rear (Grumman Avengers, he mistakenly believes). With no chance to turn away or pull into a loop, he pushes on with his attack, despite their tightened ranks that concentrates the rear gunners' fire:

I jammed down the firing button. Almost at the same time every gun in the Avenger [sic] formation opened up. The chattering roar of the guns and the cough of the cannon drowned out all other sound. The enemy planes were only

twenty yards from me when flames spurted from two
bombers. I felt as though knives had been thrust savagely into
my ears; the world burst into flaming red and I went blind.
(S, p. 219)

From here follows one of his book's most riveting descriptions, as the wounded pilot nurses himself and his damaged
plane home, covering an almost unimaginable time and distance. But the combat passage does make an important point,
the same one as Buell's: it is the adversary's skill that's admired.
"The willingness of the Allied pilots to engage us in combat
deserves special mention here," Sakai notes in an earlier passage,
"for, regardless of the odds, their fighters were always screaming
in to attack. And it is important to point out that their fighter
planes were clearly inferior to our own Zeros." Plus the Japanese
pilots were, at this point of the war, skilled and seasoned veterans. "The men we fought then were among the bravest I have
ever encountered," he believes, "no less so than our own pilots
who, three years later, went out willingly on missions from
which there was no hope of return." But that is far in the future,
when Americans have an overwhelming majority. Here, in
August of 1942, Sakai is just emerging from the long period of
Japanese superiority—and can sense that with Guadalcanal the
balance will change. "No longer," he admits, "was the war
entirely one-sided" (S, p. 108).

✪ ✪ ✪

TALES OF THE SOUTH PACIFIC

"I wish I could tell you about the South Pacific," James Michener begins his book of fact-based stories drawn from his experiences as an aviation maintenance troubleshooter and senior historical officer. "The way it actually was. The infinite specks of coral we called islands. Coconut palms nodding gracefully toward the ocean. Reefs upon which waves broke into spray, and inner lagoons, lovely beyond description." These first images from his *Tales of the South Pacific* (1947) become those of the Rodgers and Hammerstein musical that would beguile American audiences with this region. But there is more. "I wish I could tell you about the sweating jungle, the full moon rising behind the volcanoes, and the waiting. The waiting. The timeless, repetitive waiting" (*TO*, p. 1).

As Michener's book became a best-seller (and then a Broadway musical and a major Hollywood film), it joined an already existing canon of works on what flyers had done in this same theater of action. *Joe Foss, Flying Marine* (1943) by Walter Simmons complemented Richard Tregaskis's *Guadalcanal Diary* in providing a gripping narrative, in this case all the more comprehensible because it centered on the doings of a single man—and a familiar type at that, a farm kid from South Dakota who'd worked his way through college and managed to get himself into a pilot's career. Greg Boyington—"Pappy" to the world who would read of his exploits in newspaper accounts—had a story with even more hardscrabble effort to it, combined with a hell-raising attitude that made his Black Sheep Squadron seem properly named. To balance with Pappy, the swashbuckling Marine in his hefty Corsair, readers could move on to the story of the next great figure, the third in this progression of high-scoring aces from the South Pacific: Army Air Force flyer Richard Bong, every mother's favorite son, whose clean-cut appearance and impeccably good manners masked his deadly proficiency as a pilot of the Lockheed P-38 Lightning. The Lightning itself became legendary when a flight of these planes stalked a figure no less than Admiral Isoroku Yamamoto, commander in chief of the Japanese Combined Fleet, architect of the Pearl Harbor attack and the one strategist capable of dealing with the American advance up the Solomons. Even more critically, he was the most admired and even beloved military figure in Japan; when the plane carrying him was intercepted and shot down on April 18, 1943—an operation whose planning and timing seem phenomenal—the psychological impact was almost as great as that of the Doolittle Raid on Tokyo exactly one year before.

These four stories, evolving from the last months of 1942 through the long, hard war year of 1943, captured stateside headlines. At this time there were no great naval actions in the Pacific; in the war's other theater, a clockwork bombing of Germany had begun but produced no major narrative high points, while the windup of the North African campaign and the invasion of Sicily and then Italy promised to be a long, slow, slogging affair. Progress in the South Pacific was slow as well, but at least there was a measure, plus recognizable figures making it. As Joe Foss, Pappy Boyington, and Dick Bong took their turns being America's leading ace, their aerial victories let readers mark scorecards that gave dimensions to such distant places as Rendova, Vella Lavella, Choiseul, and Bougainville. In each location there were Japanese flyers who would block an American advance, and at the guns of Foss, Boyington, Bong, and the other flyers with them, increasing number of enemy planes fell. Looking at the papers, people at home could know just where we were and how things were going—so many American planes produced by the factories in Burbank, Wichita, Willow Run, and elsewhere across the country, and so many Japanese aircraft sent down in flames across the island chain pointing up toward Japan itself. When one of these victims became Admiral Yamamoto himself, the psychological tide had been turned.

Samuel Hynes, a torpedo bomber pilot stationed at Santa Barbara before shipping out for action in the Pacific, gives a good account of how Foss and Boyington appear to flyers at the time. Joe Foss is seen between combat tours, leading a fighter squadron, "and his presence made the Corsairs on the field seem more serious, machines made for killing and destroying other machines," Hynes describes in his *Flights of Passage: Reflections of a World War II Aviator* (1988), "and when I passed them on the field I was aware of the machine guns poking from the wings" (*FO*, p. 114). By this point in his memoir Hynes has decided there are two kinds of pilots: "Sanes" and "Crazies." The former are those like Foss, who have studied their planes, their enemies, and themselves, making a cool appraisal and working out the odds for any possible action. "From him you could learn how to survive," Hynes notes. "But his very sanity made him drab and unheroic, like a schoolteacher or a successful businessman. It was exciting to stand beside a man who had shot down so many planes, but the man himself was colorless. Without his record he would have been invisible" (*FO*, pp. 114–15). As for the other great Marine fighter ace of the time, the story is quite different:

> *We stood at the bar in the presence of Joe Foss and told each other stories about another fighter pilot, Pappy Boyington. If Foss was the greatest of the Sanes, Pappy was the greatest Crazy. He was the one who would fly over a Japanese base on a quiet day and invite opponents up to fight with him, as though he were a knight in some old poem. Only a world crazy with war could have supported a man like Boyington; yet for us he was the Hero, and I'd have liked to talk with him and drink with him. Foss was there in the BOQ [Bachelor Officers Quarters] bar, but there seemed no point in actually meeting him. What could he say? (*FO*, p. 115)*

Although Hynes's account is based on an impression current with the times, that impression is already the stuff of legend. But this is how quickly successful flyers become iconic figures. In truth, there was nothing boring about Joe Foss—it is just that in contrast to the flamboyant Boyington, his own manner is more composed. Fellow pilot Jim Flatley sums it up for correspondent Stanley Johnston in *The Grim Reapers*: "It was always a big day when Joe arrived" (*GR*, p. 213). From his ground control station in Guadalcanal, communications officer Walt Bayler can thrill to messages such as "Control from Foss. Chalk up four more for me," which means that "Captain Joe Foss, twenty-seven-year-old Marine Corps reserve flier from Sioux Falls, South Dakota, had bagged four Jap planes in one day" (*LM*, p. 252). Bayler, the last man off Wake Island and a ground officer at Midway during the Japanese attack there, finds genuine excitement as he plots the aerial engagements of flyers like Joe Bauer and Joe Foss, among the first fighter pilots to begin hitting hard against their persistent enemy:

> The out-of-luck Japs must have thought the skies were full of a couple of guys named Joe. Joe Bauer had dusted them off nicely; now in the second squadron came Joe Foss, already mentioned.
> And Joe Foss was really something. (LM, p. 303)

Comparisons are already somewhat invidious. As Hynes will find the Black Sheep leader more thrilling than Foss, Walt Bayler shows his greatest enthusiasm for the flying Marine who succeeds Joe Bauer as the hero of Guadalcanal's skies. Others, such as John Smith, Marion Carl, and Robert Galer, are "artists when it came to the smooth, easygoing killing of Japs. By themselves the trio accounted for forty-eight enemy planes in a very short period, getting a new notch on the tally stick nearly every time they encountered an enemy flight." They are the cool, methodical ones that Bayler uses for his contrast:

> Foss, on the other hand, was more slam-bang and exuberant in his methods. He was an energetic, determined seeker-out of enemy planes; when he located a flight he would smash headlong into it without hesitation and with little attempt at finesse. He would just shoot down everything that came into his sights, and sometimes raise hell if he ran out of ammunition before he had swept the skies entirely clean. (LM, pp. 304–5)

The distinction between the headline-making aces and the equally competent but quieter pilots is their eagerness to get into the action, no matter where or what it may be. Although there is an immense difference between the personalities of Joe Foss and Pappy Boyington, each feels compelled, as an icon of combat, to take on one of the other major characters in this theater: Washing Machine Charlie. Every air combat narrative from Guadalcanal mentions him; the most detailed description comes from George Gay in *Sole Survivor*, who includes not just the horribly unsynchronized motors (to throw off gunners' aims) and the annoying nocturnal schedule but also the pilot's personal identity. "His name was Charlie and he once had been a cab driver in San Francisco," Gay recounts. "He would talk to us on the radio, and we would talk back. There were loudspeakers all over the area, and these chats were aired for everybody's benefit" (*SS*, p. 200). Imagine a Foss or a Boyington, not just waking up to the sound of churning engines and falling bombs, but being taunted over girlfriends, wives, and favorite nightclubs back on the West Coast. Foss's plan is to put one night fighter behind this intruder and another—his own—beneath. The first would drive Washing Machine Charlie into a searchlight beam, while Foss would ride right up it from beneath, leaving Charlie blinded yet in clear view. The plan (as Walt Bayler describes it) doesn't work, because the enemy avoids this trap. Boyington's turn, coming almost a year later and up the slot at Munda, yields no results, either. Pappy spends four hours on night patrol above the base, during which a series of Charlies try to sneak in when the Marine ace comes down to lower altitude to get off oxygen, then turn away when he regains height to engage them. But at least this effort prevents any bombs from being dropped; as Frank Walton reports in *Once They Were Eagles: The Men of the*

Black Sheep Squadron, "A good many thousand men blessed Pappy for giving them the first uninterrupted night's sleep they'd had in a long time" (*OT*, p. 36).

The first outstanding ace story comes to readers in 1943: Walter Simmons's *Joe Foss, Flying Marine.* The war correspondent transcribes and edits the account so that Foss can speak directly—an important consideration, because personal testimony is considered the book's most valuable and interesting property. Telling how he shot down so many Japanese planes over Guadalcanal is only part of the story. His boyhood on a small South Dakota farm comes first, not just for the sake of autobiographical roots but because elements in this upbringing have figured in his combat flyer's success. "For a farm kid who always liked to shoot and who ached at the very sight of an airplane, a fighter pilot's life is the most fun there is" (*JF*, p. 9), he begins. Photos of the stark landscape on the prairie beyond Sioux Falls and of the humble clapboard farmhouse (scarcely twenty by thirty feet) make an escape into the wild blue yonder quite inviting, but there are elements of his childhood that remain essential to his wartime success. Out here on the plains, you had to know how to shoot; Joe's father was the best shot he ever saw, because the talent was needed to keep coyotes and marauding dogs from killing his sheep. "I mention these things because marksmanship is important in war, and good shooting isn't learned overnight," Foss explains. "Nearly all of our successful pilots have been boys who loved hunting as far back as they can remember" (*JF*, p. 13), a point that will be made in dozens of subsequent memoirs by other flyers, every one of them insistent that a typical country boyhood spent with a .22 rifle at hand gave American flyers an immediate advantage over adversaries unfamiliar with firearms until their induction into military service.

Half a century later—after he'd been governor of South Dakota and commissioner of the American Football League—Joe Foss writes his full-fledged autobiography, free of censorship and the guiding hand of a newspaper professional. The same photos and childhood details appear in *A Proud American*, but only after his best air combat story of all, which involves the special nature of his engagement with a Japanese air armada numbering eighteen dive bombers, twenty-four twin-engined Betty bombers, and sixty-four Zeros, with more following in its wake. The date is January 25, 1943, and Foss's prologue stops just as he is about to face this overwhelming force. But in setting up this key action (the result of which waits for the larger narrative to unfold), Foss tells an even more interesting story, something he wants his readers to know up front. "As the Operations Officer, it was my duty to organize flight and personnel schedules," he explains. "For weeks I'd been hiding eight fighter planes in reserve in the jungle instead of sending them out on missions." Because there's been a lull recently in enemy air activity, he fears his superiors won't understand his caution. "I knew if the brass found out, I would be about as popular as hair in a biscuit" (*PA*, p. 3). His own appraisal of Japanese strength differs greatly from intelligence reports. He and his fellow F4F Grumman Wildcat pilots have seen the enemy much closer than the researchers and planners: "We were the ones who'd gotten to know firsthand the personal styles that betrayed how the Japanese airmen were trained and how long they'd flown," Foss argues. "We were the ones who could tell how long those Zeros had been in action just by looking at their patches and markings—something the ground boys never saw. We knew the rhythms and personality of the Japanese command—from the receiving end" (*PA*, p. 4).

Foss, of course, is right. He knows firsthand that Henderson Field and its flyers have been the key players in the Southwest Pacific since action began there six months before. He also knows, as do the Japanese, that control of Henderson means control of the air, and that in turn means control of the war out here in the South Pacific. But a twenty-eight-year-old Marine captain—a reservist at that—has no business frustrating the orders of a brigadier general, especially when the figure in question is Brigadier General Francis P. Mulcahy, who on January 24, 1943, has discovered Foss's ruse and is calling him on the carpet for it. "Tomorrow's your last day, Foss!" he thunders. "Do you understand? Consider yourself fired!"

Will this be the end to Joe Foss's second tour of duty on Guadalcanal? The altercation with top brass isn't discussed in the 1943 book, as that volume covers just Joe's first tour. For the second, he's returned as a highly celebrated hero, although there are no prideful statements of self-justification—just the fact that he and his men know the enemy more intimately than do the staff at headquarters, a common enough attitude for any frontline fighter. But readers of the second book probably know what happens on the day after Mulcahy's eruption. January 25 may well have been the Operations Officer's last day on the job, but he does so fabulously that he winds up winning the award he wears on his autobiography's cover: the Congressional Medal of Honor.

The full story of January 23's exploits gets told in chapter 15, "Scramble Everything!" which will be Foss's message to ground control when, during his supposed last day as a leader, he sights the huge incoming enemy force. Here he takes the time to put it all in perspective: how despite headquarters' confidence that any contest for Guadalcanal has long been won, he himself cannot believe Admiral Yamamoto will be giving up on this strategic key to the whole theater. "Meanwhile, General Mulcahy had taken to running the Cactus Air Force like he was a traffic coordinator at a stateside airport," Foss complains. "He kept every available pilot busy supporting the ground troops and assailing the Japanese navy—usually some distance from Henderson—but nobody was guarding home base, where all the equipment not in use was lined up in neat, straight rows like a doggone parking lot" (*PA*, p. 149). Note the difference between a wartime memoir passed by the censors to build up homefront morale and a mature autobiography nearly fifty years later. In the first, Joe is introduced as the farmboy cradling his .22, practicing on coyotes until he gets his sights on the Japanese. Now, the first view is of a veteran of air combat, his eye ever on the enemy, having to do double duty by taking on his own brass. But thankfully he's been able to hide away those eight Wildcats in the jungle, as on January 25 they'll be needed to stop the assault General Mulcahy insists will never come.

As the first radar call from the north comes in, Foss scrambles his self-described Flying Circus "long before any official call to arms—an audacious act for a guy being sent off the island merely because of a difference of opinion" (*PA*, p. 150). He wisely declines the initial bait of a few Zeros, even though they waggle their wings to taunt him. By holding off, he makes the Japanese fighter pilots believe he has a larger force in reserve—which, thanks to Mulcahy, he doesn't. Farmboy practice with the old .22 has been one of his resources, but here's another, personalized with his nickname: "The hundreds of poker games I'd won during the long hours of military waiting were nothing compared to the extraordinary bluff I'd just pulled off—without firing a shot. Old Foos had played the greatest empty hand of his life" (*PA*, p. 153).

A *Saturday Evening Post* story on April 3, 1943, tells the story of what then happens (Foss quotes it rather than indulge in self-praise). At six-to-one odds, a dozen Marine Wildcats fight off the largest Japanese air assault in the entire Guadalcanal campaign—the enemy's last chance, using everything they had, to knock out Henderson Field. In ninety minutes, hundreds of planes are turned back, and many are shot down—all without a single fighter from Foss's Flying Circus being lost. The reporter praises Joe for "his generalship" and quotes his immediate superior, Colonel Sam Jack, that "it was only his shrewd leadership and knowledge of combat tactics that saved the Americans and their precious airfield from a hail of destruction. It was Joe Foss's farewell to Guadalcanal!" (*PA*, p. 154).

Had General Mulcahy followed through on his threat? No. Joe Foss understands that his tour is up for the same reason as that of so many other fine pilots before him—he's now needed to train 150 more Joe Fosses. But the magazine's dig about "generalship" and the pilot's "shrewd leadership and knowledge"— are these comments on Mulcahy's sourness the day before? Not at all, because all that has now sweetened; it is from Brigadier General Francis P. Mulcahy that the recommendation for Captain Foss's Congressional Medal of Honor comes.

A Proud American wears its politics on its sleeve; in postwar years Joe Foss was anything but a quietly retiring hero. But even in the Walter Simmons volume, Foss is allowed to speak graphically when his enemy is flying the colors of the rising sun. In early October of 1942, when his first combat tour on Guadalcanal has just begun, Joe scores his first aerial victory. He's gone up after a flight of eighteen bombers, but when an escorting

Zero dives in front of him he opens up. "With a great flash he blew into a thousand pieces," Foss notes. "It was my first Zero." He marvels at what would become a familiar picture of unarmored fighters with unprotected fuel tanks disintegrating before an attacker's eyes. "I was conscious of a lot of things—my hair standing up, a dryness of the mouth, and a crazy desire to stand up in the cockpit and yell," he notes. "That's the way you feel when a Zero blows up right in front of you" (*JF*, p. 34). His excitement is all the greater because of his inadvertence, leaving his radio turned off and being alerted only by visual signals from his wingman. But soon he's pulling off kills with fine expertise, picking a Zero off the tail of another Wildcat with comparative ease:

> *All I had to do was kick the plane around a little, and he was full in the sights. My touch on the trigger was as delicate as a drug-store clerk packing a pint of ice cream. The Jap's wing blew off, and he whirled into a cloud and disappeared. Afterward I saw the plane burning on the side of a mountain. It was Zero number two for me. I never got one any easier.* (*JF*, p. 40)

In both versions of his memoir, Joe Foss emerges as an individualist. On one occasion, enemy dive-bombers are spotted coming in for an attack when Henderson Field's fighters are off at high altitude engaging some Zeros. In the Simmons volume, Joe "gets permission" from Colonel Joe Bauer "to take off in the one Wildcat remaining on the field" (*JF*, p. 60). In *A Proud American*, the details are recounted differently. Permission is not asked, for it never could have been given, because the plane in question is grounded due to excessive magneto drop—that's what a ground crew sergeant tells Foss when asked why it is sitting unflown. Well, Joe figures, some malingerer has just filed a complaint about the aircraft to get off flying missions, so on his own authority he takes it up. But not for long; on its first climbing turn the engine cuts out, and instead of taking on the dive-bombers single-handedly the pilot is dealing with a crash. Foss is picked up, miraculously unharmed, in the ambulance sent out to retrieve what's expected to be his corpse. "Joe Bauer was waiting when we got back," Foss confesses. "It was the only time I ever really saw him mad" (*PA*, p. 113). It turns out Simmons would have liked to write about this scene, but the censors cut it out. "The Navy department wanted us to look totally heroic for the homefront," Foss explains, "rather than telling the whole truth about the realities of war" (*PA*, p. 114).

And so the harsher realities in the 1943 memoir are reserved for the enemy. "No words can overpicture the explosion of a Zero, or exaggerate the thrill it gives you," Foss enthuses. "The motor goes off in a crazy, lopsided whirl. The pilot pops out of his cockpit like a pea that has been pressed from the pod." The scene has dramatic composition even after the kill, for "the air is filled with dust and little pieces, as if someone had emptied a huge vacuum cleaner bag in the sky." Peas in a pod, vacuum cleaner bag—Simmons may have prompted the need for comparisons, but Joe Foss pulls them out of his mother's farm-wife housekeeping that's been described earlier in the book. As for what's happening in the skies over Guadalcanal, that's the Marine flyer's business, though he still reaches for similes so the reader can picture it: "The wing section, burning where it had joined the fuselage, takes a long time to fall. It goes down like a leaf—sailing, then almost stopping as it attacks the air, sailing again, and attacking the air again" (*JF*, p. 64). Action moments like these last half a century and more, as Foss can recall in old age:

Because I usually shot from very close range, the Zeros almost always exploded, which was quite a sight. There was a bright flash when the gas tanks blew and the engine would spin off by itself in a lopsided whirl. The pilot, usually still buckled in his seat, popped out of the cockpit and the air was showered with thousands of little pieces of the plane. What was left of the wing fell like a giant burning leaf. When a Zero blew up in front of you there was nowhere to go except right through all the debris. All you could do was duck and hope you missed any big pieces. (PA, pp. 111–12)

The leaf metaphor survives, but now it is burning. The enemy pilot, no longer a pea in a pod, is inescapably human, just as it is a plane that has disintegrated, not sweepings from a vacuum cleaner. Uncensored, Joe Foss's narration is starkly real, including a key element the wartime version has left implied: that Joe himself has closed in to make the kill and is in danger himself from the explosion.

Although Joe Foss had his "Flying Circus," it would be Pappy Boyington whose fame was enhanced by the quality of men he led. "Black Sheep Squadron" as a name would become "almost as much a legend in Marine Corps history as 'The Halls of Montezuma'" (*OT*, p. 99), Frank Walton recounts. The Corps made it the permanent designation of VMF 214, so that the name continued even after Boyington and his original fifty-one flyers were out of it. If the appellation calls up images of the outcast and the unruly, it is much tamer than the one its men first chose for themselves, "Boyington's Bastards," which officialdom wouldn't allow. As it was, Pappy and his Black Sheep not only made their mark on the South Pacific air war but shaped popular appreciation during the late 1950s and 1960s when the leader's memoir, *Baa Baa Black Sheep* (1958) was a bestseller, and through the 1970s as a popular television series of the same name (one continuing to be rebroadcast on cable TV into the twenty-first century). Unlike Foss, Boyington survived the censors—partly because his exploits came a year later, when sensibilities were less tender and morale a much less fragile concern, but mostly thanks to his flair for the dramatic exit. On January 2, 1944, after nearly a year of overseas duty, Pappy was shot down on a fighter sweep to Rabaul. For the next nineteen months he would be declared missing and considered dead, which was a much easier way for the Marine Corps to accommodate his legend. When he emerged from a prison camp, flamboyance again became a problem, lasting right to his death in 1988.

Greg Boyington's childhood in the Pacific Northwest was a negative image of Joe Foss's hard but healthy work on the family farm half a continent to the east. As a youngster, his name was Greg Hallenbeck, and he grew up in a family where alcoholism and possible pedophilia were unhappy norms. His intelligence and determination enabled him to work his way through the University of Washington, carrying a full load while parking cars at the Olympia Garage. His education led to a job at Boeing Aircraft, helping draft plans for the wheel gear assembly of the new B-17 bomber. He had married while still in college, and even though his wife was pregnant, the young man was intrigued by a career in Marine aviation. Cadets must be single, regulations stated, but while assembling the paperwork to apply anyway he encountered what his biographer Bruce Gamble calls "the shock of his life" (*BO*, p. 49): his birth certificate, which until now he'd never seen, stated that he was the son of Charles Boyington, who'd divorced his mother (on grounds of adultery) when Greg was an infant. Although stunned by the news, Gregory Hallenbeck gladly accepted the correct legal identity of Gregory Boyington, for the latter had no marriage recorded for his name. Under this pretense, he enlisted in the Marines' air cadet program.

With his training as a Marine flyer begins the legendary Boyington misbehavior. Having not just a wife but children as well to hide from the Corps makes his economic situation very difficult. It becomes impossible when his style of high living as a pseudo-bachelor among the other pilots starts piling up bills even a wealthy man would have trouble paying. What is a party atmosphere for some of his comrades soon translates into heavy drinking, problem drinking, and eventually alcoholism on Boyington's part. His biographer draws a character sketch in the manner of Oscar Wilde's Dorian Gray finally confronting reality, which for Pappy comes on a steamy Pensacola evening:

> The night of August 4 [1941] was no exception for Greg Boyington, who found himself down on Palafox Street [with its bars] simply "looking for an answer." Payday had been just a few days earlier, but already he was broke. Physically he was in poor shape, as well, thirty pounds heavier than when he was a cadet. It showed in his fleshy cheeks and nose, making him resemble Babe Ruth. He had smoked heavily for years, supporting the commonly held notion that "smokers drink and drinkers smoke." His wife and children were gone, he was deeply in debt, and many of his superiors were breathing down his neck.
>
> He carried his checkbook, but his bank account had been wiped out to pay the "nasty people" who were hounding him for unpaid bills. Lack of money couldn't stop his craving for

alcohol, however, and so he went inside the [San Carlos] hotel. (BO, p. 121)

As Bruce Gamble explains in *Black Sheep One* (2000), Boyington has a routine: he writes a bad check for twenty dollars, knowing that by the time the bartender tracks him down it will be payday and he can cover it, accompanied by apologies for the oversight. But some checks for larger amounts can't be paid, and the man's alcoholic dependency gives him no chance to catch up. Yet the choice of the San Carlos for his drinking on this night is good luck, for he learns that in a suite upstairs a recruiter for the American Volunteer Group is looking for pilots to fly in China.

In recounting the scene that follows, Boyington faces the truth of his situation. Here in the second chapter of *Baa Baa Black Sheep* he finds himself a first lieutenant with six years' flying experience, "most of it in fighters," but with little hope for advancement beyond the instructor's job he's doing at present. The recruiter is Richard Aldworth at the Central Aircraft Manufacturing Corporation (CAMCO), which is serving as a cover for Claire Chennault's maverick operation, but Boyington accepts him as a captain from World War I's Lafayette Escadrille. He's a bit skeptical of Aldworth's pitch, that his adversaries in China will be myopic Japanese flying unarmed transports. Still, the money sounds very good: "six hundred seventy-five dollars per month. But the sky's the limit, because they pay a bonus of five hundred for each Japanese aircraft you knock down" (*B*, p. 15).

Boyington balances the recruiter's enthusiasm (state of the art planes, flyers with twenty years of combat experience, the best technical support in the world) with his own financial need. "Somehow," he realizes, "I had the feeling I had to lie in self-defense in order to get along with this Group he was talking about." But a man who has been spending his night drinking on a rubber twenty-dollar check can improvise, as Boyington does:

> *The captain tried to impress me with the high character of the men who were to be over me and under me. They were people who drank like gentlemen and paid their gambling debts. Bravery above and beyond the call of duty was dripping all over his suite in the San Carlos Hotel there at Pensacola.*
>
> *But one thing was for certain. I didn't tell him that he was hiring an officer who had a fatal gap between his income and accounts payable. And because of this situation I had to account by mail to Marine Corps Headquarters each month how much money was being paid on each debt. Nor did I tell him that I was a whiz at a cocktail party.*
>
> *All this spelled but one thing. I would be passed over the rank of captain in the USMC, as surely as I was sitting there in the San Carlos. I had to convince the captain—and I did.*
> (B, p. 16)

Although no AVG recruit had any combat experience (let alone the twenty years described, which covered two decades of American peacetime), and although the planes were hardly state of the art (early model P-40s being sold to the British as obsolescent), no one in this outfit flying for Claire Chennault would be a hell-raiser anywhere near Boyington's potency. More typical of the 100-pilot intake is Ralph Gunvordahl, who with Joe Foss has hitchhiked from rural South Dakota to Minneapolis in February 1940 to enlist in the Corps. Other veterans of the AVG would return to regular U.S. service and, like Tex Hill and Charlie Bond, compile great records and retire twenty years later as generals. But not Greg Boyington. In the mercenary atmosphere of wartime Burma, he outdrinks and outbrawls all others, making his supposed volunteer service in support of Chiang Kai-shek's China against its Japanese invaders the stuff of comic strip adventure. He disagrees with Chennault, and angers him by losing a flight of planes in the jungle; to save face, Boyington clears a strip and flies one out. He squabbles endlessly with Chennault's chief-of-staff, Harvey Greenlaw, and begins an adulterous affair with Greenlaw's wife, Olga, the group's diarist. Even as the world will learn about his exploits back in the Corps a year later, this same public can read Olga's memoir, *The Lady and the Tigers* (1943), rehearsing the scene in which he angrily resigns from the AVG. "I thought of what he had whispered in my ear," Olga confides to her readers: "They're ganging up on me, Olga. Next time I'll fool 'em,—I'll resign. To hell with it" (*LT*, p. 248). For his part, Boyington would write a novel about his experience with Olga and the AVG, *Tonya* (1960), where his lover plays the field of available pilots and seduces them with lines such as "I'm rather handy with buttons . . . but not so good with zippers" (*T*, p. 66).

Boyington does in fact resign, after an argument with his squadron mates over having shown up drunk for night alert. But for six months he's been in the thick of it with the AVG, training in primitive conditions on a borrowed RAF Burmese airfield during November of 1941, engaging in combat with Japanese fighters over Rangoon in December, and making raids into Thailand in the early months of 1942. By April, however, he has had it. In a classic version of the I quit/you're fired scenario, he leaves the AVG and is written up by Chennault with a dishonorable discharge. Other pilots and ground crew had become dispirited and were leaving, too, and when in July the Army Air Corps made absorption into the regular service a disagreeable prospect, Chennault would have only a few loyalists left. Yet Boyington takes with him something even more important than the pay: credit for six victories, making him an ace before his first combat flight as a Marine flyer.

Getting back to the United States on his own resources is tough, and being recommissioned in the Marine Corps even harder. For a time, he returns to the Olympia Garage in Seattle and supports himself parking cars. But a telegram to Navy Secretary Frank Knox does the trick, and by January of 1943 he is back in the Corps and getting ready for overseas duty. In February he's sent to Guadalcanal as assistant operations officer for Marine Fighter Squadron 122, and for a few weeks in April he commands it. Duties involve escorting bombers up the slot, but no Japanese fighters appear—heavy losses at Rabaul have led to a lull in activity, as enemy forces rebuild. Boyington notes how his squadron "patrolled the Canal skies for hours each day but never saw so much as the vapor trail of a single Japanese plane" (B, p. 127). Yet a different kind of action soon develops—in print. War correspondents eager for anything at all to describe fix on this new commander's Flying Tiger background and experience, accepting Boyington's claim for six enemy kills. In fact only two were in the air, the Marines' and Navy's criterion, and three and three-quarters were credited as his share of Japanese planes destroyed on the ground; rounding up the fraction would be the least of Pappy's exaggerations during this war. To the delight of newspaper readers back home, here was another ace to cheer along. No matter that he had yet to fire at the enemy as a Marine.

An additional item will contribute to Greg Boyington's marketing in the United States. Joe Foss was certainly newsworthy, and his exploits had made great copy. But Foss did it all in an

F4F Wildcat, a prewar fighter that had to struggle against the superior Mitsubishi Zero. When Boyington comes back for his second combat tour a few months later, his squadron is equipped with something new: the F4U Corsair. Here was a plane to drive the public wild. As Bruce Gamble notes, even Boyington was swept away by its powerfully innovative design, including concepts that had never before been seen in a combat aircraft:

> *Just to gawk at the new plane on the ground must have thrilled the aeronautical engineer in him. With its long, cylindrical cowling, enormous propeller, and unique inverted gull wing, the Corsair exuded speed and power. The fuselage had been designed to fit like a glove around the most powerful radial engine available, an eighteen-cylinder, two-thousand-horsepower Pratt & Whitney monster that gave the Corsair a legitimate top speed of more than four hundred miles per hour at sea level. The cowling was wrapped so tightly around the engine that no space existed for oil-cooler intakes, which were mounted instead at the forward edge of the wing roots. Because of their location and shape, the intakes emitted an eerie whistle during high-speed dives. (BO, p. 218)*

If ever a fighter could be designed to match the overkill mentality of its pilot, this plane was it. There was even a special appeal in it for the Marine Corps, because the nature of its landing gear, long nose, and great distance from cockpit to deck made it far less suitable for carrier use. The F4U Corsair seemed fated for jungle airstrip work from South Pacific islands. As big and as rugged as its most famous pilot, it was the first American fighter in the theater capable of outrunning Zeros; Wildcats could only catch them in a dive, thanks to the older plane's weight. It wasn't easier to handle—pilot Tom Blackburn recalls a colleague who called it "as cooperative as a hog on ice" (*J*, p. 43)—but then neither was Boyington. Joe Foss frankly disliked it, complaining that "the Corsair was a dive bomber, not a fighter like the Wildcat" (*PA*, p. 177), while John F. Forsyth, a dive-bomber pilot himself, regretted that "fatal crashes in practice in the States were three times as numerous in the Corsairs as in the F6F Hellcats" (*HD*, p. 53), the Wildcat's replacement. New Zealand flyers such as Bryan Cox preferred it to the P-40Es they'd started with; his *Too Young to Die: The Story of a New Zealand Fighter Pilot in the Pacific War* (1987) tells a story much like Boyington's, of encountering these planes that "with their cranked wings and noses pointing steeply at the sky" remind him "of grotesque metal monsters poised to spring straight into the air" (*TY*, p. 71). Monsters were just what Admiral Halsey needed to escort bombers to the Japanese strongholds, leapfrogging from base to base and capable of flying from the roughest airfields. With the F6F Hellcat yet to be delivered and the Army Air Force's P-38 Lightning more effective as a high-altitude fighter, only the Corsair could slug it out with Zeros on these escort raids and fighter sweeps. And slugging it out would be Greg Boyington's preferred manner of combat, a style he'd learned as a collegiate boxer.

One last special element plays a role in creating the legend of Pappy Boyington. Admiral Halsey needed more fighter squadrons for his Solomons campaign, and in traditional fashion new ones were being formed back in the United States. Never before had one been put together under enemy eyes, right within the theater of combat. Six hundred miles south of Guadalcanal in the New Hebrides, the base of Espiritu Santo served as the major supply depot for the Solomons. In early May of 1942 Marine Fighting Squadron 214 was celebrating the completion of its combat tour (albeit with the loss of its commanding officer). The pilots were slated for rest and recreation in Australia, to be followed by various assignments according to specific needs. Knowing Halsey's demands, the assistant commanding general of the First Marine Air Wing, Major General James Moore, got the idea to form a new squadron on the spot. A few veterans from other outfits were on hand, awaiting reassignment, plus enough newly trained pilots had arrived from the States to fill out a roster. Moore had been hearing how a major named Boyington had been, as Frank Walton describes, "causing a furor around the fighter base on the other side of the island, demanding an assignment" (*OT*, p. 7). Moore liked this kind of style—enough not just to assign Boyington to the reborn VFM 214, but to reinstate him after an operations officer, angry with Greg since instructor days, grounded him and relieved him of his command for too much drinking.

Hence the start of Pappy Boyington's Black Sheep Squadron. The appellation had nothing to do with the character of the men. None had been rejected by other units, and none had any behavior problems—except, of course, their leader. Decades later, squadron veterans would deeply resent the premise of the television series that characterized them as misfits, for they certainly weren't. But by the 1970s mythologies from World War II had run together and overlapped, however incorrectly, to the point that Flying Tiger independence melded with Black Sheep uniqueness. The special nature of the real Black Sheep Squadron was that it was formed not in the usual methodical way, back in the United States, but right here in the South Pacific. The only true black sheep was Pappy, and thanks to his grounding he had started off right in style. But there are black sheep among the higher ranks too. Bruce Gamble notes that Moore, whose nickname was "Nuts," was a "a drinking general" (*BO*, p. 232), and he not only listens to Boyington's plea for reinstatement but lubricates it with a generous contribution from his private stock. Nor was this the last time Nuts Moore would get Pappy Boyington off the book.

Needless to say, in *Baa Baa Black Sheep* the new squadron leader tells the story differently. "I came up with an idea that would supply a temporary fighter squadron and fill the gap until the flattops arrived," he claims. "The idea was to get replacement pilots from the pilots' pool, some Corsairs used for training, and borrow a number for control purposes from some squadron not in action at the time." He ascribes his success with this plan to "Lady Luck" (*B*, p. 140), neglecting to mention Halsey's needs and Moore's way of fulfilling them. But for a legend to have currency half a generation later, some poetic license and a great flair for drama are needed. Still, the men catch his spirit quickly enough. One of them, Frank Losch, explains the chemistry of it to Frank Walton in *Once They Were Eagles*: "It was a happy combination: the stress; the dynamic leadership of Boyington; the press coverage that you [Walton] were responsible for." When it comes together, the result is impressive. "We had a team, and we all tried to live up to it," Losch recalls. "We were the *Black Sheep* Squadron. Other squadrons were individuals—we were a *team*" (*OT*, p. 123). "Close-knit" is another term these pilots use, along with "tremendous morale." "We had a leader who was experienced," Perry Lane points out, "and we had faith in him. He was one of the boys on the ground, but he knew what he was doing in the air, and we knew he was on the level with the rest of us. If you got a lousy aircraft, you figured, well, he's got one, too" (*OT*,

p. 173). It's a fact that Pappy's style was to choose the worst plane available for each mission, a reminder of Jimmy Doolittle's way of demonstrating maneuvers with half the power cut or in tighter circumstances than any of his men would face. Boyington is a moral factor, too, as Denmark Groover confesses. "I came from a section of the country where prejudice was the order of the day," he admits, adding that flying for Pappy "knocked a lot of that prejudice out of me." He tells of selling some whiskey to the mess attendants, "who were black, for $60. Boyington found out about it and made me give the $60 back *and* let them keep the whiskey, which was a damn good lesson to me" (*OT*, p. 184). Rounding out the team concept is the statement Boyington himself gives Walton to end his old colleague's book: "My job was like a coach" (*OT*, p. 190).

Boyington also saw his job as a vindication of honor. He'd left the Flying Tigers in a huff (and with a lover to write about it the very next year in her book). To make it worse, Chennault—now a general in the U.S. Army Air Force, even as his men continued as irregulars—followed up on the dishonorable discharge with the advice that Boyington be denied transport home and drafted at once into the Tenth Air Force, as a shave-tail second lieutenant. It was this insult that provided the motivation to swim all the way back to America, if necessary, get reinstated in the Marine Corps, and start "shooting down a thousand Japs" (*B*, p. 115).

Guadalcanal was the place to do it. Fellow Marine ace Marion E. Carl writes in his memoir, *Pushing the Envelope* (1994), that "it was a flight leader's war" taking place in the theater at this time and place, "with four-plane divisions usually fighting their own battles in their particular slice of the sky." As far as any mastery of grand tactics, "nobody could control so many aircraft simultaneously" (*PE*, p. 47), and thus Pappy's brawling style worked perfectly where in other circumstances a more cool and level-headed style of command might have been called for. He led by example, which in this case meant fighting by example—at the worst odds, in the poorest plane, and often in a physically debilitated condition, hung over from any number of nights' drinking. In doing so, he did not win the admiration of more refined flyers like Marion Carl, who years later would still debate the rankings for leading Marine ace, a status Boyington received, together with his Congressional Medal of Honor, when he emerged from captivity at war's end. "The medal was deserved—Greg was a talented aviator and an aggressive combat leader—but I've been rankled by the 'top gun' title ever since," Carl complains, especially since it steals glory from a preferred model:

> *Even allowing the two unsubstantiated claims from his last mission, he couldn't match Joe Foss's total of his score in Marine Corps service. To my knowledge, Joe has never made any fuss over the situation—he's too much a gentleman for that—but for the Marine Corps officially to recognize Boyington as its top ace, despite documentation to the contrary, defies logic. I suspect it's a bureaucratic inability to admit a long-standing error.* (*PE*, p. 48)

Publicity, not bureaucracy, is more likely the Corps's motive. In 1943 the country needed heroes, and to be effective in the morale wars, heroes needed publicity. Greg Boyington was the type reporters loved and people back home liked to read about. In a technologically complex war of great, faceless movements, he was one of the few who were acting not only individually but with a striking personality that matched his measurable achievements. That he'd done it all when coming from the wrong side of the tracks and making any number of mistakes along the way simply proved he was human. In a day in which alcoholism was yet to be recognized as a disease—when it was too often considered a comic attribute, or one of swashbuckling bravado—Boyington actually made it look like he flew better drunk. Because the Japanese stronghold of Rabaul never had to be captured, there could be no conclusive triumph for a leader like Pappy; Japan's greatest base in the theater was simply bypassed, with the action heading on north while the enemy garrison was left to wither on the vine, so to speak, beyond the range of supply. But before that might happen, Bougainville and its five protective airfields had to be knocked off the map, and it is here that the Black Sheep did their greatest work. As a campaign against great odds and superior strength, it was reminiscent of what the Flying Tigers had accomplished in Burma and China, at least for a time. And so this was the image of Greg Boyington that prevailed.

Pappy's fighting career comes to an end on January 3, 1944, on another of the seemingly endless missions to Rabaul. Newspaper correspondents have been hounding him about breaking Joe Foss's record for enemy planes shot down, and a combination of mechanical failures and intermittent bad weather have been costing him easy opportunities for the one-to-tie and two-to-go-ahead victories. But on this day, seventy Zeros climb from their base on New Britain to intercept Boyington's four-plane division. He should have seen them above; instead, his eyes are on a formation of six Zeros below him, cruising at fifteen thousand feet—bait for a classic Japanese trap. Bruce Gamble, who has studied the man and his career as thoroughly as any subject can be investigated, describes Pappy dropping for the kill:

Here at last was the opportunity he had been waiting for, try-
ing too hard for, but he was neither patient nor deliberate.
Like a hunter with buck fever he opened fire at twelve hun-
dred feet, almost a quarter of a mile behind the Zeke. Nor-
mally the tracers would alert the Japanese pilot, who would
instantly Split-S and be gone, but this Zeke held its course.
Boyington closed the distance rapidly, and at three hundred
feet his converging rounds occupied the same space as the
A6M. The lightly built Zeke shuddered under the impact of
the slugs, some of which had ignited as they exited the Cor-
sair's gun barrels at more than twenty-eight hundred feet per
second. An instant before the Zeke's high-octane fuel torched
off, the pilot jumped free. Several pilots from VFM-223, along
with [division members] Matheson and Chatham, saw the
Zeke's demise. Boyington had more than enough eyewitnesses
for his twenty-sixth victory. The record was tied. (BO, p. 305)

Heading down farther after more prey, Pappy is jumped by twenty Zeros and is hit, both himself and his plane, forcing him to ditch. After drifting in his rubber raft for eight hours, he's picked up by a Japanese sub, commencing an imprisonment that lasts until war's end.

Although his account has been challenged, a Zero pilot named Masajiro Kawato writes in *Flight Into Conquest* (1978) that he was the flyer who brought Boyington down. His description follows Pappy's in *Baa Baa Black Sheep* (a dramatic low-altitude bailout) rather than Gamble's account corroborated by historical records (a ditching), but begins with an accurate picture of squadron mate George Ashmun's demise. "I saw an unusual sight," Kawato mentions during a combat patrol over York Island: "An F4U Corsair was after a Zero and right behind the F4U another Zero was followed by another F4U." Although it looks like a trailing formation exercise, the business is deadly. The first Zero and F4U each fall in flames. Kawato joins the chase, catching up with the second Corsair:

> *I kept my cool and waited until I had the right distance. After fifteen or sixteen rounds of 20 millimeter gunfire, some hitting the cabin near the cockpit, it started to smoke a little, but no flames. He rolled over to the right and went in for a dive but I was able to stay with him because of my speed. I was relaxed. As he was going on over Rabaul, where our case was located, I was thinking how long this Corsair F4U would be able to escape me. I did not have much of a chance to use my guns because of his manipulations to the left and right, turns and rolling dives. We both reached sea level with high speed, as low as 1,000 meters above the water. Suddenly, his canopy opened and I saw a figure jump out. I guess he thought that his last effort of avoiding us was fruitless. I stopped chasing him and brought my plane up, watching the F4U Corsair go down, skimming the surface of the ocean, and yet, our Zeros kept chasing and shooting this pilotless plane. This particular plane stayed in my mind vividly. (FI, p. 76)*

Gamble disputes this account but also rejects Boyington's description of leaving his plane. If you believe Pappy, however, Kawato's story corresponds, not to mention the inevitable contrasts in even the most reliable memories of opponents, such as those of Harold Buell and Saburo Sakai facing off in the same skies. Suffice it to say that Kawato had a postwar career too—immigrating to America, writing his book, and selling it at the same airshows where Boyington hawked copies of *Baa Baa*

Black Sheep and *Tonya*. Pappy's legend was the most secure. Although he made as much a mess of his civilian life as he had of his prewar experience in the military, his public was forgiving. As Bruce Gamble judges near the end of his squadron history, *The Black Sheep* (1998), Greg Boyington's memoir had a "self-deprecating message" (*TBS*, p. 420), and this candor guaranteed him a warm place in his country's heart. The last line of *Baa Baa Black Sheep* speaks frankly of the type of person needed to fight a nation's wars and then be thrown upon his own resources to survive the peace. "If this story were to have a moral," Pappy Boyington concludes, "then I would say: 'Just name a hero and I'll prove he's a bum'" (*B*, p. 384). A lovable bum, it is true—and a hero nonetheless.

Dick Bong was anything but a bum. Compared to Greg Boyington, he was much more like Joe Foss: a hardworking farm kid from a wholesome family who wanted to fight hard, win the war, and build an even better America afterwards. He was in the process of doing that, helping test the plane that would bring his country into the jet age, when he died on August 6, 1945, a date that also marks the world's entry into the atomic age. Bong's business was half a world a way, back home in the States, piloting a test flight of the Lockheed P-80 Shooting Star, the plane destined to be America's first operational jet fighter. Losing power on takeoff from Lockheed's Burbank facility, Bong's P-80 crashed less than a minute after leaving the ground, a mile and a half from the runway. Controversy still exists over possible causes, centering on the aircraft's auxiliary fuel system. In any event, a jet without power was radically different from any propeller plane, and there was no chance for what in a conventional craft could have been a dead-stick landing. At the height of his fame and at the moment his country was taking the dramatic move to finally win World War II, Dick Bong died, departing a life that had seemed to have only more great promise.

There was to have been a major military airfield built in his home state of Wisconsin: Bong Air Force Base, near Kenosha, and just thirty miles north of what would become the world's busiest commercial airport, Chicago's O'Hare Field, named for another hero of the Pacific theater's air war, Navy Lieutenant Edward H. O'Hare. Butch O'Hare had gained fame on February 20, 1942, when during an early air assault on Rabaul by the carrier *Lexington* he shot down five Japanese bombers single-handedly. For this, he won the same medal as Joe Foss and Greg Boyington, the Congressional Medal of Honor—but more than a year ahead of them, making him one of the theater's first distinguishable heroes and anticipating the fame of Bong himself, who would receive this award from General Douglas MacArthur in the Philippines in December 12, 1944. Butch O'Hare was an early casualty, and hence could not establish records as did Foss, Boyington, and Bong. But his development of a weaving tactic for defense against attacks by Japanese Zeros made him a cornerstone contributor to the war effort, especially as continued by Dick Bong.

What was to be Bong AFB became, thanks to budget cuts late in 1959, a recreation area instead, a landmark in the holding pattern today for flights stacked up over O'Hare Field. The undisputed title of leading ace, however, belongs to Major Richard I. Bong. Unlike the controversy over the Marine Corps record between Foss and Boyington, Bong's forty kills as an Army Air Force pilot led all American services in World War II. His actual count probably exceeded sixty, giving him more than double the number contested between the two Marine aces. But his was a different plane and a different style of conflict. The Lockheed P-

38 Lightning, with its two engines and twin-boomed tail, performed better than anything in the theater at high altitude and was brilliant at sweeping down on its prey. And Dick Bong's air war had greater dimensions than the conflict fighting its way north from Guadalcanal in late 1942. Instead of fighter sweeps, he was called on most frequently for escort missions, taking on enemy fighters as they sought to pick off Army Air Force bombers. By 1944 the action was in the Philippines, when the Japanese were hurling their last resources into the fray, destroying much of their naval and aerial assets in the process and swelling Bong's record of kills. In Dick Bong, Americans had a flyer whose heroics demonstrated the growing momentum toward victory in this war.

Bong's first biographer would be his commanding general, George C. Kenney. In *Dick Bong: Ace of Aces* (1960), the general enjoys telling of his first encounter with this young man: not in the South Pacific, but much earlier during the war. "My introduction to Dick Bong took place in July, 1942, at my headquarters in San Francisco, where I was commanding the Fourth Air Force" (*DBA*, p. 3), Kenney begins. Low-ranking trainees don't meet generals for routine reasons, and this one hadn't yet shot down any Japanese planes. But he was indeed getting write-ups, even though his assigned duty was to become familiar with the new P-38 Lightning, as Kenney explains:

> *I had just finished reading a long report concerning the exploits of one of my young pilots who had been looping the loop around the center span of the Golden Gate Bridge in a P-38 fighter plane and waving to the stenographic help in the office buildings as he flew along Market Street. The report noted that, while it had been extremely difficult to get infor-*

*mation from the somewhat sympathetic and probably con-
niving witnesses, there was plenty of evidence indicating that
a large part of the waving had been to people on some of the
lower floors of the building. Streetcars had stopped, taxis had
run up on the sidewalks, and pedestrians had fled to the
nearest doorways to get indoors and under cover. There was
even a rumor that the insurance companies were contemplat-
ing raising the rates. The fire and police departments both
seemed quite concerned. (DBA, p. 4)*

This is serious business. Standard procedure was to court-
martial the culprit, strip him of his commission, and turn him
over to the draft for infantry service. From Bong's letters edited
by his brother, Carl, *Dear Mom—So We Have a War* (1991), there
were other flyers involved, with Dick's part limited to a buzz job
in San Anselmo, over the house of a recently married comrade.
But this in fact is the part that has Kenney concerned. A woman
from the neighborhood has complained that her laundry was
blown from the line. Her complaint gives the general a solution.
Bong will report to her address, apologize, and redo her laundry.
"Then you hang around being useful—mowing a lawn or something—and when the clothes are dry, take them off the line and
bring them into the house. And don't drop any of them on the
ground or you will have to wash them again. I want that woman
to think that we are good for something besides annoying people" (*DBA*, p. 8).

Kenney's discipline is instructive for those who want to know
about the real Dick Bong. The young man standing before
George Kenney looks like a cherub—it's hard for the general to
imagine any talent for genuine wrongdoing in the lad. But this
same pilot has just put a P-38 through paces that would do a vet-

eran combat pilot proud. Men like him were needed in the South Pacific, and needed desperately. As happens so often in such situations, the commander has to balance the misbehavior of a fighter pilot with the value of this same spirit in carrying the war to their enemy. It really does seem that you can't have one without the other. But there is something more to the fresh lieutenant: a boyishness and charm that says he'd like nothing more than to be back home for a day, helping mom with the chores. As a commander, Kenney could hardly have known better. Late in the war he'd have to use similar judgment in getting the man back home safely before he tried to shoot down every enemy airplane still flying. These were the two sides of Richard Bong.

Dear Mom—So We Have a War shows readers how much of a loving son and dutiful family member Dick Bong was. From training fields in the States to bases across the Pacific, this ace flyer proves a most dutiful son. His letters mention his own exploits, of course, but are equally devoted to queries about home. Has it been a good deer season? Will everyone be home for Christmas? What's the crop rotation for this spring? Poignantly, Bong will refer to the upside down nature of his calendar in the southern hemisphere and remark how this must be the week his mother and sisters are gathering gooseberries, and the like. He worries for his sister who has moved down to the big city, Milwaukee, for war work in the Allis Chalmers plant. He mentions transiting through Chicago and liking it even less than Milwaukee. Finally, there are descriptions of his air combats, as specific as the censor will allow. But then he will write about postwar plans and hopes, including a dream house he wants to build for all of them, with quarters for himself and his bride, a huge living room with lounge chairs for each family member, a bowling alley, and a hangar at the end for his airplane. A pipe dream? Surely so, but indicative of a young man who would much rather be at home.

Dutiful son, but also a flyer with an exceptional sense of duty, not just for shooting down enemy planes but for carrying the ace reputation with both dignity and inspiring flair. In the U.S., newspaper readers counted his kills like numbers in a home run race. In theater, commanders knew of his reliability and fellow pilots respected his expertise. How this all looked to men in the field, such as a responsible but otherwise unexceptional P-39 pilot named Edwards Park, is described in Park's memoir, *Angels Twenty: A Young American Flyer a Long Way From Home* (1997). Top-scoring aces attract war correspondents, Park understands, and he does not begrudge Bong's advantage of having a special flight of his own (flashily decked out) and his willingness to "put on his own private air show for new pilots and VIPs." On one of these latter occasions the press provides a movie starlet for photo interest, and Bong takes her along for the flight, "crammed into a makeshift seat behind him." This stunt draws Park and other young flyers "not just to see Dick fly, which was old stuff, but to catch a glimpse of the starlet, a radiant little thing with perfume that nailed us half a mile away." And what a show it is:

> *Extremely mindful of his soft, aromatic cargo, Bong edited his usual wild-ass performance down to a most gentlemanly flight—only one loop and a couple of easy barrel rolls. Then he came in for his usual showboat landing, designed to quell the fears of P-38 kids who doubted the capabilities of the big plane if and when an engine quit.*
>
> *He howled over the strip, down on the deck, then pulled up sharply, killing both engines and feathering the props. On*

momentum alone, he coasted up and gradually over in a lazy, eerily silent loop. While inverted, the plane sprouted wheels and flaps, then whistled down in a controlled dive toward the end of the strip. With a couple of sideslips and a fishtail, Bong killed off his speed and kissed the matting. His plane rolled along the runway, slowing fast. It had just enough life left to turn toward the assembled brass, gathered outside the alert tent. And as it finished its roll, Bong touched the brakes so the nose bobbed down, making a little bow to us fans. (AT, pp. 167–68)

He gets a big round of applause. The movie starlet stays put, waiting until the crowd has left to rise from the cockpit. Not surprisingly, she has wet her pants. But everyone who's seen the show and read about Bong's high scores knows something for certain that, when the heroes were Joe Foss and Pappy Boyington, was only a hope: America is going to win this war.

Like Foss in his stubby Wildcat and Boyington in his gull-winged Corsair, Dick Bong's image is linked to the P-38 Lightning, Lockheed's new generation of fighter plane that brought refinement to a new level. In *New Guinea Skies: A Fighter Pilot's View of World War II* (1992), Wayne P. Rothgeb writes of the plane's instrumentation and finely tuned controls and adds, "She had graceful power; her two synchronized engines didn't roar—they purred like kittens." Lifting off from the runway, the aircraft's wheels do no clunk into the wheel wells. "Rather, like a refined, elegant lady, she slowly lifted her gear and very discreetly tucked them out of sight. Seated in the cockpit, you became the master of this mistress of the sky" (*NG*, p. 142). As General Kenney could see from the start, Dick Bong had the perfect talents for flying this plane. With grace and style, he could put it anywhere. And once put there, the special nature of its guns did the job. As P-38 pilot Henry C. Toll explains in *Tropic Lightning* (1987), its armament was arranged uniquely. Unlike that of a single-engine fighter, whose guns had to be well out on the wings, beyond the arc of its propeller, the P-38 was able to have its four .50-caliber machine-guns and its 20-millimeter cannon firing straight forward. Instead of a convergence of fire at two hundred yards, "it had a maximum concentration from zero to maximum range. It was like playing a fire hose. If you could hit it, you could cut it to ribbons" (*TL*, p. 2). Dick Bong was never a good shot—but in a smartly flown Lightning, it didn't matter.

The Dick Bong story shows how a combination of brilliantly trained pilots flying powerfully destructive aircraft would tip the balance against Japan. The P-38 Lightning was a devastating plane, plus it had great range, and was thus the aircraft of choice for a very special mission on April 18, 1943, when Admiral Isoroku Yamamoto, not only the leader but the essential spirit of the Japanese war effort, was shot from the skies over Bougainville. It was the longest successful fighter intercept mission of the war, a round trip from Guadalcanal that even with external fuel tanks would allow just fifteen minutes for engagement with the enemy. Timing had to be perfect. But because the admiral was compulsively punctual, the intelligence report of his schedule let the squadron of P-38s arrive right on the money. Visiting the theater to encourage his forces that had been driven from Guadalcanal and who were now in danger of losing the Solomons, Yamamoto could never have suspected that his trip could lead to the greatest demoralization of all. But such was the efficiency of American air power building in the region that the strike, surgical in nature and infinitesimal in terms of its target, could be made, and made with absolute success. Joe Foss had clawed down Zeros with his Wildcat, and Pappy Boyington would bully even more of them from the air, even as Dick Bong began methodically clearing the skies with his breathtakingly slick flying. Using this same air weapon to take down a single figure, the man who by virtue of his planning of the Pearl Harbor attack had come to be the very personification of Japan's threat to America, would demonstrate precisely how the tables were turning in favor of the United States.

It is totally coincidental that the attack on Yamamoto would happen one year to the day of Jimmy Doolittle's raid on Tokyo, another small yet psychologically powerful accomplishment. But the happenstance of planning on the admiral's part determined the day, and American efficiency did the rest. The mission would be possible thanks to three factors: an ability to break the enemy's code and read his messages, including details of Yamamoto's schedule, to the minute; the possession of a plane like the Lightning with the range to take it all the way from Guadalcanal to Bougainville and with the firepower to make short work of the Betty bombers carrying Yamamoto and his staff, then fly all the way home; and pilots so superbly trained in navigation that such a flight could be almost routine, yet carried out with a spirit of initiative that let them take advantage of changing circumstances. Not coincidentally at all, these were the very factors the enemy lacked. In the mission against Yamamoto the consequence of this imbalance are demonstrated in the most personal way possible.

The plan for it all is simple to recount. From Guadalcanal, eighteen P-38s of the 339th Fighter Squadron (USAAF) would fly to Bougainville, keeping to just fifty feet above the water and holding their planes at the precise airspeed to conserve fuel and intercept the Admiral's transport at the key moment in its own flight so many miles to the north. At this point, four Lightnings would move in as a killer section while the other fourteen planes climbed to provide top cover. Among the attack section flyers are two pilots, Tom Lanphier and Rex Barber. It is their actions and the contrasting nature of accounts of their acts that make the mission controversial at the time and a matter of contention today. Joe Foss, Greg Boyington, and Dick Bong had been quite different persons, and were effective as flyers in their own, unique ways. Yet all were accepted as evolving types in the progressive story of the fighter war in the Pacific. Handling the contrast between Lanphier and Barber would be far less easy, but also indicative of what this war, now looking more and more like it would be won, meant to Americans.

Attack on Yamamoto (1990) is the most complete survey of the affair, and in it Carroll V. Glines uses nearly half a century's hindsight to draw a telling contrast between Lanphier and Barber:

> *Thomas Lanphier died in November 1987. However, he produced enough written and recorded materials in an attempt to justify his claim that there is no doubt what he would say today. He was a man with a capricious, mercurial personality, often brilliant, ambitious to a fault, articulate, and driven to desperation in his desire to defend his version of a brief combat shootout that put his name in the history books. He was an exceptionally aggressive, sometimes reckless, fighter pilot who was respected by his contemporaries for his willingness to tangle with the enemy at great risk to himself. His bravery under fire has never been questioned; his imprudence has.*
>
> *Rex T. Barber, the other pilot who claims credit, is a contrast in personality. Quiet, unassuming, and unpretentious*

on the ground, but a vigorous, aggressive fighter pilot in the air, he has no aspirations for greatness. A native of Oregon, he remained in the air force flying fighter planes during the Korean War and retired as a colonel after a full air force career. (AY, pp. xi–xii)

Given the high numbers racked up by Foss, Boyington, and Bong, the argument over a single kill would seem out of proportion, except for the monumental importance of the target. To "get Yamamoto," as the title of Burke Davis's book on the subject put it (1969), was worth any number, even the greatest, of enemy aircraft. As Davis notes, when the coded details of the admiral's in-theater itinerary were intercepted and broken, the chief of Naval Intelligence in Washington, D.C., "could not conceal his excitement," looking like "he had eaten of canary—he was obviously pregnant with a tremendous secret. He looked as if he had to do something or explode" (GY, pp. 18–19). This same enthusiasm worked its way down the chain of command until it rested with the Army Air Force pilots chosen for the mission. They, and not the Navy or Marines, were chosen simply because it was their service that had Lightnings, the only plane in the South Pacific with range for such a mission. To complete the mission successfully would deal a severe blow to the enemy—psychologically in taking out an iconic leader, but also practically in depriving the war effort of one of its most brilliant strategists. Even more so than the Doolittle Raid, the attack on Yamamoto would be an event in which the acts of a very few flyers would have tremendous impact. Joe Foss, Greg Boyington, and Dick Bong had great fame, but it came from many engagements, fought one at a time, over an extended period. The flyers in the 339th's killer section were looking at the chance for equal glory with just one mission.

The mission's execution went much like its planning: closely attentive to detail and relentless in determination to get its prey. The only hitch came just before interception, when one of the killer flight pilots, Besby Holmes, was unable to jettison his P-38's external tanks. Holmes left the formation, taking his wingman with him for cover, leaving just Lanphier and Barber to make the attack. Their targets were two Betty bombers, escorted by six Zeros. Not knowing which of the larger planes carried Yamamoto, both had to be brought down.

Here is where accounts begin to differ. In *Attack on Yamamoto*, Glines reproduces several versions, including Lanphier's, Barber's, and Holmes's, the last coming from a distance. Lanphier describes having to shoot down one of the Zero escorts, then diving on what he says to be Yamamoto's bomber (although there would have been no external sign of this admiral's presence). Approaching from the side, he "fired a long steady burst across the bomber's course of flight, from approximately right angles" (*AY*, p. 64). This sets the plane's right engine and wing alight; in moments the wing tears free, sending the Betty on a plunge into the Bougainville jungle close below. Barber describes Lanphier making a head-on pass at the Zeros, driving them off. "This was a wise maneuver on his part," Barber notes, "as it allowed me the opportunity to attack the bombers without the Zeros on my tail" (p. 68). With one Betty right in front of him, he opens fire, getting hits on the right engine, tail, wing root, and finally the left engine. It snaps left and crashes into the jungle. Leaving the scene, he sees the other Betty very low over the water, heading south. Holmes, looking back to see what is happening, hears a radio call from Lanphier that he's "bracketed by three Zeros and can't go anywhere but straight ahead" (*AY*, p. 70) and at the same moment sees a Betty plunge and crash. Having shaken off his belly tanks, Holmes calls his wingman and they return to the fray, driving three Zeros off Barber's tail. Holmes then gets in position behind the second Betty and, after giving it much fire, brings it down.

The history of an event is often a product of who holds the pen describing it. As Glines notes, the Army Air Force document written in 1943 became the official text, even though its "colorful language . . . rare for a combat action report, was typical of Lanphier's style of writing and speaking" (*AY*, p. 76). In subsequent years Lanphier sold his own narrative to newspapers and to the *Reader's Digest*. Sometimes he was on the Betty's tail, other times hitting it from the side, but always he was the key shooter, and Yamamoto the target.

At the time, the important thing was that the great Japanese admiral had been killed. There was no question about it, as his body was recovered from the wreck of what was the first Betty shot down. In the second plane was Admiral Matome Ugaki, Yamamoto's chief of staff, who survived the crash and would go on to command the Fifth Air Fleet at the war's end. In *Yamamoto: The Man Who Menaced America* (1965), John Deane Potter describes the Japanese announcement:

> It was not until 21 May, more than a month after his death and after [Captain Wasuji] Wantanabe had brought his ashes back to Tokyo, that a Japanese broadcast announced, "Admiral Yamamoto while directing general strategy in the front line in April of this year engaged in combat with the enemy and met gallant death in a war plane." Then the announcer choked and wept. (*Y*, p. 310)

For its part, the U.S. government kept quiet for the moment. It did not want the enemy to know its code had been broken, nor did it want Lanphier identified as the killer; his brother, also a flyer, was presently a prisoner of war held by the Japanese. But there was also an issue of international law, turning on the argument of whether Yamamoto was killed in combat or assassinated. America's military leaders worried about the latter. Admiral Nimitz kicked the decision up to Admiral Ernest J. King, Naval chief of staff, who in turn passed it on to Frank Knox, secretary of the Navy. Once in civilian hands, the choice to go after Yamamoto inevitably rested at the top. As Edwin P. Hoyt puts it at the conclusion of his own study, *Yamamoto: The Man Who Planned Pearl Harbor* (1990), "it was from President Roosevelt himself that Admiral Yamamoto received his death warrant," making him "the only commander on any side in World War II to be assassinated by the direct order of the chief of government of the enemy" (*YM*, p. 248).

Both controversies—over the man who killed Yamamoto and whether or not that killing was justified—involve issues of personality. Thanks to Pearl Harbor, Yamamoto had been demonized in America. In fact, his biographers find him to have been this country's friend, having lived in the United States and appreciated its ways. In the late 1930s, he was a leading opponent of any future war with the United States and even when planning the first attack warned that any conflict must be quick to the point. Were the war to last more than a year, he knew, American industrial might would overcome everything. Therefore, he suggested to his superiors, using poetic exaggeration to make his point, that the only way the United States could ever be pictured surrendering would be if Japanese forces could march to the White House door and demand it. This rhetoric may have momentarily impressed the Japanese war leadership, but in America it backfired, suggesting that Yamamoto had the impudence to suggest he himself could do this. Hence the man became a cartoon figure for righteous animosities, and the type of target any military leader or even the president himself might relish taking out.

Not that Thomas Lanphier was any less remarkable as a noteworthy personality type. In R. Cargill Hall's *Lightning Over Bougainville: The Yamamoto Mission Reconsidered* (1991), the officer in charge of fighter operations from Guadalcanal, John Condon, explains how the nature of combat changed: "when Lanphier came, it was another ballgame with that kind of aggressiveness at any altitude, down on the deck, or up at 35,000 feet. It was like turning night into day" (*LB*, p. 127). This spirit carries over into the Yamamoto mission, with Condon recalling how on the way home Lanphier radioed to base "to tell us 'that son-of-a-bitch would not be dictating peace terms to anyone in the White House'" (*LB*, p. 137). On landing, Lanphier leaps from his plane, jumps in a taxiway jeep and begins waving and shouting, "I got Yamamoto!" (*AY*, p. 82).

Given the attention paid to the likes of Joe Foss, Pappy Boyington, and Dick Bong, it is not surprising that Tom Lanphier, given his personality, would seek a piece of the same action so many high-profile Americans have already shared. *America wants aces*—this is the message World War I flying ace Eddie Rickenbacker carries into the theater on his morale-building tours, encouraging a new generation of flyers to break his own record and become the country's new ace of aces. No less a peacetime aviation hero than Charles Lindbergh visits the Southwest Pacific too, flying a P-38 to help devise new fuel mixtures for extending range—and, according to several accounts, shooting down an enemy plane. All this contributes to the atmosphere surrounding the Yamamoto mission, which itself fits right into the headline-making culture of the age.

Yet ace status does put a human face on an otherwise impersonal war. With such vast distances, great numbers, and long stretches of time involved, ace rankings also give the public a way of measuring success. The same arguments are made for the targeting of Admiral Yamamoto, a quite different kind of warfare from the type fought by Foss, Boyington, and Bong. The intersection of these two different but equally symbolic styles of air combat make for more than a coincidence. It is, as the USAAF report suggests, "almost as if the affair had been pre-arranged with the mutual consent of friend and foe" (*LB*, p. 160).

✪ ✪ ✪

ENDGAME
KAMIKAZES AND THE
BOMBING OF JAPAN

By the summer of 1944, the endgame strategy of America's war in the Pacific could commence, involving both sides in a different kind of war, the nature of which argued against any attempts at individualism. The issues were America's ability to mount mass bombing raids and Japan's unique response to this threat. Once the Imperial Navy's carrier strength was removed in the first Battle of the Philippine Sea (June 19–20), a key objective of the long campaign of island-hopping assaults, beginning at Guadalcanal, could be reached; when Saipan fell in July 1944, American bombers could begin preparations for flying to Japan, for the home islands were now within range. This reality prompted a new enemy strategy: suicide flights as a last-ditch attempt to protect the emperor and his homeland. For both sides, World War II was coming down to a case of ultimacies.

To win on its own terms, the United States had developed a new generation of weaponry and adopted tactics previously used by the RAF. The Boeing B-29 Superfortress was one-third larger than its B-17 Flying Fortress predecessor and was twice the plane in weight, bomb load, and range. Unlike the huge, high, and tight formations of the Eighth Air Force that had been hitting Germany with high explosives, these new aircraft would eventually be used successfully in two ways new to the USAAF: in relatively low-altitude (six thousand feet) incendiary raids that reduced large parts of Tokyo and other cities to cinders (as the British had done to Hamburg in 1943), and in the two missions at war's end that dropped single atomic bombs on Hiroshima and Nagasaki. Yet before either approach could be developed, planners knew their bombing forces had to be within range. With the taking of Saipan in the Marianas island chain just twelve hundred miles southeast of Tokyo, that hope was fulfilled.

Japan's reaction to the occupation of the Marianas was profound. Within days of the fall of Saipan, a protectorate since World War I and a colony rich in the culture of Nippon, Prime Minister Tojo's government fell. Some factions foresaw the war's end and lobbied for a negotiated peace. Others, however, began calling for an endgame strategy of their own, one that might do any or all of the following: disrupt the U.S. carrier fleet to the extent that the coming invasion of the Philippines would have to be abandoned, psychologically shock American morale and resolve so thoroughly as to blunt the war effort and lead to a détente within the present situation, or, in a worst-case scenario, allow the empire's defeat to assume heroic, even mythic proportions. This strategy created the kamikazes, suicide pilots taking their collective name from the "divine wind" that turned back Chinese invasion fleets in 1274 and again in 1281, frustrating Kublai Khan's intention to dominate Japan. Looking back to the *bushido* tradition of a thousand years before, the kamikaze ideal would face off against the imminence of a new era, the atomic age. The first kamikaze attack against American forces took place on October 15, 1944, when a plane piloted by Rear Admiral Masafumi Arima plunged into the carrier *Franklin* off Luzon.

Just a month before, Lieutenant Colonel Paul Tibbets of the U.S. Army Air Force had welcomed his new 509th Composite Group to Wendover, Utah, where its eighteen hundred men began training for the missions that would carry atomic bombs to Japan on August 6 and 9, 1945. Hence the philosophies of two distinct ages, separated by nearly one thousand years, were set to collide head-on.

Precipitating this collision was the B-29 itself. Rushed to production and given its final modifications in the field, it allowed U.S. strategy to be accelerated by more than a year and one half. Original plans called for a slow but steady advance from the South Pacific to the Central, with the Marianas to be taken early in 1946. With Superfortresses flying missions from China in June 1944, planners decided to bypass the Japanese fortress islands of Truk and Yap and to strike directly at Saipan. Mounting heavy bomber raids from China was a logistical nightmare: each B-29 had to make six trips across the Himalayas from India to its staging area at Kwanghan to amass enough fuel and explosives for a single venture to Japan, but the short-lived experiment made an impact on enemy thinking. Combined with the threat to Saipan, it put the Japanese in a new, defensive posture, as Saburo Sakai explains:

> War came to Japan in June of 1944. The effect on our population was unmistakable. On June 15 the people of Japan were shocked to hear that twenty bombers, tremendous giants of the air which dwarfed the powerful B-17, had flown an incredible distance from China to attack a city in Northern Kyushu. The raid did little damage, and twenty planes were hardly enough to cause national excitement. But in the homes and the stores, in the factories and on the streets,

everywhere in Japan, the people talked about the raid, dis-
cussed the fact that our fighters had failed to stop the
bombers. They all asked the same questions. Who was next?
When? And how many bombers would come?

The newscasters gave them something else to worry about.
The Americans had invaded Saipan. In more ways than one,
the war had come home. (*S*, p. 275)

Japan's response to this threat would create the conditions that made kamikaze tactics necessary and the atomic bombing of its mainland inevitable. To confront American forces in the Marianas, Japanese air elements assembled on Iwo Jima and the remnants of Japan's once great carrier fleet prepared for a major engagement. The plan was to launch carrier-borne planes from outside American range, have them make their attacks, then land in the still-held Marianas for refueling and a flight back to their flattops. The American hope was to keep these enemy air-fields bombed out, a strategy that worked so well it created what pilots called "The Marianas Turkey Shoot," in which seemingly endless streams of Japanese planes were fed into a virtual target range, where they fell by the hundreds. As Harry A. Gailey assesses it in *War in the Pacific* (1995), the ensuing air battles "showed clearly the superiority of the American pilots and planes. The F6F Hellcat, in the hands of a skilled pilot, was more than a match for Zeros operated by green, relatively untrained pilots" (*WIP*, p. 313). Close to four hundred enemy aircraft were downed, with the loss of just forty American planes, many of their pilots being rescued. U.S. submarines sank two Japanese carriers. Daring raids by American planes at the limit of their range sank another and damaged three more. Returning to their own task force in the moonless dark, they were saved by Admiral Marc Mitscher's brave decision to illuminate all eleven U.S. carriers with truck lights, running lights, and deck-outlining glow lights. Night fighters served as guides to the returning planes, while star shells burst and hung above the fleet.

American exuberance was hard to contain. It was from this battle that Ensign Wilbur "Spider" Webb's call for assistance would emerge as he approached Guam in his single F6F: "Any American fighter near Orote Peninsula, I have forty Jap planes surrounded and need a little help" (*DH*, p. 25). Harold Buell, leading his unit of six dive-bombers in an attack against the *Zuikaku*, relishes the fact that it is the last of the carriers that had raided Pearl Harbor to survive. It doesn't matter that the surrounding Japanese task force sends up so much antiaircraft fire that "I felt like I was diving into an Iowa plains hailstorm" (*DH*, p. 254). He closes his dive brakes to shoot ahead of it and drops his two bombs, then opens them again to slow his rapid descent. His plane takes a direct hit but gets him back to the carrier, leaving the *Zuikaku* so badly damaged that it will be nearly half a year before it can return to action, only to be sunk almost at once as a casualty of an Imperial Navy now bereft of its air cover.

Such was the outcome of this first Battle of the Philippine Sea, or "Marianas Turkey Shoot": that Japan's carrier-based war was over, while American forces were free to mount their assault on Saipan. On Saipan an air base could be built for the launching of B-29s against Japan. The first such attack would happen in November 1944. By March of 1945, the massive firestorm raids were under way, with Iwo Jima soon available as a fighter base for escorts and as an emergency strip for damaged bombers unable to make it all the way back. Four parallel runways on Tinian, just three miles south of Saipan, would send off B-29s in huge numbers to devastate Japan's ten largest cities, saving just Kyoto (for religious reasons) and Hiroshima and Nagasaki (where the full destructive force of America's new secret weapon could be measured). Meanwhile medium bombers (B-25s) would disrupt enemy shipping while older heavies (B-24s) destroyed Japan's Indonesian sources for oil, starving what remained of the empire's now land-based air power, the naval and army elements of which were becoming an increasingly kamikaze force, for the simple reason that nothing else seemed to work.

Aerial bombardment, a cornerstone of the European war, had been slow to find its place in the Pacific theater. At Pearl Harbor, Navy Lieutenant Clarence Dickinson could see from the Japanese attack how bombing had its limits:

> *For years I had been questioning statements about how a man could dodge a bomb dropped from an airplane and there we were, doing it! We would see one leave a Jap plane possibly fifteen hundred feet above the ground. Each time we stood fascinated. Suddenly the bomb would appear to be swelling; slanting towards us in its fall it would actually seem to grow bigger and bigger. At some point in its fall we would have to make up our minds whether it would fall on our side of the battleship or beyond it; if beyond it, we would stand and watch. Out of this experience I became wholly convinced that high altitude bombing (20,000 feet or more) is futile against ably handled ships on the open sea, unless there are such swarms of bombs falling in pattern as to make a change of course futile. Later experience was to confirm this conviction. (FG, p. 35)*

Like so many other prewar fantasies, the likelihood of B-17 formations blasting enemy fleets from the sea quickly evaporated in the new atmosphere of carrier-borne air assaults countered by dive and torpedo bombing. For the heavies, the early months of 1942 had been an ignominious tale of retreat and reorganization. Starting with the campaign from Guadalcanal, however, things improve, as written about by a pilot's wife, Priscilla Hardison, who in *The Suzy-Q* (1943) notes that not until October and November would the chance develop to mount the kind of raids their planes were designed for, pounding enemy installations at Rabaul. "Thinking back to some of their wild and lonely dashes out of Java, even early in the Australian fighting," she remarks, "they found it pretty wonderful to participate in missions where there would be as many as forty planes. It was wonderful at the time, and even more it was a foretaste of what could be expected for the future of our air forces in the Pacific Southwest" (*SQ*, p. 153). Their future would be as a long arm of artillery, hitting airfields, docks, harbor installations, and shipping at anchor. As far as bringing the war to the imperial fleet at sea, that was the business of smaller planes flown from carriers.

To deal with enemy shipping, whether of supplies or of troops, the closer tactics of medium and attack bombers were needed. Here is where two planes, the Douglas A-20 Havoc and the North American B-25 Mitchell, enter the fray, all the more prominently for the way they are modified by the first man to become individually prominent in this phase of the war, Paul Gunn. Pappy, as he'd been known through his aviation career, had been a Navy flight instructor and an operations manager with Philippine Airlines, and—beginning on December 8, 1941, Manila time, within hours of the Japanese attack at Pearl Harbor—became a captain in the USAAF. His family didn't escape the Japanese onslaught; for the war's duration, they were interned as prisoners of the enemy. But Pappy made it to Australia, where he became General George C. Kenney's right-hand man in the Fifth Air Force. Here he began modifying Kenney's planes in such an unorthodox manner yet with so much practical success that the general would write a book about him, *The Saga of Pappy Gunn* (1959). First to get his treatment was the Douglas Havoc, a twin-engined, mid-winged plane sold to the French (with a mind to the threat from Germany) and subsequently used by the British for the RAF campaign against Rommel's tanks in North Africa. However, there were no tanks in the South Pacific, and Gunn's reaction to their presence in this radically different theater was emphatic, as Kenney recalls:

> *When the A-20s had arrived, he had let anyone who would listen to him know in definite and highly profane terms what he thought of everyone from Washington to Australia who had anything to do with sending airplanes to "his" outfit without guns or bomb racks to fight a war. Some of his listeners were staff inspectors. While they may have admired Pappy's command of language they didn't seem to appreciate his comments and so noted in their reports.*
>
> *To add to his predicament, Pappy had by equally unorthodox methods managed to get hold of some .50-caliber machine guns, designed a package mount of four of them, and by rebuilding the entire nose of an A-20 had installed them. He tested the installation himself by conducting a one-man raid at treetop level on a Jap airdrome on the north coast of New Guinea. He had done a good job, too. A couple of Jap airplanes that had just landed had gone up in smoke, a gasoline dump was left ablaze, and from all the explosions after*

Pappy had finished his strafing run, it looked as though he had also hit an ammunition dump. (SP, p. 48)

Thus modified for treetop (or wavetop) attack, the A-20 Havocs helped Kenney's Fifth Air Force make an impact in the Pacific Theater even ahead of the Guadalcanal campaign. Armed with parafrags, small bombs descending by parachute and with delayed-action fuses, these planes could swoop in from nowhere, drop their ordnance right on shore installations or barge formations, and be out of sight before the bombs exploded. Ships themselves were hit with skip-bombing. Rather than aim at a moving target from high or even medium altitude, Pappy's A-20s could come right down to sea level and skip a delayed-fuse bomb across the surface like a stone, striking the enemy vessel broadside just where it met the water, its most vulnerable point. B-25 Mitchells underwent similar modifications, with the bombardier and his nose position replaced with eight forward-firing fixed machine guns operated by the pilot, who also released the bombs being aimed directly into the target in front of him.

Air power's redesigned role in the South Pacific got its best, and grisliest, demonstration on March 2, 1943, when more than 130 of Kenney's planes attacked a twenty-ship convoy en route from Rabaul to Lae on the north coast of New Guinea. Pappy Gunn's modified B-25s made their debut here, skip-bombing four cargo vessels and two destroyers in the initial fifteen minutes of battle. Before this engagement, to become known as the Battle of the Bismark Sea, came to a close, the convoy was in shreds, its waters turned red by the blood of so many thousand Japanese troops blown out of their transports and strafed mercilessly. The carnage was such that Pappy's pilots were sickened by the job they had to do; one returned from the mission and committed suicide. But reinforcements and supplies had been denied to an important obstacle in the American progress northwest from Guadalcanal, and attacks like these would speed the way toward the taking of the Marianas sixteen months later, well ahead of even the most optimistic schedule.

Not all flyers were sickened by the nature of their new air weapon. One B-25 pilot, R. E. Peppy Blount, knew enough about the other side's ability to inflict horror that he could take positive pleasure in the physical power Pappy's modifications had provided. In *We Band of Brothers* (1984) he sorts out his own feelings in making war this way:

> *Flying the strafers was the nearest thing to hand to hand combat without actually being on the ground facing the enemy with a rifle in your hands. At twenty feet you saw the expression on a face, the fear in the eyes, the frantic dive for cover, the figures sprawling and crawling in the mud all in the streaking fraction of a second's glance at an enemy taken completely by surprise. That feeling was good! It was when you had waited too long to get down on the deck, when you'd blown your surprise, the enemy knew you were coming and you felt all hell about to break loose, with no place to hide— that's when you got sick! I learned quickly that the ground, the trees, the natural or man-made obstacles, the topography and terrain were the best, closest, and most appreciated friends of the strafers. That was a game of the quick and the dead and only the quick were still alive.* (WB, p. 10)

Fighter pilots like Edwards Park liked the speedy job these B-25s did. It made escort duty much easier, "a job we liked because they were fast and sure, thundering in very low, blasting everything in sight, then gone in a flash, and we with them" (*AT*, p. 119). For his part, Peppy Blount feels that once he can get in there, nothing can survive his onslaught, given that he's so close it feels as if "I was shooting *up* into most targets! With this concentrated firepower I could bust a building, neutralize and sink a ship, wipe out a gun revetment, disintegrate a train or rolling stock and give myself the edge of that critical fraction of a second when I could reach out to silence or out draw the guns of the enemy" (*WB*, p. 125). Two B-25s, wing to wing, could destroy an enemy destroyer, its superstructure melting in their fire and its decks chewed up as if by termites. His plane's armament, as modified by Pappy Gunn, provides "the most destructive firepower that I saw in World War II. It could only be matched, in intensity, by the collective firepower of a warship of the destroyer or larger class" (*WB*, p. 293). In a theater where the Navy was delivering most of the destruction, Pappy Gunn's little B-25s did more than hold their own. Pappy himself would not only make the modifications but would dream up missions and want to fly them himself. Meeting Wayne Rothgeb, he tries to talk the P-38 pilot into escorting five of his B-25s to Lae, where they would land on the airstrip "and then turn the planes towards those bastards in the caves. That will fix them! We'll blast them out!" (*NG*, p. 147). This mission never happened. But when Hap Arnold, chief of the Army Air Forces, learned that Gunn's changes had worked so well at the Battle of the Bismark Sea, he ordered the man assigned to temporary duty at Wright Field in Dayton Ohio, "to teach my engineers something" (*SP*, p. 61). From this point on, Pappy Gunn's radically improvised field modifications became a standard for future manufacture.

With A-20 attack bombers and modified B-25 mediums inter-
dicting supplies and tearing up the Japanese bases standing in
the way of the long advance up from Guadalcanal and the
Solomons, the American offensive would find its most useful
long-range air asset in the B-24. Why not B-17s? The Flying
Fortresses arriving at Pearl Harbor during the December 7
attack had taken the enemy's first blows, and the few that were
able to fight their way south from the Philippines to Java
astounded Zero pilots with their size and heavy armament. But
by 1943 the mighty Eighth Air Force was on its way to commanding the skies over Europe; there, the B-17's higher ceiling
helped flyers cope with the powerful German antiaircraft guns,
while its ability to maintain tight formations allowed a concentration of firepower against Luftwaffe fighters. For the war to be
fought by the Fifth Air Force, starting from Australia and heading up across New Guinea to the island chains stretching across
the South Pacific toward Japan, flak was less of a problem than
range. And range was what the B-24 Liberator had, more than
was needed in missions from England, where a prime require-
ment was to be able to sustain heavy battle damage and limp
home over the occupied countries and the Channel, something
at which the Flying Fortress was better. Theater commanders in
Europe were willing to let more B-24s be assigned to the Pacific,
if that meant they would have the lion's share of new B-17s.

Hence the Consolidated B-24 became the Pacific's heavy
bomber of note until the Boeing B-29 could begin hitting the
Japanese mainland from the Marianas. Because so many of its
early missions involved crossing the Owen Stanley Range, these
Liberators became icons of the war in their discovery as wrecks
nearly half a century later. "There are more planes missing in
Papua New Guinea than in any other country on earth, many of

them in the mountains, at sites never reached by the Australian and American Graves Registration teams that searched shortly after the Second World War" (*MP*, p. 14), writes Susan Sheehan in *A Missing Plane* (1986). Equipped with identification technologies developed during the Vietnam War and motivated to honor the memory of the American servicemen whose stature had been compromised by the problematics of this more recent military conflict, recovery units during the 1980s reaped a large harvest of crashed Liberators, often with the remains of their crews. Such work, fitting and important for its own sake, may also have contributed to the renewed interest in World War II that reached great proportions in the 1990s (with its various fifty-year anniversaries) and has not subsided yet.

For two years, running up to and through the summer of 1944, the Pacific theater's B-24 Liberators had bombed the jungles, taking a necessary but second-place role to the medium and attack bombers that chewed up more specific targets. Sometimes their work was even more functional, such as to draw up enemy fighters for the likes of Pappy Boyington and Dick Bong to dispatch. Even the taking of Morotai, just four hundred miles from Mindanao (the southernmost of the Philippines), failed to give Liberator crews a more clearly defined sense of purpose. For as pilot John Boeman puts it in *Morotai: A Memoir of War*, "I was reconciled to the idea that neither my crew nor any other was likely to win the war in one great heroic mission from Morotai." Instead, he could pledge himself "to do the best we could on each mission whether or not we ever met any Japanese. After all, it finally had sunk in to me, our job was only to put our bombs where we were told to put them. It was somebody else's job to decide where that was and whether or not there were any Japanese there" (*MO*, p. 162). Unlike the bombing missions flown by B-24s from England in the Eighth Air Force and from southern Italy in the Fifteenth Air Force, early years in the Pacific campaign provided little in the way of strategic targets, and many crews shared John Boeman's frustration.

During the fall months of 1944, however, even as bases in the Marianas were being readied for the new B-29s and their raids on the Japanese homeland, a plan for the B-24s was put into practice that gave them a more dramatic role in helping bring about the enemy's strategic defeat. The inspiration came from the Fifteenth Air Force's destruction of the oil refineries in Ploesti, Romania—a long and difficult but eventually successful operation that created major fuel shortages for the Wehrmacht and Luftwaffe. As Germany looked to Romania for oil, so did Japan depend upon its supplies from the Dutch West Indies— obtaining these sources had been one of Japan's major induce- ments for going to war. American submarines had quickly inter- dicted the shipment of crude oil back home, but Japan had countered by expanding refineries in Borneo to produce fuel on the spot, from where it was available to ships and planes in the area. The huge installation at Balikpapan was capable of provid- ing all the petroleum Japanese forces would need to defend the Philippines. General Douglas MacArthur, however, wished to deny them that fuel, and so asked that B-24 Liberators destroy this target, even though it was eleven hundred miles from their base in New Guinea. His challenge was a tempting one, as he explained to Colonel Tom Musgrave, the B-24 commander: "For the first time, you'll be on a target that parallels the kinds of tar- gets they have in Europe" (*DSS*, p. 15).

The difference was that by this time the B-17s and B-24s in Europe were being given fighter escort. In the Pacific, such help from the bombers' "little friends" was still six months away. Yet in five raids from September 30 to October 18, the Balikpapan refineries were taken out, meaning that MacArthur's long-sought retaking of the Philippines could be launched against an enemy starved for fuel. In the last major naval action of the war, Japan's surface fleet was effectively destroyed; the Battle of Leyte Gulf on October 23, 1944 marked the end of a campaign dating from the Coral Sea and Midway. Now would begin the endgame strategy that prompted each side to put radically new pieces into the game: for America, B-29s that would bring fire and eventually nuclear fission to Japan, and for the Japanese themselves, their own expression of the ultimate act in warfare, the kamikaze.

In a new millennium when suicide attacks have become an instrument of terror, memories of the Japanese kamikaze warfare of over half a century before have become complicated by the very real nature of such a threat to everyday domestic life. Yet even in 1944 and 1945, when its targets were strictly military, the kamikaze phenomenon eclipsed Americans' ability to comprehend the nature of this act. This lack of understanding continues to the present day, to the extent that the campaign's effect remains seriously underestimated. Today even Americans with a good historical sense acknowledge the terror of these kamikaze acts but fall short of appreciating the numbers. How many such attacks were there? Several hundred, people suggest, rarely suspecting that there were over five thousand, nearly half of which successfully hit their targets. American losses were not just great—they were staggering, and threatening to the war's progress. At one point, there was even consideration given to suspending the Philippine invasion, so great was the carnage. As Raymond Lamont-Brown computes it in *Kamikaze: Japan's Sui-*

cide Samurai (1997), "The truth was that more US warships had been sunk in three months of operations in the Philippines than had been lost or damaged in the previous Pacific naval battles including Pearl Harbor" (*KJ*, p. 82). Indeed, by the war's end the United States Navy would lose more vessels to the kamikazes than to any other foe in its history. Making the ordeal even worse was that the nature of these losses had to be kept secret, lest stateside morale plummet at the thought that a war so close to being won might be prolonged or end in a stalemate.

The Empire of Japan could never win World War II with kamikazes, but the immensity of these suicide attacks gave the enemy hope that an acceptable form of peace might be negotiated, short of the unconditional surrender that had been Allied policy since the Casablanca Conference early in 1943. Also, with its surface fleet destroyed and its air forces too short of fuel to allow the high proficiency training needed for conventional forms of attack, a kamikaze assault was the last remaining option. In terms of planes available and young men to fly them, the numbers were there. And even more effective would be the psychological nature of the assault. Here is where the very special nature of the kamikaze's act made its impact.

The idea of going down in flames while taking an enemy along is far from foreign to American combat sensibilities, and quite early in the war such actions were justly celebrated. In the Battle of the Coral Sea, Navy Lieutenant John J. Powers took out a Japanese carrier by guiding his dive bomber to point-blank range—surviving antiaircraft fire and holding his Dauntless SBD in perfect position for a key hit, only to perish (with his gunner) because he was unable to escape the blast area. Yet he was trying to escape it, putting his plane into recovery for normal flight before the explosion caught up with him. At Midway,

Captain Richard E. Fleming's obsolescent Vought SB2U Vindicator (from the only squadron to take this old plane into a major battle) was crippled by Japanese gunners as it dove on the cruiser *Mikuma*. As Walter Lord describes in *Incredible Victory* (1967), "Somehow he kept his lead, made his run, dropped his bomb. Then—a blazing comet—he plunged into the turret of his target" (*IV*, p. 261). To Mitsuo Fuchida, observing the act from below, Fleming's act fits in with Japanese tradition of *bushido*, qualifying as "a daring suicide crash" (*M*, p. 226), but even here there could be no sense of premeditation, because Fleming and his back seat man were goners anyway. Instead, losses were easier to bear if they made some tactical sense, and so it was the idea of accomplishing something, rather than dying for nothing, that characterized accounts of such early sacrifices. In 1942 some enemy pilots did the same thing when fatal crashes were inevitable.

With the bona fide kamikaze attacks that were first launched in the Philippines, beginning in October of 1944, an entirely new style of warfare would be brought into play. *The Divine Wind* (1958) is an important volume coauthored (with individually signed chapters) by Rikihei Inoguchi (senior staff officer to Vice Admiral Onishi, originator of the kamikaze forces) and Tadashi Nakajima (operations and training officer for the first kamikaze units). Its foreword by an American naval officer from the Philippines campaign, Vice Admiral C. R. Brown, explores the "mixed emotions" evident when watching "a man about to die—a man *determined* to die in order that he might destroy us in the process." There was, naturally, "a hypnotic fascination to the sight so alien to our Western philosophy," a "detached horror" in the witnessing of such a spectacle, even though the viewer was an intended victim. "We forgot self for the moment,"

Brown explains, "as we groped hopelessly for the thoughts of that other man up there. And dominating it all was a strange admixture of respect and pity—respect for any person who offers the supreme sacrifice to the things he stands for, and pity for the utter frustration which was epitomized by the suicidal act" (*DW*, p. v). How could so many men, thousands upon thousands, be so motivated? Brown finds a possible answer by distinguishing the nature of their act:

> *It is certainly not that the enemy was more courageous than we. One of the earliest lessons one learns in battle is that courage is a very common human quality. Mute evidence is the story of our Torpedo Squadron Eight at Midway, and the unforgettable picture I once observed on board the Essex when I watched the 20-millimeter gun crews stand unflinchingly to their guns until enveloped in flames, in an effort to beat off a kamikaze.*
>
> *But there was a fundamental difference in the heroism of the opposing warriors. The Japanese resolutely closed the last avenue of hope and escape, the American never did. To the Western mind there must be that last slim chance of survival— the feeling that, though a lot of other chaps may die, you yourself somehow are going to make it back.* (*DW*, pp. v–vi)

By late in 1944 the Americans and Japanese had learned some things about one another, yet a fundamental sense of dislike grounded mutual appraisals. And at the center of it was a cultural contrast displaying its highest profile in the opinion one takes regarding the kamikaze. Consider Walt Bayler's attitude, quoted earlier in this volume: "We said, truthfully enough, that for Japan to pick a scrap with us would be equivalent to committing national suicide, forgetting that kara-kiri, or as they more correctly call it, *seppuku*, is a favorite indoor sport of the little saffron-colored so-and-sos" (*LM*, p. 12). Other books published at the time were even more outspoken in their disdain for Japanese traditions, misunderstood as they were. Nor were Japanese judgments about their enemy more accurate, as Yasuo Kuwahara, who would train as a kamikaze pilot, notes in his memoir, *Kamikaze* (1957). The occasion is a conversation between brother and sister during the final winter of war, as Kuwahara, a champion glider pilot, prepares for military service. The two wish for summer, then turn to wishes for peace. When his sibling expresses wonder that there can be people who hate them, who wish to make conquest, the young pilot reasons with her. "Why not?" he offers. "We hate them. We want to conquer them, don't we?" To the reader, he summarizes the Japanese view:

> *The Allies were big people, pale-skinned, with strange hair. Red hair, some of them—others yellow. They were selfish, prodigal and lazy, wallowing in luxury. Their soldiers were savage and guttural-voiced. "Do you believe what they say about American marines, that they are required to kill and eat their grandmothers? That's what half the people are saying at school." (K, p. 31)*

His sister scoffs at the idea, insisting that these notions are ridiculous beyond belief. But Kuwahara knows they are shared by some of his friends in school and counters that "No doubt the Caucasian concept regarding us was just as extreme." He quickly runs down the checklist so familiar to Americans at the time, that the enemies "were yellow-skinned, slant-eyed monkeys, dwelling in paper houses," bereft of originality and capable only of making copies. All of them were "sneaky, treacherous and fanatic," with "Dirty Jap" a popular epithet. "Often I have wondered since," he recalls, "just how much such forms of ignorance (on both sides) have contributed to wars" (*K*, p. 31).

Thus the two sides would face off for the final year of World War II. The first genuine kamikaze attack was one that jumped the gun, so to speak. On October 15, 1944, Rear Admiral Masafumi Arima took to heart the plans being laid by Vice Admiral Takajiro Onishi that a dedicated corps of suicide pilots be created from available naval air forces and directed against the American ships approaching the Philippines. The carrier *Franklin* would be his target; to the great surprise of his own men, and to the even greater consternation of the personnel aboard, Arima crashed his plane into the *Franklin*'s flight deck, setting off fires that spread to its powder magazines. Close to sinking, the carrier was withdrawn for repairs. This was Onishi's hope for the more properly organized kamikaze campaign beginning with the Battle of Leyte Gulf a week later: that a relatively few but effective strikes could take the American carrier force out of action. Such a knockout never happened, but the war was prolonged; even General Curtis LeMay, the most optimistic proponent of strategic bombing, reckoned that it would take until November 1945 for Japan to be brought to its knees, and more conservative planners believed an invasion would be required to do the job. That hostilities ceased in mid-August was only due to an even newer style of warfare being introduced—at which time, according to Robert C. Mikesh in *Broken Wings of the Samurai* (1993), there were no less than 10,500 aircraft prepared for kamikaze use, double the number that had already been used (*BW*, p. 7).

During this final year of warfare, two kamikaze forces evolved. The first, consisting of piloted rocket-propelled glide bombs to be dropped from mother ships, was developed in the summer of 1944 and given rush priority after the Marianas Turkey Shoot made carrier-based aviation a thing of the past for Japan. The craft, called *Ohka* (for "exploding cherry blossom") by the Japanese and derided as *Baka* ("stupid") by the Americans, was still in a testing phase when Vice Admiral Onishi, ready to assume command of the First Aviation Fleet in the Philippines, decided that conditions were so desperate as to require a stop-gap measure. In this decision was born the kamikaze corps, flying conventional aircraft and named for the divine wind of Japanese history, signaling the hope for a miraculous intervention in the face of grave national danger.

From the harsh controversies that surrounded the kamikaze notion during the war and that have continued in years afterward—even into the twenty-first century when kamikaze pilots whose numbers were never called survive as honored veterans—several key facts emerge. The first and most important truth is that the idea of mounting out-and-out suicide missions originated among pilots themselves, especially within the lower ranks (relatively few flyers were commissioned officers, especially toward the war's end). Second, even once the kamikaze corps were officially established, service in them was volunteer—strictly so in the navy, and ostensibly so in the army, although many young pilots in the latter branch learned to their dismay that volunteering was expected. Third, initial hopes were that the entire kamikaze campaign might achieve its goal in the Philippines, knocking out the American carrier force and keeping the Japanese homeland secure, at least until an acceptable peace could be negotiated. The fourth truth about kamikazes was kept quiet during the war: that their attacks were very costly to the U.S. Navy, so costly that intelligence forces feared that a revelation of the kamikazes' effectiveness would encourage even more such attacks (and perhaps weaken morale at home). The fifth and last element ties in with the first. Given that the kamikaze spirit was genuinely indigenous to so many young Japanese flyers now fighting this war, prospects were that Japan would not surrender easily. Inspired by a heritage dating back to their country's mediaeval period, these pilots were motivated to the extent that their kamikaze campaign was kept alive far longer than planners on either side might have expected— through the Philippines debacle, through the bloody defense of Okinawa, and right up to the day in August of 1945 when the emperor counseled his people that fighting on would be wrong. A mediaeval strength had just collided head-on with the ethos of a new, postmodern age: atomic warfare. Afterwards, neither country would ever be the same.

Memoirs from the opposing sides of this kamikaze campaign read like accounts from two different worlds. From the American point-of-view, the impression is horrible indeed. Seaman First Class Pete Burt survived four kamikaze attacks in the Philippines; his first ship, the escort carrier *Ommaney Bay*, was sunk, while the cruiser that rescued him, the *Columbia*, sustained three extremely serious hits. *Kamikaze Nightmare* (1995), written by his brother Ron, contains Pete's descriptions of just what being targeted by a kamikaze was like. Typical in this account from January 6, 1945, when as it approaches the Lingayen Gulf the *Columbia* comes within range of no less than seventy enemy airfields, with attacks possible from any and every direction. From his position on deck Pete sees a destroyer hit by a suicide plane. Then a dive-bomber, perhaps attempting a conventional attack, sweeps in low over the *Columbia*, clips the ship's radio antenna, and dissolves in an explosion just beyond the other side:

The plane passes within thirty feet of Jack, Alvin, and me. We duck inside the gun sight tub. Aviation fuel sprays all over the bridge around our G. Q. [General Quarters] station.

The damage control parties jump into action quickly. They prevent fires from starting as they spray water all over the exposed areas. We are fortunate to have only one casualty reported. (KN, p. 78)

A near miss, Burt reports, can cause almost as much trouble as a hit. Gas can spill and ignite across the decks. Even the sight of an approaching plane can be unnerving, the kamikaze plunging through antiaircraft fire seemingly untouched. The *Columbia* has survived the event he has just described, but three hours later the attacks resume, with the battleship *California* taking a serious hit and the *Columbia* in the sights of another suicide plane. Vice Admiral Onishi had calculated rates of fire and compared them with the space covered; odds were very heavy in the attacker's favor, something Pete Burt could see for himself. On America's side, Vice Admiral John S. McCain stepped up gunners' training to achieve a greater density and higher rapidity of fire. He also combined four task groups into three, allowing for more screening of the carriers by destroyers, plus replaced dive-bomber squadrons with more fighters, so that air patrols could keep a lid on activity from the many Japanese airfields scattered throughout the islands. Yet more than half of all incoming kamikazes still managed to get through, as does the one Pete Burt has been watching in the distance, stalking the cruiser from just outside the range of fire and then setting course.

"He puts his sights on the *Columbia*," Burt notes, and imagines how the full-throttle dive raises an engine scream that blots out all sound of exploding antiaircraft shells. "He appears invincible," the seaman admits, and shudders as the plane crashes into the main deck. A bomb the kamikaze has carried penetrates below, starting infernos on the first and second decks and puncturing the hull in several places. Fires are everywhere. "Screams of dying men screech from below decks as the damage control people seal the compartments, trapping many unfortunate sailors" (*KN*, p. 79). It is Burt's unceasing nightmare that he is unable to save these men, among them several of his closest friends.

Postwar research by Pete's brother Ron has come up with the identities of five Zero pilots, one of whom wrought the devastation just described. The five flew from the air base at Mabalacat on Luzon. Two of them were technical school alumni, while another pair was just minimally trained in a flight course for noncommissioned officers. About the fifth, Yoshiyuki Taniuchi, nothing is known beyond his name and rank. None returned from the mission, and so nothing can be known of their personal feelings. But from accounts of those who trained with the kamikazes, and from the memoirs of suicide pilots who survived because their missions were canceled, there emerges a story of another world entirely. Contrary to popular belief, it is not a world of crazed vengeance or of robotlike obedience. Instead, the qualities that emerge are quite surprising ones.

"The philosophy of *Bushido* brought a mental calm to the kamikazes" (*KJ*, p. 22), Raymond Lamont-Brown explains. Its modern equivalent, of course, had been put to militaristic purposes, refabricated as "a medieval emotionalism that Japan was superior and that it was a divine mission to liberate the Orient from Western influence" (*KJ*, p. 20). To Occidental temperaments, this historic revival seemed at best atavistic and at worst a style of maniacal brainwashing that had created an enemy force of senseless robots. Nevertheless, evidence suggests that the pilots who flew these one-way missions were anything but throwbacks or automatons. Having studied historical records and personal accounts, Bernard Millot concludes in *Divine Thunder: The Life and Death of the Kamikazes* (1971) that "as soon as the Philippines were threatened, the Japanese propensity for self-sacrifice reappeared spontaneously" (*DT*, p. 232). Their task "did not spring from a frenzied collective insanity," but rather was "the logical outcome of a whole national psychology reacting to a specific situation," very much as if "the fruit of a two-thousand-year-old tree had been abruptly ripened by the electric atmosphere of a storm" (*DT*, p. 233).

Ripened on that tree are flyers such as Ryuji Nagatsuka, whose *I Was a Kamikaze* (1974) tells of his career in conventional air combat and training for one last act as a kamikaze. Hiroshima and Nagasaki intervene, and so he survives the war, but with memories of something other than futile sacrifice. Recounting the story of a small kamikaze group in the Philippines that aborts its mission three days in a row when it cannot locate the American task force, he contrasts his colleagues' tearful humiliation with their eventual success, when on day four they locate their enemy. The pilot in command, Navy Lieutenant Yukio Seki, does not hesitate to act:

> At 1040 the lieutenant's formation chanced upon some American aircraft carriers about 850 nautical miles off the island of Leyte. Seki waggled his wings as a signal to attack, dived, and skimmed just above the waves towards one of the carriers. Before the ship could begin evasive manoeuvres, or the anti-aircraft guns could open fire, he had crashed into the carrier, exactly between the flight deck and the hull. The bomb he was

carrying exploded, making a huge hole in the side of the ship. Another Zero followed Seki and, with consummate skill, plunged into the hole already ripped open in the side of the ship. The carrier fled, zigzagging as it went. Pilots in the other Zeros saw flames and black smoke billowing to a height of 3,000 feet. Another Zero crashed into a second carrier and set it on fire. Yet another hit a heavy cruiser, which belched smoke and was presently shaken by secondary explosions. The Shikishima group had finally carried out their suicide-mission! (*IW*, p. 152)

As Nagatsuka admits, it is a "horrifying spectacle, but, at the same time, a historic event." And not just because this particular group had been frustrated in its earlier attempts. Throughout his own training, which has involved diving at ground targets and pulling out only at the last second, the author has fought the inclination to close his eyes at what in real action would be his own destruction. In view of the *Shiskishima* group's success, he now appreciates how the act can be done. "The heroes of this first suicide group had undoubtedly kept their eyes wide open right to the fatal moment of the crash," he avers, "as if they wanted to watch their own lives vanish forever" (*IW*, p. 152).

Ryuji Nagatsuka's penchant for the poetic image is characteristic of his background, one shared with many other kamikaze pilots. The best flyers—those with career military training and many hours of combat experience—were saved for escort duties, getting the kamikazes through the American combat air patrols, then themselves returning to escort more missions. They were too valuable to be routinely expended in crash dives, though many fought for the privilege. Nor were the ranks of future kamikazes filled with young men with scientific or engineering backgrounds; these were needed at home for the war industries. Instead, great numbers came from law schools and graduate programs in the humanities. Nagatsuka's schoolboy hopes were to be a scholar of French literature. Throughout training and service his dearest possession is a two-volume edition of George Sand's *Les Maîtres Sonneurs*. It is from a literary perspective, then—one shared with so many of his colleagues—that he can assess the nature of his work. His initial training flight is thrilling, of course, but he also knows that "this first step in the air was leading me to my death" (*IW*, p. 44), given that any aerial adventure involves calculated risk. When Vice Admiral Onishi briefs the first kamikazes, including Lieutenant Seki's *Shikishima* group, senior staff officer Rikihei Inoguchi can observe in these men "a composure and tranquility which comes to those who are aware of their own significance and power," even though he finds it "impossible to suppress a feeling of protest against our country for having come to such dire straits, against the spirit of the young men themselves, against Admiral Onishi, and against my own involvement in these circumstances" (*DW*, pp. 19–20). Half a year later, when the defense of Okinawa has sparked an even deadlier kamikaze campaign, Commander Tadashi Nakajima can still marvel at the calm exhibited by an *Ohka* pilot, Lieutenant (Junior Grade) Saburo Dohi. From the crew of Dohi's mother ship, Nakajima learns how the young man spent his final hours en route to battle, saying "he wished to nap and asked to be called 30 minutes before arrival in the target area. He had stretched out on a makeshift canvas cot and gone to sleep. Upon being awakened he had smiled and said, 'Time passes quickly, doesn't it?'" (*DW*, pp. 153–54). Shaking hands with the bomber's crew, Dohi climbs into his rocket-propelled craft and begins his one-way mission.

At the end of it, the destroyer *Stanley* is hit. As for Dohi's last moments, one can consider Hatsuho Naito's general appraisal in *Thunder Gods: The Kamikaze Pilots Tell Their Story* (1989) that "not any" of these flyers "shouted 'Long Live the Emperor!' as they dived their bomb-filled planes into the enemy." Instead, "They agreed to die for the sake of their families and their relatives in the firm belief that their death would contribute to their well-being" (*TG*, p. 189).

How the kamikaze campaign ever happened is owing to the conflux of several forces. Tactically, the interdiction of fuel limited Japanese operations to just those guaranteeing immediate results. Strategically, the loss of Japan's carrier-borne air power in the Marianas Turkey Shoot meant that the last remaining hope was for land-based planes to do the job. Navy flyers were good at it, Army pilots less so (because they were less likely to be true volunteers and because they had no training in recognizing and approaching nautical targets). Emotionally, there was a great impetus to defend the homeland, once Japan came within range of American bombers. There is no doubt about the spirit for this campaign arising from the pilots themselves. But in Vice Admiral Takajiro Onishi, this spirit found an able director who was quite literally in the right place at the right time. Instructed to keep Admiral Halsey's carrier fleet from supporting the Philippine invasion, he knew only one way how. As Edwin P. Hoyt observes in *The Kamikazes* (1983), "For the first time he was actually in control of a tactical situation" (*KS*, p. 34). And the tactic he chose was that of the suicide mission, simply because nothing else had even the slightest chance of working. Since the death of Admiral Isoroku Yamamoto, Takajiro Onishi had emerged as the leading voice for Japanese air power, and with the need to defend the Philippines and then Okinawa, a new style of aerial warfare had been convincingly articulated. The vice admiral's proof came as early as October 25, the first day of heavy kamikaze action, when the death plunge of a single Zero resulted in the sinking of the *St. Lo*, an escort carrier that had previously survived the eighteen-inch guns of the super-battleship *Yamoto* and fought off any number of conventional air attacks. The Zero and its bomb had plunged through the *St. Lo*'s wooden flight deck, exploding on the hangar deck below. Here American planes, already armed with their own bombs and torpedoes, exploded, tearing the vessel in two. It was an awesome spectacle, all the more so because it had been accomplished by a single pilot and his aircraft. There could be no arguing with the material cost-effectiveness of a kamikaze assault, and with his flyers' ready consent, Onishi's path was clear for directing the considerable air resources that remained.

To American pilots flying from the carriers these enemies were attacking, the kamikazes were less of a terror than another foe—a more outrightly aggressive one, but still part of the mechanics of flying. For John F. Smith, whose F6F was part of the fighter complement aboard the escort carrier *Suwannee* during the Battle of Leyte Gulf, kamikaze hits can be described with precision. In *Hellcats Over the Philippine Deep* (1995), he notes how an approaching plane does it: hiding in the radar's blind spot just above the carrier, rolling over into a steep dive, and hitting just forward of the elevator, a spot where the flight deck is weakest. It penetrates to the hangar deck, "leaving the front silhouette of an airplane" (*H*, p. 139). In his own *Skipper: Confessions of a Fighter Squadron Commander, 1943–1944* (1985), Navy flyer T. Hugh Winters describes a kamikaze "on final" (*SK*, p. 143), technical language more appropriate for an aircraft on final approach for landing. True, there is a pilot in the plane, and his body survives the crash into Fly Control II on the carrier's bridge, where it is left to hang from the superstructure—"No one volunteered to cut him down. A sad day for *Lexington*; a glorious day for him" (*SK*, p. 144). By the time of the Okinawa battle, Hellcat pilot Hamilton McWhorter considers kamikaze assaults a matter of grim routine:

> There were so many attacks during this time that it seemed as if general quarters was sounded whenever we turned around. Quite often, we just stayed at general quarters for hours at a time. We actually started to become conditioned to it—just like lab rats. It got to the point that as long as the *Randolph* was firing her 5-inch guns, we pretty much conducted business as usual, figuring that the bogey was still 4 or 5 miles away. When the 40mm guns opened up, we became a bit more concerned, because that meant the bogey had closed to maybe just a couple of miles. If the 20mm guns started firing there would be a mad rush to get down to the wardroom, below the armored deck. (*FH*, p. 200)

Yet each hit was fully appreciated. "What a weapon it was!" exclaims Harold Buell, by now coordinating fighter-bombers with his dive-bomber squadron to clear the ocean of Japan's last ships. "Here was a flying bomb with a perfect guidance system—human mind and eyes for radar and human hands to move the controls." Beyond even the mental terror was the material consequence: more vessels lost than in the entire history of the U.S. Navy, all of them sent to the bottom or taken out of battle just as victory seemed within reach. "The destruction caused our naval forces by this weapon during the coming months was to have horrible consequences," Buell explains, "and it most certainly helped to make the decision to use the atomic bomb an easier one for American leaders in the summer of 1945" (*DH*, p. 295).

In Honolulu, where for America World War II began, there is a narrative set in stone that highlights the developments of this long conflict. Appropriately, it is located in the National Memorial Cemetery of the Pacific that occupies the crater of a long extinct volcano known as Punchbowl. The story portrayed on carefully crafted mosaic panels starts with the attack on Pearl Harbor and continues with maps and brief narratives of the naval and island-hopping campaigns that occupied the next three years. The last panel, however, tells of events concluding in March of 1945, when the island of Iwo Jima was secured. As Kathy E. Ferguson and Phyllis Turnbull indicate in *Oh, Say, Can You See? The Semiotics of the Military in Hawai'i* (1999), as far as the memory of the memorial is concerned "the war ends at Iwo Jima; there is no representation of Hiroshima or Nagasaki" (*OH*, p. 123). The omission is greater than that, because in terms of endgame strategy the capture of Iwo Jima was in fact the beginning of a final move, not the conclusion of it. Iwo Jima was taken not simply as part of the island-by-island advance toward Japan (many outposts of the empire had been bypassed), but as a fighter base for P-51 Mustangs (which could escort B-29s on bombing raids to Japan) and as an emergency landing strip for damaged bombers unable to make the long haul back to Saipan, Tinian, and Guam in the Marianas. Even more so than the capture of Saipan, the fall of Iwo Jima exposed the enemy's homeland to devastation from the air. In this same month of March, the very effective firestorm raids began, setting a style of warfare that would climax with the ultimate destruction from the skies, atomic bombs. Iwo Jima was not the end, but just the beginning of it.

Why then is the strategic bombing of Japan omitted from the Punchbowl memorial? Perhaps for the same reason that the Smithsonian's Air and Space Museum was forced to modify its exhibit of the plane that carried the atomic bomb to Hiroshima. Warfare may at times be popular, but heavy bombing never is. In such raids, whether undertaken with incendiaries, high explosives, or atomic weapons, the casualties are high and horrific. Mass bombing does not distinguish soldiers from civilians or military installations from cultural treasures. Its effects are intended to be psychological as well as material, and in this very effectiveness lies both its value and its bane. The Axis powers— Italy in Ethiopia, Japan in China, Germany in Poland, the Netherlands, and England—had begun with tactical bombing. None of these countries ever had long-range aircraft capable of carrying a heavy load of explosives. The London Blitz, for example, which killed twenty-five thousand people, was accomplished by two-engined medium bombers carrying a small fraction of what planes like the British Lancaster and American B-29 could eventually drop on Germany and Japan. Nevertheless, as Arthur Harris, the future leader of RAF Bomber Command, said of the Luftwaffe bombers raining their destruction on London in 1940, they were sowing the wind. By war's end the enemy's home cities in both the European and Pacific theaters lay ruined.

Ruins themselves would be strategic bombing's monument. In Berlin, the gutted main tower of the Kaiser Wilhelm Church has been left standing as it was at war's end, just as in Hiroshima the skeletal frame of that city's Industrial Promotion Hall, one of the few structures to survive the atomic blast, remains today as a sentinel to nuclear holocaust. As for the war's victors, remembering the bombing campaign can be awkward. In Britain, the flyers of Bomber Command remain the only veterans without a medal for their work, while their leader, Air Marshal Arthur Harris, was notoriously unrecognized when it came to postwar honors. And although Japan has memorialized its kamikazes in the Yasukuni Shrine near Tokyo, the United States continues to be diffident about its own flyers in the endgame act of World War II. As late as 1994, forty-nine years after the first atomic bomb was dropped, a controversy over how the plane that dropped it should be displayed rocked the Smithsonian's National Air and Space Museum in Washington, becoming a major issue in the midterm congressional election—a story told by the museum's director (who lost his job in the process) Martin Harwit in *An Exhibit Denied: Lobbying the History of Enola Gay* (1996).

The *Enola Gay* is surely the most famous bomber in history. Named (at the last minute before its key mission) for the mother of its pilot, Colonel (later General) Paul W. Tibbets, it has become an icon for factions on any and all sides of the debate over nuclear warfare. Martin Harwit tells how he intended to rise above specific issues in the exhibit as he first envisioned it, a presentation titled "The Last Act":

> *This is not an exhibit about the rights and wrongs of war, about who started what and who were the bad guys and who were the good. It is about the impacts and effects of bombing on people, and on the strategic outcome of conflicts.... What are the losses to humans who become the victims—civilians or military, it doesn't matter. (ED, p. 13)*

It is this lack of distinction on Harwit's part that became controversial. No matter that the men in Tibbets's plane could not differentiate combatants from noncombatants, and that the bomb itself could not be sufficiently smart to make such distinctions either. The mission was strategic, not tactical, and such was the way strategic bombing worked in 1945, whether conventional or atomic.

In the more than half century afterwards, debate over the *Enola Gay*'s accomplishment has taken a turn away from its immediate practicality toward its long-range effects. No one today argues with the fact that using the atomic bomb on August 6, 1945, and again three days later, saved lives. Against the immediate death toll of approximately seventy-five thousand people (and even thrice that number if effects on health are considered) must be weighed the one million American casualties expected in the planned invasion. As the image of Japanese persons as enemies faded, two million of them were added to the ratio, for that's how many may have died defending their homeland. As the postwar decades advanced and the new Cold War with China and the Soviet Union ran its course, arguments over the United States' decision to use atomic weapons at Hiroshima and Nagasaki took on a larger dimension. Did America's decision to use the bomb inaugurate that Cold War, or at the very least set the terms for it on a level previously unimaginable? In any event, the culture of containment that characterized the American 1950s and early 1960s was underpinned by two terrifying facts: that both sides held the power of total annihilation and that there was a precedent for using this awesome might.

The most interesting perspective, however, is one that conflates all strategic bombing, both conventional and atomic, into one view. It is the position taken by Curtis E. LeMay, whose career spans the techniques' full development. As a young flyer in the prewar Army Air Corps, he had an early view of how imprecise the application of this weapon was, and how intensive training would be necessary to make it work. As a Wing commander during the early phases of the Eighth Air Force's campaign against Germany from England, he pioneered the notion of close formations (for aerial defense), tight bomb patterns (for concentrated, effective destruction of the target), and better navigation and target spotting by lead crews. The rigors of such training and a steel-willed application of his techniques made him initially unpopular with his men. Once they saw his method's effectiveness, these same flyers became his advocates—not because they liked the risks but because they appreciated how any less effort would simply be a waste of life. Even his harshest critics had to yield the grudging admiration that he flew lead on the toughest and most dangerous missions, never asking his men to do anything he wouldn't do himself. This success brought him to a higher command in the China-Burma-India theater, from which he did his best to launch strategic bombing attacks on Japan—and where he also determined that the logistics of long-range supply were simply not worth it. Given command of the bombing campaign from the Marianas, he introduced more innovations, including corporate maintenance, and more efficient support, including the replacement of bomb dumps with direct supply of ordnance from dockside to hardstand. By early in 1945, he had the strategic bombing campaign against Japan well under way.

The problem was that even under LeMay's tougher leadership the campaign was not working. The reasons were many, but nearly all pertained to the radical difference between the European and Pacific theaters. Distances from Saipan, Tinian, and Guam to Tokyo were more than twice that from the Allied airfields of East Anglia to Berlin. The new B-29 was certainly built for this longer range, but it had been rushed into service, with developmental modifications taking place along the way—not that these modifications always worked, for the plane's engines remained a constant source of frustration. Until Iwo Jima fell, there was no place to land in between, safe or otherwise; if a Pacific theater B-29 went down on one of these runs, that was virtually the end of it and its crew, unless it could ditch off the Japanese coast where American submarines might be on station. LeMay could see that the Japanese fighter force at this late stage of the war was no Luftwaffe; but then the B-29 was not as dependable as the European theater's B-17, nor was there the solid earth of France and the Low Countries (or neutral havens of Sweden and Switzerland) for emergency landings and possible escape. Then there were the targets themselves: in Europe, identified on maps available for decades and given close study in any number of prewar exercises, but in Japan a matter of terra incognita that was too often obscured by rain clouds. What information there was came from a single fortuitous reconnaissance mission flown at a moment's notice on October 13, 1944. Japan's fall and winter overcast prevented subsequent photographic flights, and this same bad weather made visual bombing from high altitude, the B-29's intended strength, a wasteful liability.

LeMay's solution was dramatic: increase bomb loads by eliminating some of the B-29's defensive weight, change those bomb loads from high explosives to incendiaries, and send the planes in under the weather at the frighteningly low altitude of six thousand feet (or even less). It was, as Air Force historian and public information officer Major Gene Gurney says in his study of how the B-29 was used, *Journey of the Giants* (1961), "probably the greatest one-man military decision ever made" (*JG*, p. 210). LeMay's biographer, Thomas M. Coffey, explains why, citing the trust Army Air Force chief Hap Arnold had placed in the young commander and the warning issued by Arnold's top aide, General Lauris Norstad:

> *Unless LeMay soon figured out how to make better use of this expensive weapon Arnold had entrusted to him, Norstad had bluntly informed him that his future would be as cloudy as the skies over Japan. If he didn't get results pretty soon, not only would he be fired; the strategic air offensive against Japan would probably be cast aside; the mass invasion would go on as scheduled in November, and perhaps half a million Americans would be killed in it.* (IE, p. 147)

Coffey's *Iron Eagle: The Turbulent Life of General Curtis LeMay* (1986) and LeMay's own *Superfortress: The Story of the B-29 and American Air Power* (1988, coauthored with Bill Yenne) do much to sort out fact and mythology regarding both the man himself and the larger nature of strategic bombing. The most problematic thing about the LeMay myth is that it is based on a falsehood. The general's most famous quotation is most likely the famous "bomb them back into the Stone Age" imperative that was said to characterize his opinion, as a retired Air Force officer and soon-to-be vice-presidential candidate, on the Vietnam War. Thomas Coffey acknowledges the phrase, but attributes it to the proper author: popular novelist MacKinlay Kantor, ghostwriter of *Mission with LeMay* (1965). Whether because of careless proofreading or because he just didn't care at all, Curtis LeMay let the words stand, even though they were Kantor's creation, not his own. As the war worsened and LeMay's partnership on a third-party ticket with former governor of Alabama George Wallace heated up politics all the more, strategic bombing came to have powerfully negative connotations for a new generation. Regarding the North Vietnamese and their Viet Cong allies in the south, Kantor put these words in the general's mouth: "My solution to the problem would be to tell them frankly that they've got to draw in their horns and stop their aggression, or we're going to bomb them back into the Stone Age" (*MW*, p. 565). By implication, they became the public's understanding of what his mission had been in World War II, first over Germany and then in the skies above Japan. Nothing could be further from the truth.

No amount of bombing could have ever done that to the Reich or to the empire—cities and their suburbs were too large, and strategic targets were too diffuse, thanks to the decentralization of industry in armaments and munitions minister Albert Speer's Germany and the use of widely scattered cottage industries for military production in Japan from the very start. What was needed was an instrument that could disrupt and eventually prevent a society's ability to wage war, and to do it effectively. For LeMay, the target would not be a product—an aircraft factory here, a rail yard there, or even this or that city—but rather a process, the very process by which the enemy had organized itself to maintain a state of belligerence with the United States.

To take an adversary's country out of the war not by means of an invasion but through air power alone would be strategic bombing's ultimate test. It was a test that failed in Europe, as witnessed by the need for land armies to seize the very last domicile in Berlin—Hitler's bunker—before V-E Day could be declared. That the Soviet Union's Red Army was the one that accomplished this task was of great significance to the war in the Pacific, because in this theater the Allies were just two, the United States and Britain. Until almost the very end of World

War II, Russia and Japan were not at war. Neither wanted to be—the Soviets for fear of an untenable second front to their East, the Japanese for fear of a postwar Communist state in their country should they lose. Nor did anti-Communist factions in the American government fancy sharing the rehabilitation of a defeated Japan with Stalin. Therefore it was essential that the empire fall, and as expeditiously as possible.

Falling to air power alone had another implication. Just as international politics were influencing the war's larger course, interservice rivalries had created a politics of their own. Once victory in the Pacific became more likely, attention of some military planners turned toward postwar battles. These would be fought not with a foreign enemy but among themselves, as the Army and Navy battled for congressional appropriations, the Marine Corps argued for its continued existence, and the Army Air Force sought to emerge as an independent, coequal military branch. If Japan fell to the USAAF alone, the likelihood of a postwar USAF was a much stronger possibility. Hence the Navy's desire to get into Japanese air space, something LeMay resented (immediately, because of its diversion of resources, and perhaps in the long run because of the postwar interservice politics to come). Between February 15 and 25, 1945, LeMay felt obligated to turn his B-29s against Japanese airfields to protect the carrier action of Task Force 58 taking place against the mainland within range of Tokyo Bay. In return, he received an assurance from Admiral Spruance that Iwo Jima would be taken, giving these same B-29s the emergency landing field and base for escorting P-51 fighters that they so desperately needed to bring their own style of warfare more effectively to Japan.

Thomas Coffey's appraisal of this situation, admittedly from Curtis LeMay's point of view, shows the dynamics at work.

Seven months of missions from China and the Marianas hadn't been very effective, but they had brought the war to the enemy's homeland—a public relations coup for the Army Air Force. The Navy, which had in fact carried the battle all the way across the Pacific, felt it would lose out in the competition for future congressional appropriations if this junior service were allowed to tell America it alone was winning the war. "Now that the Japanese fleet had been eliminated," Coffey reports, "it was about time, the Navy decided, to show the American public that it, too, as well as the headline-hunting Air Force, was capable of direct attacks on Japan" (*IE*, p. 141).

On the virtual eve of LeMay's decision to change bombing tactics, this distraction with the Navy actually served to refocus his attention on the need for his weapon's ultimate success. There had been earlier indications of how different the Navy's approach was. Even an exchange of courtesies could be embarrassing, such as when LeMay had to accept Admiral Nimitz's invitation to a formal dress dinner wearing the only uniform he had, a set of poorly pressed khakis (when returning the favor, the general could offer the admiral and his staff just Spam in a Quonset hut). A more detailed example comes from the memoirs of a navigator on the way to join LeMay's command—Earl Snyder, whose *General Leemy's Circus* (1955), named for the Japanese propagandists' denigration of the Twenty-First Bomber Command, characterizes the differences as such:

> *Eniwetok was a beautiful little island well kept by the navy. It was typical of the contrast of the navy with the air force, if you compared it to Kwajalein. Kwajalein was an air-force island. Food was poor, living conditions were poor and recreational facilities were poor. When the air force moved in, its*

primary object was to get planes in and out on schedule; living was secondary. By comparison, the navy, once it had secured an island, seemed to be primarily interested in enjoying life on it. They did that to the fullest extent. The navy had ample ships on which it could store and transport building materials, food, drink, ice-making machinery and the like; the air force had only airplanes, and they were not allotted to handling these supplies. The navy had the Seabees, whose primary mission was construction. The air force had their engineer troops, whose primary mission was construction—of runways and air depots and maintenance buildings. I was to learn, in months to come, even more forcefully the difference between the navy and the air force in this respect. (GL, p. 36)

While there is a tone of interservice resentment to Snyder's assessment, his details add up to a fundamental difference in the kinds of war waged from air and sea, including the most basic of practicalities, supply. Yet on an individual level there could be the most heartening examples of cooperation: a group of Seabees noticing the terrible state of General LeMay's quarters and rebuilding them, unasked; soldiers, sailors, Marines—just about anyone who was available—hauling bombs from docks to hardstands, even though it wasn't their job. In the least likely of circumstances, it was the spirit of Pearl Harbor, defending itself on December 7, 1941, all over again. Just two years later a Navy veteran named James A. Michener would base his first novel, *Tales of the South Pacific*, on the greater sense of purpose that emerged from these sometime squabbles.

With facilities, supplies, and equipment finally available, LeMay could turn his amazingly fine-tuned force against enemy cities in a terrifying new way: low-level firebombing. Two years before, in March of 1943, the advantages of using incendiary bombs over explosives had been demonstrated at the Dugway Proving Ground in Utah, where a simulated Japanese town had been constructed and then destroyed in a manner that let the DuPont Company, Standard Oil, and the National Research Defense Council determine just what type of weapon would be best. By late in 1944 they had it: an incendiary bomb with a base made of jellied gasoline called napalm. The question remained how to deliver it on target. LeMay's answer was to go in low, between five and eight thousand feet—beneath the weather, lower than the enemy's flak defenses, and close enough for manual release over a visible point of attack already aflame in the darkness.

This was not how it had been done in Europe, but that method had failed out here in the Pacific. Doing it LeMay's new way seemed impossible. "However," the general reminds his readers in *Superfortress*, "we realized that the Japanese *also* considered it impossible and that they were not expecting it." This lack of enemy expectations worked to LeMay's specific benefit. "We knew that the Japanese early warning network was greatly inferior to that of the Germans," he writes, "that the Japanese night-fighter threat was virtually nonexistent, and that the Japanese antiaircraft gunners had their shells fused to explode in the high altitude environment where they were used to finding the B-29s" (*SF*, p. 122).

The first low-altitude incendiary raid took place over the night of March 9–10, 1945. LeMay's memoir relishes the facts: 325 of the huge Superfortresses led by a pathfinder force that ignites a 500-by–2,500-foot section of Tokyo, creating a fire that, fed by subsequent incendiaries, destroys an area of the city unimaginable by previous standards. In retrospect, there is an irony to this raid's dimensions. Tinian, the island from which so many of LeMay's B-29s flew, was about the size and shape of Manhattan, and when constructing its roads and facilities the engineers had named them after streets and sites ranging from the Battery to Central Park—almost exactly the equivalent area of Tokyo destroyed in this single attack. Brutally honest, the general does not address this material dimension but instead computes the human cost. "When the conflagration finally burned out," he writes, "267,171 buildings had been destroyed and 83,000 people were dead, the highest death toll of any single day's action of the war, exceeding the number of deaths caused by the big Allied raids on Hamburg and Dresden, or the nuclear strike to come in August on Hiroshima." Just as candidly, he admits the fact that "millions of homeless found themselves facing an uncertain future with little or no food and clothing in the freezing cold" (*SF*, p. 123).

Figures don't lie—LeMay cites these and many others for their crushing effect, which is just the truth about strategic bombing he wishes to convey: not the sledgehammer effect of creating a new Stone Age but the careful science, both military and physical, necessary to take an entire society out of combat. In Japan's case, popular mythology had created the picture of just such a culture that was supposedly willing to defend its homeland down to the last man, woman, and child. This was the view American planners projected when accepting strategic bombing as an alternative to invasion. And while from their position it may well have been a reductive stereotype, militaristic factions among the Japanese leadership were drawing a stereotype of their own, based on dictates of religion and national spirit. Therefore the air war that developed from this confrontation would be different from the blitzkrieg effect of the initial German aggression and the attempt at demoralization undertaken by the Royal Air Force's Bomber Command in Europe. Over there, tactics had expanded to include psychology but remained tactics nonetheless. Here, in the last stages of war in the Pacific, truly strategic bombing would be given its most complete test.

At their new, lower level of bombing, LeMay's Superforts were devastating. Once Iwo Jima could become a base for P-51 Mustang fighters, skies would be swept clear of adversaries. One of these Mustang pilots, Jerry Yellin, would have little problem with the idea of bringing destruction to Japan—until a generation later, when one of his sons married a Japanese woman and settled there to raise Yellin grandchildren in the culture of this pilot's former enemies. Learning about the war all over again gives him a special perspective, as when early in *Of Wars and Weddings: A Legacy of Two Fathers* (1995), he makes a new friend and hears his description of a raid as experienced from the ground:

> *"I remember one raid in particular. It was in April and began in midmorning. The bombers were escorted by American fighters for the first time. They came in much lower than before and we could see wave after wave filling the entire sky for hours. Again the fires started and then the winds began to blow. The fire spread from section to section and by evening were lighting the night sky like daylight. I lived many miles from the fires, but at eleven that night I could read a newspaper in the street in front of my house. That's how light it was. On that day 80,000 Japanese died and that was only the beginning."* (W, p. 19)

In other theaters, such a ground-based perspective would stand in high contrast to observing strategic bombings' effect from on high—where, except when complicated by flak and enemy fighters, the experience could be surreally detached. Over Japan, however, American flyers get a sense of what Jerry Yellin's future friend has experienced. Consider Earl Snyder's approach to another, smaller city, which still makes for a horrific scene, even from a distance. "As we drew near the coastline of Japan," the B-29 navigator writes, "we had little difficulty in determining where the target was. Osaka's burning lit up the sky so that it could be seen easily from the air for miles and miles. Our bombing altitude was eighty-one hundred feet" (*GL*, p. 115). Coming up to the flight deck, Snyder looks forward from the plane's Plexiglas nose and is awestruck by the approach to their aiming point. "The holocaust that met my eyes required seeing to warrant believing," he notes. "There was one huge bonfire with flames licking almost to the altitude we were flying." Plunging into this towering inferno of smoke and fire, he heeds the pilot's warning that "This is gonna be rough" and holds on for dear life. Looking out the windows to the side, he's not surprised that the inboard engine to his left, just fifteen feet away, can barely be seen:

> *The smoke became dense, the fumes almost overpowering. I got some satisfaction out of realizing that what I smelled burning was Japan. The heat began to grow uncomfortable and our plane was being buffeted around violently by the convection currents caused by extreme heat. Had the pilot not had his safety belt fastened tightly he could not have controlled the plane. I grabbed for the arms of the pilot's and co-*

pilots's seats and braced myself firmly. I was thrown back and forth as though I were a cork in a child's bathtub. I began to fear that I might be thrown against either the pilot or co-pilot or one of the control columns. I lay down on the flight deck and hooked my feet in behind some metal panels. With my hands I held tightly onto the legs of the pilot's and co-pilot's seats. (*GL*, pp. 116–17)

From the immensity that Jerry Yellin's friend-to-be experiences on the ground and that Earl Snyder experiences from a mile and a half above, Curtis LeMay is able to calculate his success. "The March 10, 1945, incendiary attack was easily the turning point in the air war against Japan and quite possibly of the entire war in the Pacific," he writes. "The decisive effect of this and the raids that came during the following nights was due largely to our ability to send truly large masses of B-29s against the target on a consistent basis" (*SF*, p. 124), and that consistency was achieved by mastering the technology at hand. For this air strategist, the path to victory was anything but a matter of using nuclear weaponry to bomb an entire country back into the Stone Age, the reputation his ghostwritten Vietnam War era autobiography would so falsely create. From the B-29 itself to the maintenance and supply methods LeMay developed to the style of attack he devised, there was no quantum leap in warfare—just a perfection, to an ultimate degree, of what had been available, in theory and in practice, since the war's start. The fire raids on Japan were a climax to all that, and with that climax came the possibility of a denouement in which the general could foresee a Japanese surrender.

Firebombing raids would continue through spring and summer of 1945, with just a few cities left untouched—for reasons that after August 6 and 9 became apparent to all. Japanese casualties from these raids were enormous; over three quarters of a million civilians, equaling the number of combat deaths among Japanese troops for the entire war (the atomic bombings would put homefront losses even higher). With the quantum leap in destruction yet to come, Japanese flyers had already reached their own ultimate state, evident to Saburo Sakai when the Army pilots gave up trying to intercept the incoming B-29s and retired their planes for kamikaze use against the expected invasion. For a time, Sakai is pleased that the new Raiden fighter gives him and his fellow Navy pilots an advantage. But not for long:

> *The enemy's answer was to send swarms of Mustangs over Japan during the daylight raids. The swift enemy fighters tore savagely at our planes and slaughtered them. Where the Raiden shone against the B-29, it was helpless before the swifter, more maneuverable Mustang. Almost every day our new fighters plunged burning from the sky, their wings torn off, their pilots dead. (S, p. 365)*

Therefore, kamikaze tactics had to take to the air: not to crash into American ships, or to be readied for suicide action against invasion forces, but to ram the mighty B-29s in flight. Zeros and other planes were stripped of their armor plate, their bomb racks, and their guns. This left them light enough to reach even the B-29s' highest altitude. Once there, options were still available: early on, before air defense had been relinquished to Navy flyers, some Army pilots would undertake a head-on approach, lock the controls, and parachute to safety at the last moment. Others scoffed at such mere brushes with suicide and opted for the real thing, as Gene Gurney describes in *Journey of the Giants* when a Superfortress named "Uncle Tom's Cabin," piloted by Major John E. Krause, leads the lower elements of a formation in a bomb run against the Musashino Aircraft Company near Tokyo. Thirty enemy fighters dive in attack, the leading one just missing the first two planes of Krause's element before slamming into his own, breaking open a gash from which padding and equipment stream into the sky, followed by a sheet of yellow flames. Krause fights to control the huge B-29, giving his gunners a platform from which to shoot back. "Jap planes were falling and exploding," Gurney notes, "but whenever one fell, another roared in to take its place" (*JG*, p. 167). One of these pours gunfire into the bomber's No. 4 engine, just before another crashes into the wing and engine No. 3. "The bomber staggered and shuddered, but Krause gained control and brought it back to its bomb course," amazing crewmen from other B-29s in the element looking on:

> *Then came the third ramming; a Tony firing away at the Cabin's underside failed to pull away in time and drove straight into the plane's belly. The bomber broke into a spin, fighters following it down. At 500 feet Krause again got control, and his gunners made their ninth kill.*
>
> *But the Cabin had flown its last. Still firing defiantly, it flew level for a moment; then its nose dipped and it dived straight down into Tokyo Bay.* (*JG*, pp. 167–68)

The image is a powerful one: down in flames and firing all the way—but still taken out of action. Kamikaze fighters are in this case effective against their B-29 adversary, "super fortress" that it is. Expanded to its greatest hypothetical dimensions, the situation plays out as a war of gruesome attrition: which would exhaust itself first, LeMay's conventional forces, or the kamikazes' ultimate resources, which were their planes and themselves?

LeMay, of course, believed he would finally win, for this had been the pattern of the war since its inception. But it would take time for the Empire of Japan's last resources to be depleted, even as they'd be flung, one at a time, against the limitless armadas of B-29 Superfortresses. Kamikazes could fight fire. But could they fight fission? Of the countless descriptions of the August 6, 1945, atomic bombing of Hiroshima, one account sticks out, coming as it does from Yasuo Kuwahara, the young kamikaze pilot in training whose life is one of the putative three million saved by the event. His suicide mission is scheduled for August 8, preceded by the luxury of a two-day pass that on the fateful date has taken him to Hiroshima. Walking its streets in the morning bustle, he hears the air raid sirens and glances up—"a small concern to me, since two planes had already passed over while I was on the streetcar" (*K*, p. 174). The single B-29 now visible is flying unmolested, able to "meander at will like a grazing animal." Conditions are so clear that Kuwahara can even see the point of release, when "a tiny speck separated from the silver belly above, and the plane moved off, picking up speed. No bigger than a marble, the speck increased to the size of a baseball." What could it be? Passers-by see it, too, and speculate: the best guess is, "more propaganda pamphlets—more of the same thing." In the minute that follows, conversations continue, the stuff of city life in a land at war but so far spared from the devastating fire raids that have destroyed so many urban centers in Japan. Then comes the unthinkable, as a huge flash and surge of heat suddenly fills the surrounding world:

I threw up my hands against the fierce flood of heat. A mighty blast furnace had opened on the world.

Then came a cataclysm which no man will ever completely describe. It was neither a roar, a boom, nor a blast. It was a combination of those things with something added—the fantastic power of earthquakes, avalanches, winds and floods. For a moment nature had focused her wrath on the land, and the crust of the earth shuddered.

I was slammed to the earth. Darkness, pressure, choking and the clutches of pain . . . a relief as though my body were drifting upward. Then nothing. (K, p. 175)

What follows becomes familiar from so many other narratives, including those collected by John Hersey for his *Hiroshima*, originally appearing in the *New Yorker* on August 31, 1946 (an issue that immediately sold out) and published as a volume in November that the Book of the Month Club considered so important as to distribute for free to all its members. How World War II in the Pacific came to this ending is a story of vast geopolitical and moral complexity, but that America's air war climaxed this way is a fact whose import can be grasped by heeding the forces that brought it to be. Some were political, to be sure, and overriding all were the forces of scientific discovery and a very human drive toward practical application. Yet a simply helpful way to understand how this new style of aerial warfare came about is to listen to the voices involved with it.

Consider Tom Ferebee, the mission's bombardier. In *Duty* (2000), he recalls for author Bob Greene his first impressions after making the release and handing back the plane's controls to pilot Paul Tibbets. "I couldn't see the bomb any more after he started turning," Ferebee reports. "But then, as we flew away . . .

it was like something I'd never seen before. Parts of *buildings* were coming up the stem of the bomb—you could tell that something strange was going on, because you could see parts of the city, pieces of the buildings, like they were being sucked toward us." Having forgotten to pull on his protective goggles, he sees the same flash that nearly blinded Yasuo Kuwahara: "It was the brightest thing you'd ever seen, underneath us" (*DU*, p. 262). What caused all this? Like the people down below, every member of the crew except Tibbets and the specially trained electronics officer, Jacob Beser, could only guess. For nine months of training, the weapon's nature had been kept secret from them. Only after takeoff had they been told, and then so in only very general terms. "Colonel, are we splitting atoms this morning?" (*FT*, p. 242), tail gunner George R. Caron would ask, and the answer Tibbets provided meant no more than the speculation taking place down on the ground, where (as noted by John Hersey) a missionary priest surmised that "The bomb was not a bomb at all; it was a kind of fine magnesium powder sprayed over the whole city by a single plane, and it exploded when it came into contact with the live wires of the city power system" (*HI*, pp. 78–79). In fact, the weapon's effect would be so far beyond any previous measure that to a person's imagination it could be *anything*, as indeed it was to the men in Paul Tibbets's B-29 who flew back to Tinian, wondering just what they had wrought.

President Harry Truman's announcement to the world that an atomic bomb had been dropped was remarkably candid in its details, but words alone could not convey the nature of what had taken place. Three days later, with full knowledge of the news about Hiroshima, P-51 pilot William P. Wyper is on a routine patrol mission when he witnesses a replay of the event, as noted in his *The Youngest Tigers in the Sky* (1980):

While flying over the northeast part of Kyushu a couple of days later, we saw a gigantic blinding flash to the west of us. It was truly an eerie sight, like nothing any of us had ever seen before. On countless occasions we had seen the shockwaves radiating from the conventional bombs dropped by our heavy bombers, but the shockwave we saw on that August ninth morning was unlike anything we had ever seen before. It gradually traveled through our formation. I know it was an optical illusion, but the skin on the next airplane seemed to ripple as the shockwave went past. We knew that we had just witnessed the detonation of a second atomic bomb. (YT, p. 181)

Wyper's conclusion is the same drawn by most other airmen, including those in the atomic mission crews: "There was no possible way that a country could endure for long the relentless pounding that our mighty air force was inflicting upon Japan." Having escorted LeMay's bombers, heard about Hiroshima, and now witnessed the devastation unleashed against Nagasaki, this P-51 pilot can say he's seen the pattern developing. "First it was military installations, then factories," he reflects, "and finally entire cities that were being literally blown off the face of the earth" (YT, p. 181). In the face of all this, surrender seemed inevitable.

Fewer than nineteen hundred air force personnel were involved with bringing these two atomic bombs into the Pacific theater. Formed as a special composite group and trained secretly in the isolation of Wendover, Utah, they enjoyed a unique sense of privilege within the military establishment. Just flying B-29s made them special, for all such models were under the direct command of General Henry H. (Hap) Arnold, Army Air Force chief of staff. Unlike the B-17s and B-24s that were up for grabs among the various air commands around the globe, Super-fortresses were his personal domain; there was no way any of them could be diverted to purposes not directly concerned with the defeat of Japan. In similar manner, authority for developing and delivering the atomic bomb was vested in another individual, an Army engineering officer: Major General Leslie R. Groves. Once Hap Arnold picked Lieutenant Colonel Paul Tibbets as a pilot in charge, the way was clear for unfettered development. Groves gave Tibbets a code word, "silverplate," to use when anything regarding personnel, material, or procedures threatened to block his way. Virtually running his own show in a remote corner of Utah, Tibbets had only to deal with the bomb itself being built by scientists and engineers in New Mexico. Otherwise, shots to be called were his.

At age twenty-nine, Tibbets might have seemed young to assume such an important command—full colonels were in charge of groups, much less composite ones with such a demanding mission. But like Curtis LeMay, Tibbets had distinguished himself among the B-17 forces in the European theater. LeMay, just eight and three-quarters years older, had made his everlasting mark with bombing effectiveness. Too low in the command structure to design such missions, Tibbets flew them, and in these circumstances emerged as a leader. In the popular lore that followed the war, he'd become famous as a character in not just one but three major motion pictures: *Enola Gay* (1980), in which he's played by Patrick Duffy; *Above and Beyond* (1953), where Robert Taylor takes his role; and most interestingly in *Twelve O'Clock High* (1949), where the character portrayed by actor Dean Jagger is based on Tibbets's own work in reorganizing a demoralized bombardment wing. In his autobiography, *The Tibbets Story* (1978), he describes the trouble at his base in

England, where those in charge had neglected their duties in favor of hobnobbing with the local aristocracy. To remedy this situation, the commander is replaced by Colonel Frank Armstrong, "a no-nonsense officer who quickly straightened things out. If the image struck is that of Gregory Peck in an Army Air Force uniform, the impression is right, as Tibbets relates this situation at Polebrook with the subsequent screen classic:

> *Part of the problem was described by Beirne Lay and Sy Bartlett in their novel,* Twelve O'Clock High *[1948], which became a popular movie. The fictional general in that story, Frank Savage, is based on the real-life Frank Armstrong.*
>
> *Those who read the book or saw the picture may remember that, when Savage arrived to take command, security on the base was lax, many of the key officers were absent, and no one knew where to find them. He found a squadron commander, with the rank of major on duty. In reality, I was that major, having been promoted from captain during our stopover in San Antonio earlier in the year.*
>
> *Armstrong promptly appointed me his executive officer. From that time on, morale and efficiency improved at Polebrook, although the Rothschilds and other party-givers in the neighborhood lost some interesting American guests.* (*TB*, p. 70)

Like LeMay, Tibbets had been groomed for his role. Combat success in the European theater made him a natural for testing and modifying the B-29, and his extensive work with the Superfortress made him the most likely person to fly it into combat carrying the atomic bomb. Just getting the plane ready for such a job required considerable innovation, as a load of this size and shape had never been imagined by Boeing's designers. For a time, it seemed the British Lancaster would have to be used; as happened, the B-29's bomb bay could be modified, but only by borrowing bomb hooks from the Royal Air Force plane that had been dropping 22,000-pound "Grand Slam" explosives on the Reich. Yet equipment and even the bomb itself were the lesser parts of Tibbets's duty. He had to devise a way of breaking away in a breathtaking maneuver, more suitable to a hot fighter than a lumbering heavy bomber, in order to escape the A-bomb's blast waves. He had to find key personnel with the necessary skills for all this and wound up ignoring the checkered pasts of some people (including one with an outstanding warrant for murder) so that the work of his 509th Composite Group could continue. Plus all of it had to be done in secret, hidden away in this desolate corner of northwest Utah where security forces would have to shadow his flyers any time they ventured off base. As with so many other American successes during the war, this work in getting an atomic age outfit into shape was a matter of combining technical resources with the proper mix of human beings—of finding a way not simply to produce something but of making it function effectively. With less than a year to work with, this is what Paul Tibbets was able to do.

Of the entire composite group that trained all winter and spring in Utah and then shipped out to the Marianas for a summer of practice runs (with single conventional explosives) over various Japanese targets, only two crews eventually carried atomic weapons to enemy cities: Paul Tibbets's men in the *Enola Gay* and, three days later, the crew of pilot Charles Sweeney's borrowed Superfortress, *Bock's Car*. For each mission there were other B-29s for weather reconnaissance, scientific measurements, and observation. Flying the weather plane in advance of the *Enola Gay* was Captain Claude Eatherly, the man who in postwar years would become much more famous than Tibbets, Sweeney, or anyone else involved with the atomic bombings, thanks to his controversial protest of the events. The group's security chief, William "Bud" Uanna, had worried about Eatherly's wild escapades in Salt Lake City and his tendency to run off at the mouth, although much of what he said bore little relation to reality, let alone the specifics of the group's complex work. In *Ruin From the Air* (1977), authors Gordon Thomas and Max Morgan Witts note that there was more than one such extrovert in the outfit, but this flyer seemed the worst:

> *Claude Eatherly had also established his image among his crew as a tough-talking, hard-drinking, girl-chasing gambler who would wager odds on anything.*
>
> *He continued to romance about his background and war record.*
>
> *He was a man, in Uanna's words to Tibbets, "with a problem." The security officer again urged that Eatherly should be transferred.*
>
> *But Tibbets stubbornly refused, for once, to listen to Uanna. He insisted Eatherly's fine flying record was all that mattered.*
>
> *Uanna never again raised the matter. And Eatherly continued to weave his fantasies.* (RA, p. 141)

As a manager of men, Tibbets was justified in keeping Eatherly on the job. Neither immoral behavior beforehand nor high moralism afterward was the issue in August of 1945. Ending the war was this flyer's single objective. That is the theme of Bob Greene's thoroughly atypical but brilliantly insightful book. Getting to know Paul Tibbets in the late 1990s, when Greene's father, a World War II vet himself, was dying, the author of *Duty* learns how that singleness of purpose could motivate just a relatively few men to get World War II over and done with. Had Tibbets felt anger on this mission? No. His motivation lay elsewhere, as he explains to Bob Greene:

> *"My mother was a very calm, pacific individual, and I learned from her to be the same way. You get a lot damn further by being calm when you're doing a job. Our crew did not do the bombing in anger. We did it because we were determined to stop the killing. I would have done anything to get to Japan and stop the killing."* (DU, p. 19)

Get to Japan and stop the killing—such is the motive of typical American flyers in this theater, a commitment evident among all service personnel from December 7, 1941. Good planning was essential, deep resources were a blessing, and genius of production proved critical. But foremost in the effort were acts of initiative by individual Americans, from the civilian dock workers at Pearl Harbor who leapt aboard ships to man antiaircraft guns to the culminating example of Paul Tibbets. Emblematic of the way he helped end the war was the decision he took to move his composite group overseas—not just because discipline and morale at his godforsaken base in the wilds of Utah were approaching breaking points but because he feared the atomic scientists at Los Alamos had reached a point of diminishing returns in fine-tuning the bomb. Better to get the show on the road, he figured, or the last act would never be staged. General Groves exploded in anger when learning the lowly lieutenant colonel underneath him was using his extraordinary authority to do this, on his own—and then commended Tibbets for his initiative, realizing that this was the only way to get things done. In sum, it was a spirit consistent with how the war had been fought since the first P-40s rose from Wheeler Field, without formal permission, to engage the Japanese planes attacking Pearl Harbor.

Remarkably, two Japanese flyers central to the first acts in this war were still on the scene for Paul Tibbets's closure of this terrible drama. Less like a character in a *Noh* drama from Japan's Middle Ages than an actor in the denouement of one of Shakespeare's history plays, Mitsuo Fuchida—flight leader of the aerial attacks on Pearl Harbor and now chief of air operations for the Japanese navy—is scheduled to visit Hiroshima for an invasion defense conference on the morning that the first atomic bomb explodes. Near the end of their study, *Enola Gay* (1977), Gordon Thomas and Max Morgan Witts picture him flying in on the following day and wondering "what force had created the strange force over the city":

> *He called the airport's control tower. There was no reply.*
>
> *As he got closer, Fuchida saw that Hiroshima, the city he had left only the afternoon before, "was simply not there anymore. Huge fires rose up in all quarters. But most of these fires seemed not to be consuming buildings; they were consuming debris."*
>
> *Fuchida would have no conscious recollection of landing his plane on the runway . . . . His next memory would be walking toward the airport exit, immaculately dressed in his white uniform, shoes, and gloves, and coming face-to-face with "a procession of people who seemed to have come out of Hell."*

Horrified, Fuchida walked into Hiroshima. The dead and the dying clogged the gutters, floated in the rivers, blocked the streets. Near the city's center, whole areas had simply disappeared; for at least a square mile, "nothing remained." Utterly depressed and exhausted by what he could see, Fuchida wandered aimlessly through the wasteland. (EG, pp. 268–69)

On a more abstract level, Fuchida could reason out the conclusion: "In flattening Hiroshima, the United States had given Japan the opportunity to acknowledge defeat with dignity. It had also taken upon itself the responsibility to end the war promptly" (*GS*, p. 150). But his country would have to accept such closure on the enemy's terms. The difficulty was dramatic, resolved only by the emperor's words broadcast to a nation that had never before heard his voice. Even then, some Japanese people, famous flyers among them, resisted the notion of abject surrender. One such person was Saburo Sakai. In *Samurai!* he talks of a final mission on the night of August 14–15, 1945, in which he brings down a B-29 (*S*, pp. 370–74). In *Winged Samurai* (1985) he tells historian Henry Sakaida that the event never happened, having been invented by his coauthors for a dramatic ending to their book. The truth, he reveals, is more fascinating. His last mission of the war would take place on August 17, 1945—also after the surrender, but in more interesting circumstances. "Our commander told us that the war was over and that we were not going out looking for trouble," Sakai reports. "But he also added that should the Americans dare fly over us and we wanted to get them, he wouldn't stop us. Then around noon, we received word that some American bombers were flying over Tokyo. That really provoked us and we said, 'Let's go get them!' and piled into our planes" (*WS*, p. 134).

Turning their backs on a career of close military obedience and acting, in fact, like some of their American adversaries, Sakai and his comrades take off on their own—resolved, like those P-40 pilots from Wheeler Field in 1941, to protect their own airspace. The planes they encounter are not bomb-laden B-29 Superfortresses but rather a flight of aptly named B-34 Dominators (built by Consolidated Aircraft to replace its B-24 Liberator, a workhorse of the European Theater where so many Nazi-occupied countries had to be freed). The Dominators are over Tokyo Bay on a photographic mission and are attacked by ten fighters, one of them Sakai's. Fire is exchanged, but no one is injured and no planes on either side are lost. Acknowledging their own sense of closure to this war, the Japanese flyers head back to base, ready to begin the long, awkward, but eventually rewarding process of becoming allies with their former enemies.

★ ★ ★

CONCLUSION
DIMENSIONS MORAL AND MORE

Air war in the Pacific skies of World War II ends with the introduction of atomic weaponry, and hence it initiates more concerns than it solves. There were moral dimensions to the act that
would not only continue but grow in importance, so that two
generations later the problem seemed less resolvable than ever.
Political dimensions were even more wide ranging, encompass-
ing one era's struggle with superpower coexistence and
another's anguish with terror. Yet it is no accident that these
matters were introduced in the Pacific theater. Other dimensions from this air war show up in narratives as equally unique,
including the fact that so many flyers from this war front
became important religious figures after hostilities ceased—flyers on both sides, American and Japanese, plus one major
British figure whose official role of witnessing the Nagasaki blast
from an accompanying U.S. aircraft prompted his virtual on-
the-spot conversion from a perfector of strategic bombing to a
pacifist dedicated to the most humble service of humanity possible. As religious figures, many of these former adversaries
would meet, bridging another dimension unique to this theater:

unlike in Europe, adversaries in the Pacific skies found it next to impossible to view their opposition with customary chivalry or even pity. Finally, even the language to describe this particular air war would be different, reflecting these concerns and others that made combat over the Pacific a different world entirely.

Bob Caron, tail gunner on the *Enola Gay*, had the clearest view of the world's first hostile atomic explosion. The official photographs he took of it would not just show the world what had been accomplished but serve as an icon of destruction for generations afterwards; his was the first mushroom cloud, and hence the most memorable. In Caron's autobiography, he highlights a comment from Secretary of War Henry L. Stimson about the gravity of this act, how the invention and availability of such weaponry had created "a revolutionary change in relation of man to the universe" (*FT*, p. 199). Being involved in its use would be something every participant had to reckon with. From the scientists who developed the weapon and the technicians who built it to the flyers who delivered its first two types to Hiroshima and Nagasaki, an entire literature has been created from their reactions. Indeed, the picture has become a much larger one, taking in the responses of combatants in general and people on the home front—as it should, given that in such a democratic effort as America's role in World War II, every citizen becomes complicit. Most flyers took it as a matter of course. For Jimmy Doolittle, presently in charge of the Eighth Air Force that had been fighting from England since late in 1942, it meant his great armada would not be shifted to the Pacific theater. "Of the 8th's units scheduled to be in place by August 15 [1945], two bomb groups had begun to arrive on August 7, the day after the first A-bomb drop," he writes in his autobiography. "However, according to the plan, we were not scheduled to be at full strength until February 1946" (*IC*, p. 453). That's his answer to how he felt about the atomic missions. Given the chance to put his early units in action just two days before the surrender, he declines, telling his superiors that "if the war's over, I will not risk one airplane or a single bomber crew just to be able to say the 8th Air Force had operated against the Japanese in the Pacific" (*IC*, p. 454). For Hamilton McWhorter, first Hellcat ace of the war and flying against the enemy since November 1942, it's a case of reasoning that without the bombs "even I would have had to do another combat tour" (*FH*, p. 213).

Vengeful statements are few and far between. Among the airmen especially, consensus reads in favor of closure, the spirit Paul Tibbets expressed when saying all he wished to do was "get to Japan and stop the killing" (*DU*, p. 19). The conscientious objector to all this would prove to be Claude Eatherly, pilot of the weather plane that preceded Tibbets's flight and indicated acceptable bombing conditions over Hiroshima. Eatherly voiced no objections at the time. Instead, his reputation in the composite group was one of a swashbuckler and hell-raiser—popular with his men (whose rights he fought for) and respected by everyone in the outfit, from top to bottom, as an excellent pilot, but a person whose manner of aggression proved colorful, to say the least. He stayed in the service through the atomic tests over Bikini Atoll in 1946, but left in 1947 as an unhappy man, his application for a regular commission having been turned down and, according to his Air Force record as investigated by William Bradford Huie in *The Hiroshima Pilot* (1964), clouded by "cheating on [a] written examination" (*HP*, p. 68) for meteorology school, something Eatherly saw as his last chance in a downsized postwar USAAF. Thereafter, the man's life became especially problematic. Huie, a novelist with an interest in what he calls "several true, offbeat stories about Americans who served in the Second World War" (*HP*, p. 7), depicts these problems harshly and remains deeply suspicious of the flyer's motives in emerging as an antiwar activist. But even Eatherly's most committed defenders, including the Austrian philosopher Gunther Anders and the liberal American journalist Ronnie Dugger, blanch at the ruin he made of his own life. To what extent is guilt over participating in the first act of atomic warfare responsible for a broken marriage, failed career, alcoholism, and a rap sheet of crimes committed so pointlessly as to invite apprehension and conviction, much less several years of psychiatric confinement and a series of sanity hearings?

Anders accepts the hypothesis first proposed by Secretary of War Stimson and extends it to this person's case, a person whom he posits as representative of anyone and everyone living in the post-atomic era. For a philosopher, the fundamental change in how humankind relates to the universe creates a terrible dilemma for the individual. In *Burning Conscience* (1962), a collection of letters Eatherly and Anders exchanged between 1959 and 1961 when the weather-plane pilot was at the peak of his popularity in the international peace movement, Anders advances a thesis meant to explain Eatherly's behavior:

> The 'technification' of our being: the fact that to-day it is possible that unknowingly and indirectly, like screws in a machine, we can be used in actions, the effects of which are beyond the horizon of our eyes and imagination, and of which, could we imagine them, we could not approve—this fact has changed the very foundations of our moral existence. Thus, we can become "guiltlessly guilty," a condition which

has not existed in the technically less advanced times of our fathers. (*BC,* p. 1)

This may indeed be the case for America's first atomic generation. In more general terms, it has been propounded by philosophers far more famous than Anders, as they add nuclear anxieties to the general sense of *angst* they see pervading the modern condition. In practical terms, comrades find Eatherly's position hard to understand. In Ronnie Dugger's *Dark Star* (1967), Paul Tibbets's complains that "I'd have to stretch things real far to see how he could arrive at a guilt complex. He didn't do anything but look at the weather. He wasn't within a hundred miles of where it happened. His imagination would have to be pretty broad to tie himself with responsibility with all the people that were casualties." As for where responsibility lies, Tibbets is precise: "The only thing he did was to tell me what the weather was. He had nothing to do with the decision making" (*DK,* p. 214). Decisions Claude Eatherly did undertake, before and after the Hiroshima mission, make for bizarre reading today. On one of the conventional raids designed to give flyers from the composite group experience over Japan, Eatherly found the target obscured by clouds, and so instead had his bombardier aim for the emperor's palace (had this sacrosanct and strictly off-limits target been hit, the entire course of the war and the occupation would have changed catastrophically). Shortly after leaving the Air Force in 1947, Eatherly took part in arrangements for a raid on Cuba by American adventurers hoping to overthrow the government; here the former weather pilot's responsibilities would involve a flight of bomb-laden P-38 Lightnings obtained as war surplus. The plot was uncovered, and Eatherly was arrested and prosecuted, serving time in jail for this offense. In light of all this, Tibbets would remain generous, only saying in his own book that "this irresponsible pilot was one of the few in my out-fit whose behavior was impossible to predict" (*TB*, p. 193). And of course the *Enola Gay*'s pilot acknowledges his own role, but only as an appointed job whose necessity he accepts. Having studied both cases, Dugger balances them in terms that had become necessary for the times: "This is what each of these men has done with his life among us. In that plain light, Tibbets is the dutiful officer, and Eatherly is the dutiful human being. The one denies personal liability for what he does, and the other seeks this liability. These days one must choose between these two courses of action" (*DK*, p. 244).

Thanks to the almost literal media circus that Eatherly's case created, it is hard to draw conclusions from his individual response to atomic warfare. Because of some confusion in the original reporting of his behavior problems, the world came to know him as "the Hiroshima pilot," assuming that it was he who dropped the bomb. With such a confused focus, debate over the morality of atomic warfare had little chance of reaching any sense of resolution. Cold war politics made it all the harder. Yet as problematic as they are, Eatherly's objections fit a general pattern of other flyers, more socially responsible in their behavior, turning to religious pacifism following their experiences in the skies over this ironically named ocean, an ocean that had seen some of the most brutal combat in the history of humankind.

A prime example of how much action sprang from the Pacific rather than European theater is the experience of Leonard Cheshire, Group Captain in the Royal Air Force and holder of Britain's highest and extremely rare award, the Victoria Cross, for bravery in action as a bomber pilot. *Bomber Pilot* (1943) is the title of his first memoir, written as a squadron leader in the thick of air combat over Germany. The argument he makes here for strategic bombing is as enthusiastic as anything from Curtis LeMay, presently doing similar work in the same European skies as a lieutenant colonel in the United States Army Air Force. "Well, everybody is the same," Cheshire notes of this general enthusiasm among the Allies to bring the war back to Germany; "after all, Berlin is the reason for most of us joining Bomber Command" (*BP*, p. 58). Like LeMay, he combined improvements in navigation and innovations in target marking to make strategic bombing effective. By war's end he had so distinguished himself as to be in the RAF's logical choice to represent Britain as the atomic missions were flown. Sent to Tinian, Cheshire became one with the world of B-29 Superfortresses lumbering off by the hundreds, headed for Japan. Some carried conventional explosives. Others bore missives of peace. Appropriate to the beliefs he then held regarding the importance of demonstrating strategic bombing's ultimate effectiveness, Cheshire shared the consensus prevalent among the American flyers, as noted by his biographer, Andrew Boyle, in *No Passing Glory* (1955):

> *When the bombers left Tinian carrying leaflets as well as bombs, they feared that the Allies were giving the people of Japan too broad a hint of their impending fate. Copies of the ultimatum and warnings that their city would be next on the target list were being dropped on a score of places. Would they take the hint, would their rulers let them, before the atom bombs could be assembled and used? That was the paralyzing obsession that gradually laid hold of Cheshire and others.*
>
> *"During the final days before the atomic attacks," Cheshire wrote to me five years ago [in 1950], "a more authoritative*

rumor began to circulate. It said that the Japanese were on the point of surrender. We learnt later that it had been true. Far from causing us to hope that the attacks would be postponed, it only served to aggravate our obsession to see the bombs explode. Indeed I and the majority of the others were determined that if the surrender took place, some means should be found of keeping the war going until the attacks had been launched." (*NP*, p. 256)

When logistics denied Cheshire a seat on the Hiroshima mission's observation plane, he was irate. Only a chance to see the second blast over Nagasaki mollified him. The sight of it, however, changed him forever. "How pale by comparison Wilhelmshaven; how insignificant Bergerac," Cheshire states in the very few words of his subsequent memoir, *The Face of Victory* (1961), devoted to the atomic attack. The effect is so far beyond that of these massive yet conventional raids he'd flown in Europe that he finds himself almost speechless. But not completely. He can make the comparisons, adding, "Yes, and with such utter devastation before our very eyes, how imperative to do something to see that it should never happen again" (*FV*, p. 51). While keeping clear of the international peace movement that consumed the hapless Claude Eatherly and perhaps exacerbated his personal problems, Cheshire nonetheless devoted the rest of his life to humanitarian causes, reducing himself to near pauperhood in the process. For this, and not his wartime service, was he made a peer of the realm by Queen Elizabeth II and given the Order of Merit in 1981.

A close parallel to what Leonard Cheshire did for his fellow humanity after war is found in the story of Jacob DeShazer, bombardier on one of Jimmy Doolittle's B-25s that raided Tokyo in 1942 and one of the five men imprisoned by the Japanese afterward. His three and one-half years as a prisoner of war provide ample materials for a classic captivity narrative, one made all the more stressful by the constant threat of execution (the fate that befell three of the eight Doolittle Raiders soon after being taken by the enemy). But imprisonment is just part of Jake DeShazer's story. Its major element is his transformation from a military to a religious figure. This act in itself produces a text, "I Was a Prisoner of the Japanese," taking form as a pamphlet written in Japanese and distributed in postwar Japan by the millions through the efforts of DeShazer, now a Christian missionary, and the Bible Meditation League. In *DeShazer: The Doolittle Raider Who Turned Missionary* (1950) by Charles Hoyt Watson, portions of this tract are translated and reproduced, none more illuminative than the passage where DeShazer describes his early confinement in a small cell packed with his colleagues and fifteen Chinese prisoners, two of whom were women:

> *One day one of the Chinese women fell down and hurt her head. [The Japanese] laughed and said she was pretending to be sick. Guards hit her on the head with a stick, which was attached to their keys. They seemed to be the very lowest type of people. Sometimes they would make us stand up during the night after they had awakened us from our sleep. They would threaten to hit us with long clubs which they poked through the bars of the cell.*
>
> *It was the first time that I had ever been in such a wicked environment. I could not help wondering why there was so much difference between America and the Orient. There is bad in America, but the bad in America does not begin to compare with that which we observed. The truth was begin-*

ning to dawn upon me—it is Christianity that makes the dif-
ference. Even though many people in America do not profess
to be Christians, yet they are following the Christian ways.
(*D*, pp. 65–66)

What follows in DeShazer's experience is something more involved than the turn to faith so characteristic of religious narratives. His story is religious, to be sure: *DeShazer* is written by the president of Seattle Pacific College, the religious institution that prepared the young veteran for his ministry; and the book is published by an evangelical firm, the Light and Life Press of Winona Lake, Indiana. Practicing Christians, especially those inclined toward a fundamentalist style of belief, find the story inspiring, as even in simply humanitarian terms it is. In a subsequent age when multiculturalism has become a new reality, some of DeShazer's activities seem outdated in their apparent lack of sympathy for other sets of values and beliefs. But even for his time, elements of true understanding emerge, elements that add a dimension (other than a strictly religious one) to the Pacific air war's impact on culture in general. For instance, once the regular routine of POW life is established, DeShazer can see how what strikes him as appallingly brutal treatment is meted out to Japanese prisoners as well, who accept it from their countrymen as a matter of course; once he himself accepts it, his situation seems more bearable. In similar fashion, this new sense of responsibility impresses his guards, and possibilities for genuine communication improve. Yes, the imperative toward Christianity is foremost, but readers two or three generations later must allow for the relatively monocultural nature of these times for American service personnel, who were serving, after all, in a military yet to be racially integrated and fighting to defend liberty that did not extend to American citizens of Japanese extraction who lived on the West Coast. Consider Lieutenant Commander James Flatley's written address to his flyers of fighter squadron VF-10, the Grim Reapers, as they prepare for heavy action off Guadalcanal:

> *Doubtless you have been raised a Christian, even though you may profess no specific belief. All Christianity vocally or audibly or tacitly acknowledges that there is a Supreme Being, usually referred to as God. The Bible tells us that God is our Maker. That He Created us. That He gave us a free will and a conscience. He also gave us Ten Commandments to guide us in our daily relations with our fellow men. He told us that if we obeyed these commandments to the best of our ability we could be rewarded after death by being received into Heaven, and conversely, if we deliberately disobeyed them, we would be justly punished . . . .*
>
> *What is this all leading up to? Only this. We are fighting a war today against enemies who for the most part are not Christian, who deny the existence of God—the Nazis and the Japs. . . .*
>
> *What's the answer? The answer is a return to God. How can we return? By getting down on our knees and praying, or just praying if we don't believe in kneeling. By professing anew, or maybe for the first time, our belief in God. By asking for His aid. . . . (GR, pp. 121–23)*

From a chaplain, to troops attending a service of their own faith, and doing so of their own free wills, these words would be (and still are) standard. But as these flyers of VF-10 prepare for battle, each and every one of them is given this message from their commanding officer—and not for religious comfort, but as an encouragement to take on the enemy. Flatley confided to the war correspondent writing his unit's story that conveying this message makes him feel better and his men feel better too. As well it might; in *Pilots Also Pray*, an especially popular wartime memoir published in 1944, Tom Harmon makes frequent religious references in the manner that Flatley employs. So does Marine pilot Thomas Moore Jr., whose writing of *The Sky Is My Witness* (1943) is motivated by a monsignor's counsel that "it was only by the grace of God that you've come back to us" (*SM*, p. 6). Both men make frequent references to a mother's rosary beads and a strength they find in the faith of their upbringing. Religion is part and parcel with America, they suggest. Consider Harmon's socially narrow yet nonetheless heartfelt definition of what "America" means:

> *It's simple and good and wholesome. It means home, and then it means the ones you love, and the thrill of a football game in the fall with the stadium full and the boys running out on the field and the bright colors in the bleachers, and it means taking your sweetheart to the Junior Prom all dressed up and looking so pretty you are prouder of her than ever, and the campus all white with snow in the middle of the winter, and standing in front of the library chewing the fat with the boys—and you say Apple Pie. Okay. That's what Bob [his squadron mate] and I were thinking about. America, that great and varied thing we couldn't describe but were proud and eager to fight for.* (*PP*, p. 103)

As for the specifics of DeShazer's reawakening, they too follow a familiar pattern. A copy of the Bible that has been allowed for the prisoners' reading offers comfort and inspiration, especially after the death of co-pilot Robert J. Meder, who has wasted away from malnutrition and untreated beriberi. For Charles Hoyt Watson, president of a Bible college, the effect on DeShazer is seen as divinely transformative. But even military historian Carroll V. Glines, in his study of the entire group's experiences, *Four Came Home* (1995), acknowledges religion's influence. "While Jake DeShazer was the only one of the four survivors to enter the ministry," he writes, "the other three freely admit that the message of the Bible they were given after Meder's death deeply affected their personal religious philosophies." Specifically, "they feel their survival was due to the message of hope and forgiveness they found in its tattered pages. They harbor no permanent resentment against their captors and are grateful to God for their survival and eventual release" (*FC*, pp. 161–62).

This religious impulse, bound so tightly to such popular ideals as football, college, prom dates, and apple pie, is for DeShazer something less mystical than commonly practical. As another icon of these times, news commentator Lowell Thomas, puts it, "Jake heard a voice telling him that it should be his mission to teach the Japanese how to treat human beings decently" (*D*, p. 131). The motive may seem quaintly patronizing today, but its sincerity must be admired in light of the way opponents in the Pacific theater had dehumanized their visions of each other. An example even more dramatic than DeShazer's is that of Mitsuo Fuchida. His case is the most prominent one that historians Donald Goldstein and Katherine Dillon can cite at the start of their introduction to Gordon W. Prange's *At Dawn We Slept* as an example of all the "amazing changes in Asia since that historic day in December 1941" when Fuchida had been flight leader of the Pearl Harbor attacks. "After enough adventures for ten men," Goldstein and Dillon marvel, "Fuchida watched the surrender ceremonies aboard *Missouri* in Tokyo Bay. Thus he whose '*Tora! Tora! Tora!*' initiated the Pacific war witnessed its ending." But that is hardly the end of the story. As the historians continue, "Later he became a convert to Christianity. Until his recent death [in 1976] he served the Prince of Peace as a nondenominational evangelist, frequently testifying in the United States" (*AD*, p. x).

Prange himself, as Fuchida's biographer, studies this man's conversion (and the motive for it) with great care. In *God's Samurai*, the arguments are less religious and more humanitarian. The Japanese flyer's story spans a greater range of emotions than does DeShazer's. In the 1930s, for example, Fuchida not only admired the Luftwaffe's achievements, but personally idolized Adolf Hitler, sporting a small moustache trimmed in the Fuehrer's manner. Hence the pilot who directed the two air attacks on Pearl Harbor did so while proudly emulating the appearance of the Allies' enemy number one. A more obvious candidate for damnation in Lieutenant Commander Flatley's religious exhortation could not be imagined. Nor did Japan's defeat tame this man's aggressive hatred for those he still considered his enemies; the fate of his countrymen held as prisoners of war by Americans concerned him deeply, and his concern was mollified only by two revelations—that the child of an American missionary couple killed by the Japanese (as purported spies) had dedicated her life to making things more comfortable for enemy prisoners, and that Jacob DeShazer had not only endured so nobly the atrocious conditions of his own imprisonment but had dedicated his postwar life to missionary work for the benefit of his former adversaries. "This second example of love overcoming hatred hit him with an even greater impact," Prange says of his subject, "DeShazer having been a tough airman. Fuchida knew the breed well and could identify with him. He determined to read the Bible and find out what this was all about" (*GS*, p. 207).

The new Mitsuo Fuchida emerged into a postwar world ready for conversion stories. In 1949 the Association Press, under the auspices of the Young Men's Christian Association (YMCA), had published a short volume titled *I Attacked Pearl Harbor*. Its author, Kasuo Sakamaki, had been the ensign in charge of one of the five two-person midget submarines sent to infiltrate Pearl Harbor in the hours before the air attacks Fuchida would be leading. Of the ten men involved, all but one perished. Upon capture, Sakamaki had begged to be executed. Instead, he was processed as the Pacific theater's first prisoner of war. "The Americans had yet to learn that for a Japanese warrior being taken prisoner meant disgrace," Michael Slackman explains in *Target: Pearl Harbor* (1990). "Lest Sakamaki be thought eccentric on the subject, one need only note the glory showered by Japanese propaganda on the 'nine' midget submariners in the Pearl Harbor attack. By allowing himself to be taken alive Sakamaki becomes a nonperson" (TP, p. 277). Recovering this lost personhood is what the young ensign's book would be about. Of his call to duty at Pearl Harbor, he speaks in the willfully assenting voice of any sincere Japanese military personnel: "I, Kazuo Sakamaki, was being buried as of that moment" (*IA*, p. 18). What happens during his long stretch as a POW, beginning at Camp McCoy in rural Wisconsin, is nothing less than a rebirth into a new world of different cultural values. Beforehand, his adult life had been one of "strict conditioning," the accomplishment of a "complete separation from understanding of other human beings except those of my own kind in the services." In captivity, however, his spiritual senses reawaken, particularly with regard to "the humanness of the Americans I came in contact with." A slow and subtle process, its "tremendous effect" (*IA*, p. 56) is held in abeyance until it becomes as fully realized as his initial disposition not to commit suicide but to accept what life might offer instead. As in so many religious narratives, the moment is a special one when full awareness comes:

> *I cannot recall exactly when this transition to a desire to live took place. But when I became conscious of it, the realization was like a sudden stab in my chest by a sharp knife. It was a stab against me, but it was more than that. It was a powerful hammer-blow against the heart of my whole past, the past that represented the entire history and culture of Japan out of which I, Kazuo Sakamaki, had been born and created. This was in reality the rebirth of reason. Reason! Where did I have it? Where inside of me had it been until then? (IA, pp. 56–57)*

The distance Mitsuo Fuchida had to travel for understanding is even greater. Listening to the emperor's counsel of surrender being broadcast on August 15, 1945, he finds it impossible to understand the concept being proposed: "to pave the way for a grand peace for all generations to come." Prange pictures him puzzling it out, questioning, "How could human beings establish a permanent peace? The idea flew in the face of history. Man could not achieve perfection, hence there would always be wars. At that moment he wanted peace so that Japan could rebuild. When the time was ripe, the nation could wage war again, shining with imperial radiance" (*GS*, pp. 166–67). As long as this attitude prevails, the flyer remains frustrated and unhappy. But like

Leonard Cheshire, another man on the brink of conversion to a different set of values, he knows that "whether or not everlasting peace was possible, the atomic bomb left mankind no choice but to try and achieve it" (*GS*, p. 178). And so, like still another flyer, P-38 Lightning pilot Heath Bottomly, whose *Prodigal Father* (1975) details plenty of air combat in the Southwest Pacific, Fuchida doesn't so much change sides as do what his American counterpart describes, which is to "align myself with the power that controls the universe" (*PF*, p. 111).

Religion has its own power, and the theological aspects of that power are matters for a different type of discourse. How it figures into narratives from the Pacific air war, however, relates directly to the special nature of this conflict. Operations in this theater were conducted over great distances and across a huge expanse of seeming emptiness. What land there was below impressed flyers from both sides as exotic—American and Japanese stories alike are filled with details of life among uncivilized savages in exceedingly primitive conditions, the harshness of it all relieved only by the lushness of nature. Such a primeval world lying between the adversaries only reinforced their cultural differences; for all practical purposes, opponents in the Pacific might just as well have come from the other side of the moon. Little wonder, then, that all campaigns came down to a single ultimate: kamikaze warfare for the Japanese, atomic warfare for the Americans. Rather than narrowing the gap and allowing bridges to be built, World War II as it was fought in Pacific skies only increased the distance, until each side had exhausted its willingness (if not its abilities) to fight in conventional terms.

Such ultimacies raise moral questions, opening the door to religious considerations. And once the religious is entertained, cultural bridging suddenly becomes possible. Christianity is Jake DeShazer's bridge to humanitarian purpose, just as it becomes Mitsuo Fuchida's way of overcoming such deep-seated hostility to his enemies, people at the time he could not ever imagine having the status of "former enemies." But Christianity is not the only force that can bring such diametrically opposed interests into harmony. Jerry Yellin, the P-51 Mustang pilot flying from Iwo Jima, is Jewish, and will in later life find peace and satisfaction in the practice of Transcendental Meditation. His combat experiences, as described in *Of War and Weddings*, are typical of any flyer's from this theater, and his motivation to fight the Japanese is the one most commonly held: we didn't want a war, but they treacherously started it, and so we'll end it. From February 15, 1942, when he enlists in the Army Air Force, to the war's end, he hates the Japanese. Then, for over half a lifetime afterwards, he forgets them. A business trip to an entirely transformed postwar Japan in 1982 reawakens his interest, particularly when he meets and becomes friends with a Japanese man who shared some of Yellin's experiences, not as a flyer but as a ground target.

This startling reversal of perspective prompts some rethinking. Significantly, Yellin relates the challenge of his new friendship to something he'd learned as a young man, a very proper lesson his mother taught him about human respect that he had, quite naturally, turned into hatred of the enemy. The mother's intention had been a good one, asking how he'd feel if someone molested his sister and then saying any young woman he dated would have a family with equally protective feelings that he surely must respect. Should he do anything offensive, they'd be understandably enraged. But then Pearl Harbor is attacked, young Jerry Yellin prepares to serve, and reapplies the lesson:

That is how I felt about the Japanese. They had invaded my home, my country, and I would have to make them pay. All of the stories we began to hear from Corregidor and Bataan, the indignation fueled by American propaganda that depicted the Japanese as "monsters," all contributed to my hatred for an entire nation of people. Now I had to look at them, and at me, from a different perspective. (W, pp. 33–34)

Seeing Japanese people as individuals—as people he speaks to, who speak to him, men and women with whom he can share meals and develop friendships—is what begins Jerry Yellin's process of understanding. Coming as it does more than a full generation after the war, that process is not exceptional; time can heal differences between even the most bitter of adversaries. What becomes the real test for Yellin is when his youngest son, David, not only begins studying Japanese culture but chooses to live there, marrying a Japanese woman and starting a family. "Slowly I had begun to accept the Japanese as people, even though the memories of war surfaced from time to time," the author considers. "But my family? I was beginning to understand Japan, the culture, but a son married to a Japanese? I just didn't know" (W, pp. 66–67). It doesn't help that the neighborhood in which David is establishing his new life was, as he tells his father, "completely untouched by the American bombers. . . . The roads didn't need to be rebuilt. This is one of the older parts of town, and the roads are as narrow as when they were used by wagons and carts." Yellin doesn't tell his son that "I had strafed the rail station and boats in the harbor nearby" (W, p. 67).

Jerry Yellin's initial aversion to the Japanese was prompted by familial sentiments. For him, the Pearl Harbor attack and the taking of the Philippines had been assaults on something as personal as his family, and in 1942 he responded accordingly. Throughout his life, family remained an important principle. But now "family" would be including something besides "American." As he tells his wife, just walking the streets of his son's new country gives rise to contrary emotions. He loves the beauty and serenity he feels in this part of Japan but also worries that "the older women never seem to look directly at me. And when they do, I wonder what they might be thinking." Do they picture him as the P-51 pilot he was? They might, because "when I look at Fuji I see it through the rings of my gun sight, anti-aircraft fire bursting in the background. I just can't shake the war and what I felt then" (*W*, p. 96).

Strangers in the street, a friend made on the train, even his new in-laws: these are not the first Japanese people Yellin has met face to face. From his wartime memoirs, readers learn of an earlier occasion:

> *One afternoon, I hit a Zero pretty badly. As I closed in, I saw that the plane was falling apart. The pilot bailed out and came within a few feet, literally, of hitting my airplane. I could see the startled expression on the pilot's face, the disbelief that this was happening to him. For a split second he floated by me, hanging in the air, his plane in flames and shattering in the background. I didn't see his chute open, I was going too fast and really wasn't concerned. His plane was on fire and that is what mattered.* (*W*, p. 134)

This last sentence is one of the most familiar from World War II air combat memoirs from any theater. Despite possible motives for vengeance, the target in a dogfight always turned out to be the plane itself and not the individual flying it. Making such deadly technology work for yourself and surviving in the process meant visualizing the machine and not the man. Over Europe, where there might be less cause for personal animosity between USAF and Luftwaffe flyers and even the British and German pilots could be known for occasional acts of chivalry, the sight of a person emerging from the cockpit of a damaged plane would often prove startling to the adversary who'd just raked it with fire, so focused had attention been on the aircraft. Victories were always described as against a Messerschmitt or a Focke-Wulfe (or a Spitfire or a Hurricane), never against a personal flyer; "kills" themselves were registered if the plane went down, regardless of whether the pilot parachuted to safety. An ace was someone who shot down five or more enemy aircraft, not someone who necessarily killed that number of enemy flyers. State-of-the-art air combat in World War II stood right on the dividing line between individual contact and technical depersonalization. Hence the rare but still possible occurrence that Jerry Yellin describes when he shoots down this particular Zero and faces, for a split second, its suddenly recognizable pilot.

The depersonalization of air warfare is one thing, as common in the European and Mediterranean theaters as in the Pacific. But when the enemy is Japan, a further alienation takes place, as Yellin recalls from testimony received in May 1943 by the Kirk Committee, convened by President Roosevelt to consider America's postwar position regarding this nation he now believed would be defeated. More than a generation later, this old P-51 pilot, about to become father-in-law of a Japanese woman and later grandfather of children who are half Japanese, finds it hard to explain sentiments put on the record by the U.S. Navy, especially in the presence of a new Japanese friend who has been attending to details of the forthcoming wedding. Here is what Jerry Yellin reads him from the committee's proceedings:

> *The Japanese are international bandits and not safe on the face of the earth. The only way to ensure peace is to destroy them. Japan should be bombed so that there is little left of its civilization, and so that the country cannot begin to recuperate for fifty years. . . . Such drastic measures were necessary because this was a question of which race was to survive. White civilization was at stake. We should kill them (the yellow race) before they kill us. . . . The Japanese accepted western civilization only recently and should not be dealt with as civilized human beings. The only thing they will respect is force applied for a long period of time. Because Japanese domestic conditions had created the country's aggressive behavior overseas, the only way to eliminate the threat would be to destroy it entirely; or possibly turn it over to China. In either case, Japan as a culture and as a power should cease to exist. (W, pp. 200–1)*

These sentiments, though presented to the Kirk Committee, were hardly official views. And everyone, including the memoirist who quotes them here, knows they are as distant as possible from the policies and practices of MacArthur's occupation government, whether formal dicta of military authority or the behavior of American soldiers on duty in postwar Japan. Why are they cited in *Of War and Weddings*? To show the distance that existed between the two cultures in World War II, and how from that perspective harmonious existence was off the scale of imagination. Yet harmony would come. In Yellin's case, it's a matter of not just facing his own fears but realizing that his future in-laws have precisely the same types of fears. These worries begin with harsh memories from the war, but then take a new cast as concerns about the future. In neither case are they abstract. Yes, Jerry Yellin once strafed the area in which his future daughter-in-law was born. And yes, the future father-in-law of Yellin's son had "wanted desperately to fire a gun at my enemy, to kill one before I gave my life to our Emperor" (*W*, p. 245). And yes, their fears so many years later are grounded in fact. Will the respective son and daughter, by virtue of their cross-cultural marriage, be lost to each of their families?

Hence a bond is formed in their common concern, a commonality only at first based on the status of having been adversaries. Where for other American and Japanese flyers Christianity provided a link, Jerry Yellin finds peace in a Universalism for which Transcendental Meditation provided a catalyst. The very practical application for his beliefs is found in his family, which now includes grandchildren being raised as Americans and grandchildren being raised as Japanese. What a tragedy it would be, he considers, if one grandchild were ever put in the position of having to take up arms against the other. When the mothers-in-law embrace, Yellin appreciates the act, given how it is "an entirely out-of-character gesture for a Japanese person" (*W*, p. 268), yet one that does the job of signifying acceptance. What moves him most, however, is the salute he receives from his son's father-in-law as Jerry and his wife head back to America:

I did the same to him, and we turned away and left. I must say that it was extremely emotional for me. I couldn't believe this last gesture of respect from my former enemy, now my family. The years of hatred and anguish dropped away, I was relieved of the burdens of guilt for living through the war. I

felt I could get on with my life and live in peace with myself.
(*W*, pp. 268–69)

From the very start of Japan's war with America, reconciliation was the furthest thing from any combatant's mind. In the Pacific theater, matters were at once so different from Europe. Over there, RAF and Luftwaffe flyers could meet with a sense of mutual respect that from time to time suggested chivalry and sport. Narratives from the Battle of Britain and onwards rebound with incidents of courtesy and humanity as exceptions to the more routine business of killing. In the Pacific, there are extremely few such stories. Above Germany, involvement of the American Eighth Air Force dramatically increased the levels of both vulnerability and destruction. But being captured was not the end of things. As the cliché developed, it was a matter of "For you, now the war is over," with the chance for human elements to resume, even if they be nothing more than the base struggle for survival. No such return to simple human issues would happen when adversaries in the Pacific were taken out of combat and met face to face. Consider this episode from the Pearl Harbor attack, as reported by Walter Lord:

> *A dive bomber crashed near Ford Island, just off the dock normally used by the* Tangier *. . . another into the main channel near the* Nevada *. . . another off Pearl City, not far from the destroyer-minecraft* Montgomery. *Chief Machinist's Mate Harry Haws sent Seaman D. F. Calkins in the destroyer's whale boat to investigate. The pilot was sitting on the wing, but refused to be rescued. As the gig drew alongside, he pulled a pistol. He had no chance to use it—Calkins shot first.* (*DI*, pp. 125–26)

Throughout the war, the gap between these sides seemed uncloseable. Race, religion, culture—the distance measured by the Pacific Ocean seemed so much more vast than that of the Atlantic, an ocean spanned since 1492 with increasing frequency, climaxing with waves of European immigrants in the nineteenth century and reaching its denouement in 1927 with Charles Lindbergh's solo flight across an expanse that no longer seemed beyond easy measure. Warfare, that most intimate of human acts, sometimes unites opponents. In the Pacific, no such opportunity presented itself, as even the manner of conducting the war was so different for the two sides. In Europe, Hitler's blitzkrieg had been answered with the Allies' strategic bombing. In individual air combat, Spitfires faced Messerschmitts, P-47 Thunderbolts took on Focke-Wulf 190s—opposing aircraft that shared technologies and design features and that were flown essentially the same way. In the Pacific skies, the Zero was such a different plane from the USAAF P-40s and Navy Wildcats that *engagement* was hardly the word for describing how they met— the Japanese fighter designed for nimble, close-in dogfighting, the American planes more suited to high-speed dives and sudden, heavily armed hits. Both sides had aircraft carriers, but each used them differently. By the time the United States had learned the best uses of a carrier strike force, its adversary had lost so many of its own carriers that a new form of aerial attack would be needed: that of the kamikaze, another concept so alien to western thinking that the enemy became even less comprehensible than before. If anything, kamikaze actions convinced Americans that they had been right about their adversaries from the start, just as some Japanese believed the atomic bombings of Hiroshima and Nagasaki showed that their own military leaders, so shrill in their characterization of the United

States as a country dead set against the emperor and his people, had been correct.

The first Japanese attacks—on Pearl Harbor, Wake Island, and the Philippines—straightened out some American thinking. Their adversaries were not myopic, technologically primitive dolts but rather highly trained, well equipped, and sharply focused opponents. But this very skill works against any sense of commonality, as Walt Bayler suggests in *Last Man Off Wake Island*:

> *Worst of all in point of horror, the Naval Hospital had been bombed and several patients killed.*
>
> *That was the crowning infamy. We no longer questioned the accuracy of Japanese bombardiers after the demonstration they gave us the first day. Now it was clear to us they had deliberately bombed the hospital where they knew their shrapnel would find a concentration of wounded men helpless in bed, unable to run for shelter—sitting shots for Oriental hunters who just look blank and uncomprehending when they hear us speak of sportsmanship. (LM, pp. 55–56)*

Throughout the war, this alienation of the Japanese would continue, just as they themselves cultivated notions of their western opponents as an adversary sharing no human characteristics except the basest ones. *Well Done! An Aircraft Carrier in Battle Action* (1945) is a relatively sophisticated account of action in the western Pacific by Morris Markey, one of the first journalists to write for the *New Yorker* (a magazine noted for its scrupulous professionalism, including miniscule fact-checking) and by wartime a veteran author of important features. Unlike some earlier reporting by younger war correspondents, there is no demonization of the enemy in his account. But there remains a clear sense of distance from the Japanese, even as their flyers undertake the same preparations as their American counterparts:

> *Invisible to the eastward, Saipan. And invisible to the westward the Japanese fleet, planning, thinking, preparing, nursing their planes for the attack upon us, their pilots in the Ready Rooms taking orders from stiff-backed officers who spoke sharp, clipped phrases. Surely they had upon their blackboards in the characters of their odd language the same admonition which our own blackboards carried in honest English: Get the Carriers.* (WD, p. 176)

Half a century later, linguists would speculate that languages built with ideographs rather than alphabets restricted the ability of their users to think in an improvisatory manner. And it is true that just such a genius for impromptu creative thinking, whatever its cause, gave American forces an advantage in the war. But Markey's sentiments are much cruder than that; whatever its sterling qualities, English is not more *honest* that Japanese. Yet such was the perception of America's enemies even as they were being driven toward clear defeat.

Those who have studied Pearl Harbor conclude, in the words of Michael Slackman, that "responsibility for U.S. unpreparedness stemmed from institutional and cultural factors, rather than any single individual clique" (*TP*, p. 282). This same, almost willful reluctance to comprehend one's enemy continues through the adversarial confrontations during wartime and prevails in odd ways long afterward. Consider journalist Bob Greene's dismay, expressed in *Duty*, when he learns that *Enola Gay* pilot Paul Tibbets drives a Toyota. "It's purely commerce," the old veteran explains. "I bought a Toyota because at the time I bought it I was looking at cars, and I thought it was the best one for me. I looked around and I decided that American car-makers were giving you what *they* wanted to give you, not what *you* wanted to drive" (*DU*, p. 144). Tibbets's attitude is refreshing, but a shock to Greene, who had not yet been born when World War II ended. As an American, Greene presumes a prejudice against all things Japanese—even though he and Tibbets, as fellow Ohioans, are from a state that lost far more lives fighting the Confederacy (including Tennessee and Alabama, where Chevrolets and Fords are assembled) than battling the Japanese. When Paul Tibbets was born, in 1915, one was as likely to encounter a veteran of General Lee's army as of General Grant's. Yet for Greene, a postwar baby boomer for whom so much of worldly existence would be transformed, surprise that the veteran pilot would buy a Japanese automobile is an attitude rooted so deeply in America's wartime thinking that more than half a century later it would remain operable, and as damaging as ever.

"When I killed him, I hated him"—so says Tom Lanphier, the P-38 pilot initially credited with shooting down the transport plane carrying Admiral Yamamoto. "He was the only personalized killing I've been involved in. Naturally, I became interested and learned a great deal about him." Other adversaries would meet face to face after the war. For Lanphier, this would be impossible, yet his words about Yamamoto bring the admiral to life. "He was a gambler, a poet, a calligrapher, master strategist, planner, courageous man, cared for his men, didn't give a damn for his superiors, the ones who didn't agree with him"—in short, a person very much like Lanphier himself. "Altogether, a truly great man whom I admire and respect," the American flyer concludes, "and if I had the chance to kill him again, I'd do it in a minute" (*AY*, p. 151). Do flyers from the two sides meeting up long after the war still feel this way about each other? No one says so, though some reunions are chillier than others. What do get recounted are the memories, and in narratives from the Pacific air war animosities run strong. Consider the one told by Joe Foss in *A Proud American* about two opponents meeting after coming down close together in the water just off Guadalcanal. The American is Jack Conger, someone Joe has known since childhood in South Dakota (with a boyhood story as a reminder). On the tail of a Zero that has attacked Henderson Field, Jack runs out of ammunition and tries to chop off its tail. His Wildcat hits the fuselage instead, but both pilots manage to bail out safely before their planes crash. It all happens near shore, from which some Marines in a Higgins boat set out to rescue the two men. Because the enemy pilot is closest to shore, the boat heads for him—but is waved off by the Japanese flyer who points to his American rival. "Your friend back there said to pick you up first," the sailors laugh as they head over to Conger, who responds as he thinks is appropriate:

> "Well, he's a real sport," said Conger. "There's a little chivalry left in the war at that."
>
> With Conger in the boat, they turned back toward the Japanese pilot. The Marines wanted to finish the enemy at a distance, but Conger insisted on rescuing the man. I could hear the heated argument clearly from where I stood knee-high in the surf.
>
> Conger won the debate and personally reached down to grab the enemy airman's life vest to pull him into the boat. The pilot smiled and extended an arm up to Conger. As the

two clasped hands, the Japanese pilot whipped his other arm around with a cocked 8mm Nambu pistol, rammed the barrel between Conger's eyes, and pulled the trigger. (PA, p. 115)

The gun does not fire, for being water-soaked, but the message is clear: body language in the enemy's culture is quite different from that in Conger's. Foss has little doubt that his own message will be lost on the reader—a reminder, more than half a lifetime later, of Morris Markey's preference for the "honesty" of his own manner of speech. How different a scene it is from the celebrated meeting of RAF pilot Douglas Bader, the famous legless ace who when shot down near a Luftwaffe base in occupied France is honored with a formal meal in his captors' mess and given the courtesy of having a replacement for one of his artificial limbs air-dropped by his squadron mates. English and German are, of course, linguistically and historically related. But the distance between American language—even body language—and Japanese is more broadly cultural. From the Japanese point of view, their pilot was doing nothing wrong at all; had he accepted Conger's bonhomie and become a chivalrous chum, *that* would have been a cardinal sin against his people.

As it happens, Conger (with a lifetime of back problems caused by his violent reaction to nearly being shot) and Shiro Ishikawa (the Zero pilot who after trying to kill Conger spits on Joe Foss as he's led away) meet long after the war—and, as Foss reports, shake hands. "Time heals and God can give us a forgiving heart." He adds that "Subaro Sakai, the top surviving Japanese ace, with whom I often share platforms at university symposiums, recently told me that I am his best friend in America" (PA, p. 116). The old Marine fighter pilot ends his chapter there, letting blank space speak for the silence that is all he can offer in return.

For veterans of the Pacific theater, it often takes something extraordinary, such as faith or family, to bridge the gap between the old adversaries. Comradeship of the air is far less effective for them than it is for their European Theater counterparts in mending old wounds. Instead, they maintain a special camaraderie of their own. Any sporting impulses they feel are not with the enemy but among themselves. Pacific theater memoirs abound with metaphors from baseball and football—even Saburo Sakai uses language from the diamond to characterize his aerial exploits, for the summer game was as popular in Japan as in America. But these are team sports, and the emphasis is among one's cohort. No duels in the skies, no jousts between rival knights in airborne armor—just a sense of team spirit for one's own side.

There's a leveling effect to team sports that appears in these narratives, all the more so when the pilot is marked for fame or already among his culture's notable figures. Consider Ted Williams, who in 1941 had hit an astronomical .406 for the Boston Red Sox, at the same time leading the American League with thirty-seven home runs. In 1942 he led the league with 137 runs batted in, making his stellar reputation all the brighter and himself quite evident when he began training as a pilot. Aviation cadet classes have a way of greeting newcomers, chanting "You'll be sorry" as their junior counterparts march in. Arriving for preflight training, he hears a special call, as described in his memoir, *My Turn at Bat* (1969): "The cadets already there were hanging out the windows watching us, and as we passed, one guy hollered, 'OK, Williams, we know you're there, and *you're going to be sor-ry*'" (*MY*, p. 96). But from here on it's flying skills that count. In his same class is teammate Johnny Pesky, who proves less adept at shifting from shortstop to the cockpit:

Flying came easy for me. But poor Pesky. He was a great lit-tle athlete. A boxer, wrestler, basketball player, he could run like hell and he was a tiger on the obstacle courses. But he couldn't swim a stroke, he'd go right down, and he flew an airplane like he had stone arms. One time at Amherst, on a real windy day, we were flying Cubs. If you hold a Cub too tight, the wind blows you off the runway. You have to crab, or you have to slip.

Poor John lines up the runway, comes in and, whoosh, the wind blows him away. Around he goes. He tries again and the wind takes him again. He made eight approaches that day. It looked like we were going to have to shoot him down.

They finally got Pesky out of there. In an airplane he was a menace to himself and everybody else, but he was certainly officer material so they moved him into O.C.S. [Officer Can-didate School] and he actually got his rank before I did. (*MY*, p. 113)

Pesky, of course, would return to the Red Sox with Williams. But for now his place was elsewhere on the team. A new team-mate who kept his place in the same class as the Boston slugger was George H. Bush, a young first baseman from Yale and future president of the United States. As a cadet, he'd write home to tell about training with Williams. But as Joe Hyams notes in *Flight of the Avenger: George Bush at War* (1991), flight instruction and classroom work were complemented by "hours of close-order drill on the parade ground and nine sports con-sidered the most effective in developing agility and strength as well as competitive spirit: the cadets competed against them-selves as well as against one another. These were football, soc-cer, basketball, boxing, swimming, track, wrestling, gymnastics, and tumbling" (*FA*, p. 37). Though President Bush's service as a naval aviator would be most widely remembered for his Avenger being shot down (with the pilot drifting in his life raft before being rescued by an American submarine), his major contribution would be leading what biographer Robert B. Stinnett calls in *George Bush: His World War II Years* (1991) "the Bush team" (*G*, p. 1103) in producing 1,017 reconnaissance photos for the Peleliu invasion.

Before becoming vice president and then president, George H. Bush would be director of the Central Intelligence Agency, where another team member, E. Howard Hunt, had flown Avengers as well. Hunt's fact-based novel, *Limit of Darkness*, dates from 1944, as fresh as any firsthand account of this style of air war in the Pacific, and in it one of his characters explains the project at hand. It's an old fleet doctrine that the striking radius of a task force is contained by the hours of night; one must be out of the enemy's range by daylight. Air power changes that, to the extent that "the limit of darkness is pushed back to the limit of our own air cover" (*LD*, p. 104). With this new principle established, what is the aviator's role? To keep pushing that limit farther and farther. How is it done? By a teamlike organization of a carrier group's assets, including the coordinated use of aircraft for interrelated tasks, such as the newly conceived "plunge bombing" of the huge Grumman Avenger. How will it all work? "System," Hunt's character explains. "The Nips can't beat system, plus brains" (*LD*, p. 103).

Teamlike organization characterizes missions in the air, and when operating from an aircraft carrier the teamwork is all the more remarkable. In *Helldiver Squadron* (1944), war correspondent Robert Olds wonders at the finely tuned activity needed just to get these planes into the air and then back on deck again:

The efficiency and daring of the plane handlers never ceased to amaze the airmen. They wore bright colored jerseys and cloth helmets for quick identification—red for armament and refueling squads; green for those who freed the planes from the arresting gear; white for fire captains; brown for plane captains; blue for plane pushers and yellow for plane directors.

These deck crewmen, sometimes called "airdales," constantly darted in and around the closely packed planes and spinning propellers with unbelievable agility. They crawled on their bellies under fuselages and clutched at the deck gratings to keep from being blown into one prop by the blasts of another. It seemed incredible that accidents were so rare. (HS, p. 90)

This hive of activity on aircraft carriers, with so many disparate functions all closely coordinated to one general purpose, characterizes air war in the Pacific and makes the tone of narratives about it quite different from storytelling styles of the European Theater. Over there, strategic bombing was the mode from 1942 onward. Fighters swept ahead and astride of these great formations—the farther away the better, for keeping threatening adversaries well at bay; only later in the war, in the months surrounding D-Day, would tactical missions against tanks, railways, and smaller troop units bring these dynamic single-seaters into contact with ground targets. True, escort missions had to be carefully planned but nothing like the integration of squadrons working from a carrier. Torpedo planes, dive-bombers, and fighters would have to work cooperatively for any mission to succeed. And this would be just the carriers' air assets. Combine them with Army Air Force level bombers (B-17s and B-24s) operating at higher altitudes and the mediums (B-25s and B-26s) coming in much lower, with P-38 fighters flying top cover and New Zealand Air Force P-40s doing escort duty, and the mixture is complex indeed. Even Marine flyers (such as Joe Foss and Pappy Boyington) operating from land bases had to participate with other air elements in a way that their Army Air Force counterparts in Europe (Chuck Yeager, Frances Gabreski, Hub Zemke) did not always have to entertain. Hence the imagery for describing the Pacific air war is necessarily social in nature. Consider the title of John B. Lundstrom's account of naval air combat from Pearl Harbor to Midway, *The First Team* (1984), and how he describes the intricacies of Commander William B. Ault's juggling of available resources as scattered remnants of his *Lexington* Air Group prepare to strike the carrier *Shokaku* during the Battle of the Coral Sea:

> *Ault resolved to attack with the forces at hand: four dive bombers, eleven torpedo planes, and six F4Fs [Wildcat fighters]. Poor weather had effectively robbed him of eleven SBDs [Dauntless dive bombers] and three F4Fs. As his tactical plan, Ault would hit the carrier first with his SBDs to draw the CAP [the enemy combat air patrol of Zeros] away from the more vulnerable torpedo planes. With his two fighter escorts close by, Ault forged ahead with his four SBDs, arranging to approach from a different direction from that of Torpedo Two [Devastator torpedo bombers], following at its slower pace and circling around to the south. Ault's options were limited by intermittent clouds; in some spots the ceiling was much lower than 6,000 feet. (TF, p. 237)*

The resulting attack takes an additional four thousand words to describe, given the complexities of arranging complementary actions by dive bombers, torpedo bombers, and fighters made all the more difficult by bad weather and enemy interference. Two 1,000-pound bombs and five torpedoes hit home, enough to inflict heavy damage but insufficient to sink the big carrier, which was able to limp back to port. The *Lexington* would soon go down herself, prompting strategists to call the Battle of the Coral Sea a draw. As war correspondent Ira Wolfert would note in *Torpedo 8: The Story of Swede Larson's Bomber Squadron* (1943), at this stage in the war "neither side could ever put into action at one place at one time enough planes to take care of all the work that had to be done—warding off the enemy's Sunday punch while, at the same time, knocking his block off with your own" (*TE*, p. 8.). From these conditions of engagement, narrative style is clear: even more so than the air war in Europe, combat in Pacific skies would be a matter of getting many different elements working together, all the time keeping an eye on the enemy's extremely dangerous combination of these same forces.

Language to describe such complexities is often pushed to poetic limits. In his account of the new *Lexington*'s Air Group 16 during the concluding phase of the First Battle of the Philippines on June 19, 1944, *Mission Beyond Darkness* (1945), Lieutenant Commander Joseph Bryan III describes the night Admiral Marc Mitscher risks enemy attack by turning on the carrier's lights, lest the Air Group's returning planes be lost. The planes find their carrier, but bringing them in is a tortuous operation, including a terrible pile-up when a SB2C Helldiver comes in too fast and crashes into four planes just landed and not yet cleared. The slaughter is ghastly, but work must continue, and a powerful deck crane begins at once to untangle the wreckage, even as the dead and dying are carried away. For the time being, the remainder of Air Group 16 must remain aloft while the ship is blacked out (as a warning to other airborne craft) and the wreckage removed. Looking above, the flight control officer can see that "even the semblance of a landing circle has vanished. Planes were stampeding in an animal panic, blind and headlong, crowding and shoving to be the first in line when the *Lexington*'s lights went on again" (*MB*, p. 77). Aircraft approach the stern and seem to hover there, just above stall speed, before spurting away and heading back into position. A Dauntless dive-bomber "skittered along the waves only a hundred feet off the port beam, then stopped abruptly and sank. No one got out." Ten minutes later, the lights go back on, just as an Avenger slips into its approach. The landing signals officer brings it in, then glances back to see "six planes hurtling toward him. The stampede had resumed" (*MB*, p. 78).

The Helldiver that has caused all this trouble is called a "rogue plane" throughout this account. Coming in too fast and ignoring the landing signal officer's instruction would seem unforgivable, yet there is no condemnation beyond the term needed to identify its out-of-place context in the landing circle. One might assume the pilot was wounded, but that is not the issue; what matters is that the deck be cleared and operations resumed. Four months later in the same campaign, during the Battle of Leyte Gulf, Air Group 15 aboard the *Essex* faces a more personal issue: because casualties in VB-15, the Group's Helldiver squadron, have been so high, the rear-seat gunners balk at continuing to face such danger. Their sentiments are understandable; as Edwin B. Hoyt notes in *McCampbell's Heroes* (1983), they are enlisted men "at the mercy of their pilot"; specifically, "if he goofed, they died" (*MH*, p. 168), and during the last few missions the Naval Reserve officers they flew with had been making more than the usual amount of mistakes. Yet such behavior is a court-martial offense.

To prompt a solution, the squadron commander announces "that even if the gunners did not fly, the Helldivers would fly with empty back seats, but they would fly and bomb and fight the enemy. The announcement silenced the rebellion" (*MH*, p. 169). Such is the essentially social nature of this air war.

Appeals like this to a spirit of teamwork are not uncommon in any theater of war, but they do seem more frequent in the Pacific. Novelist Frederick Faust, writing under the pen name of Max Brand, would interview Marine flyers on leave in order to produce a factual account, *Fighter Squadron at Guadalcanal*, written in 1943 but not published by his estate until 1996. His insight into the squadron commander, Lieutenant Colonel Joe Bauer, is typical, drawing on Bauer's prewar experience playing football and then coaching it at the Naval Academy. "He turned sport into war," readers are told, "and he turned war into sport" (*FSG*, p. 46), using the techniques of one action as the inspiration for the other, depending on whether his men were at peace or in combat. Yet all of the sportsmanship is directed toward one's own team, with none to be shared with the enemy, other than as a target. Notice the momentary admiration a Japanese flyer receives from William M. Gaskill in *Fighter Pilot: World War II in the South Pacific* (1997) when his diary entry for September 25, 1944, describes his P-38 squadron in action, dealing with a single enemy plane:

> *Nip broke off, half rolled & down. We went to the deck where that Jap put on the most superb exhibition of flying I have ever seen. He made us with our old trucks look like bulls in a china closet—the way he maneuvered. He would half roll on the deck—split "S" at 3,000 feet . . . he would whip in and out of our sights. . . . The other boys came over & joined us & it*

was a merry rat race . . . . On one 360 [degree turn] I met him head on at 30 degree deflection—saw my cannon shell explode in his left wing—so did Col. Dusard and Col. West-brook. They picked him up & everyone I do believe got in a burst at him before Col. Westbrook slipped in and finished him off. His wing came off & he quarter rolled, hit the trees & ground, exploded & burned. We had him all boxed off & Westy had a no-deflection shot. (FP, p. 102)

"Rats" is late-war South Pacific lingo for enemy flyers, particularly fighter pilots. It appears in many narratives from this period and usually refers to the threat posed to bomber formations by these enemy planes. Here, for a moment, Gaskill is able to personalize his adversary, who has distinguished himself with such brilliant airmanship. But the P-38 pilots are a team unto themselves, and they have no problem either ganging up or sharing the kill, boxing their opponent as in basketball and then passing off to the team member who has the best shot. The "rat" is dispatched as easily as another P-38 pilot, Dick Bong, does another necessary job when assisting in a rescue mission, an episode described by Carl Bong and Mike O'Connor in *Ace of Aces* (1985): "Dick was flying cover for the rescue party as it crossed Embi Lake in a rubber raft when he spotted a large crocodile (!) tailing the raft. Dick reportedly rolled in, killed the croc with a strafing run and scared the hell out of the men in the raft" (*AA*, p. 54). Bong himself would use an animal code of his own when writing home, as the letters collected by his brother in *Dear Mom, So We Have a War* attest—not "rats" for his adversaries but rather "fish" (*DM*, p. 156) to indicate his interest in whether his father was having any luck poaching out-of-season deer for the family's larder.

In the bombing offensive, which would not reach strategic proportions until March of 1945, team solidarity—or the lack of it—is also a major issue. New Zealander Bob Spurdle, an RAF veteran of three tours in the European Theater, returns home to fly with his own Royal New Zealand Air Force, doing escort duty in the Solomons. After his experience in Spitfires, he bridles at being given an obsolescent American P-40 from Lend Lease days with which to protect the USAAF bomber formations winging their way to enemy targets. Not that he likes the bomber crews any better. He goes so far as to complain to an American Brigadier General, who is "very good about it and kept his cool while I lost mine," which is remarkable given the slur Spurdle makes against his ally's sense of democracy: "Sir," he reports, "I've checked out the names of the pilots who press on—the Schmidts, Wilsons, MacGregors and such like, but the Napolinskis and Finklebergers chicken out!" Having learned little about squadron solidarity (and the irrelevance of Anglo-Saxon names to USAAF conduct), he goes even further in *The Blue Arena* (1986) to criticize the customary livery of Yank bombers. "And another thing," he blusters to the General. "The bigger the nude painted on the aircraft, the sooner it will turn back!" (*BA*, p. 151). The outfit Carter McGregor Jr. writes about in *The Kagu-Tsuchi Bomb Group* (1981) doesn't have a Hollywood-style nude for its nose art; instead, the most characteristic emblem for these planes is that of a fanged and armored fire god hurling destruction at a fearful enemy. His chagrin with the British comes when his disabled B-29 is denied landing rights at an RAF field for fear its presence will draw a Japanese attack. McGregor and his crew land nevertheless, saving their own lives plus the plane, to which repair parts are airlifted so that after a week it can fly home. "The sequel to that mission, including the reaction from the

British, was really a comical anticlimax and did not endear us to our Limey allies, nor them to us, " McGregor writes. "The accounting of that experience with the British did not appear in any official report but was just another of those wartime incidents that is not recorded in history, only in the memory of those involved" (*KT*, pp. 164–64). Yet McGregor's memoir becomes history, and an important part of it is his belief that the entire crew, and not just he as the pilot who led them, deserved a medal for their experience. To make his point, he lists their names, a roster that might confound Squadron Leader Spurdle: "Paslay, Jennings, Krzyzkowski, Greenfield, Jordan, Tweet, Weinberg, Nordhagen, Horn, and Smith, the real heroes" (*KT*, p. 164).

Oliver Sheehan, pilot; Robert J. Rothwell, copilot; James A. Gebbie, bombardier; Wendall P. Rawson, navigator; Uhland S. Adair, engineer; John J. Haggerty, radio operator; Rocco W. Bobbora, assistant radio operator; Raymond M. Phillips, assistant engineer; Richard O. Wall, gunner; Thomas D. McNamara, gunner. These ten crew members of a B-24 bomber named *Ten Knights in a Bar Room* died when their plane disappeared over New Guinea on December 1, 1943. The plane's wreckage and the remains of the men who flew in it were found in 1970, as Americans were fighting in another war on this nether side of the world. A young firefighter, too young during the Vietnam years to be drafted, would make a study of not just the crash and the subsequent recovery efforts thirty-seven years later but of the ten flyers themselves, individuals from California, rural and urban Illinois, Alabama, Minnesota, Massachusetts, Pennsylvania, Nevada, and Missouri. Michael J. Cundiff's *Ten Knights in a Bar Room: Missing in Action in the Southwest Pacific, 1943* (1990) demonstrates the wide-ranging yet tightly drawn interrelationships that constitute a World War II bomber crew. Farm boys working side by side with city slickers; university-educated offi-cers and factory hands together in the confines of, by today's standards, a relatively small aircraft, their fates intertwined in a mutual dependency; northerners, southerners, easterners, west-erners, all sharing the identical fate. Later generations would note that there were no African Americans among them, no Japanese Americans. But otherwise it was the democratic cross-section within which Squadron Leader Spurdle had presumed to find distinctions in valor and duty. The same mixture of per-sonnel and the same rigors of an air war would characterize the lives of bomber crews in the European Theater. But here in Pacific skies a plane could disappear without a trace and remain so thoroughly lost that a chance recovery more than a genera-tion later would make headlines across the country. As Cundiff records, "a total of 241 American aircraft disappeared without a trace in Papua New Guinea, and this is only for the Fifth Air Force. The figure does not include the Thirteenth [and Twenti-eth] Air Force or the Marine Corps. For the Fifth Air Force, if we were to add those aircraft that were seen to crash, mostly into the sea, but from which the bodies were not recovered, the total would increase to at least 313 aircraft" (*TK*, p. 118). Where do the remains of their crews lie? Beneath the seas, or on terra incog-nita. The society they share is theirs alone.

Considering the immensities, air combat in the Pacific skies of World War II might seem essentially unknowable. Yet like the crash sites discovered and human remains brought home for burial today, in a world so different from the one in which these events happened, key elements can be absorbed, just as locations from this vast expanse half a world away forced their way into Western consciousness at the time. In March of 1944 radioman

Charles Furey and his reconnaissance squadron would fly to their first operational base at Munda Airfield on the island of New Georgia. In *Going Back: A Navy Airman in the Pacific War* (1997) he recalls it as "a part of the world filled with danger and mystery." But not a total mystery, for "the names of every island, and the waters that surround them, have become, in one year's time, part of the American language. We have read about, heard about, seen pictures of Guadalcanal and Savo Island and Ironbottom Bay and Bougainville—where the fighting is still going on—and Kavieng and Rabaul—where the battered Japanese wait for our troops to land" (*GB*, p. 91).

In theater, he's soon given the chance to view some Japanese prisoners. Unlike the aerial views of places otherwise known only as new words in the wartime vocabulary, this chance to view is summarily rejected:

> *I have no desire to see the face of my enemy, especially a captured one who is probably sick, depressed, weak, and hurt. I don't want to feel any sympathy for him. In the middle of this long battle, I don't want to let my guard down, even for a little bit. I don't want to acknowledge that those captives are even human beings, like ourselves. I prefer to continue it the way it has been all along, up to now. For me, the enemy is faceless. Admittedly, he mans the planes and ships that oppose us. But it is the planes and ships that are our targets, and if he is a part of them, then he has become a target himself.* (*GB*, p. 137)

Above all, this American flyer does not want to see that his enemy is a young man like himself, to risk learning that not only might he be a radioman too but a better radioman, a better person. "The way I look at it," Furey concludes, "I am on one team and he is on another" (*GB*, p. 138). If they are to meet, it will be as adversaries, each dedicated to the elimination of the other's side. Nothing personal, of course—that's just the way it is.

BIBLIOGRAPHY

Ballard, Robert D., and Rich Archbold. *Return to Midway*. Washington, D.C.: National Geographic Society, 1999.

Bartsch, William H. *Doomed at the Start: American Pursuit Pilots in the Philippines, 1941–1942*. College Station: Texas A & M University Press, 1992.

Bayler, Walter L. J., and Cecil Carnes. *Last Man Off Wake Island*. Indianapolis: Bobbs-Merrill, 1943.

Bergerud, Eric M. *Fire in the Sky: The Air War in the South Pacific*. Boulder, Colo.: Westview Press, 2000.

Blackburn, Tom, with Eric Hammel. *The Jolly Rogers: The Story of Tom Blackburn and Navy Fighting Squadron VF-17*. New York: Crown, 1989.

Blount, R. E. Peppy. *We Band of Brothers*. Austin, Tex.: Eakin Press, 1984.

Boeman, John. *Morotai: A Memoir of War*. Manhattan, Kans.: Sunflower University Press, 1989.

Bong, Carl. *Dear Mom, So We Have a War*. Superior, Wis.: Burgess Publishing, 1991.

Bong, Carl, and Mike O'Connor. *Ace of Aces: The Dick Bong Story*. Mesa, Ariz.: Champlin Fighter Museum, 1985.

Bottomly, Heath. *Prodigal Father: A Fighter Pilot Finds Peace in the Wake of His Destruction*. Glendale, Calif.: G/L Regal, 1975.

Boyington, [Gregory] Pappy. *Baa Baa Black Sheep*. New York: Putnam's, 1958.
———. *Tonya*. Indianapolis: Bobbs-Merrill, 1960.

Boyle, Andrew. *No Passing Glory: The Full Authentic Biography of Group Captain Cheshire*. London: Collins, 1955.

Brand, Max [Frederick Faust]. *Fighter Squadron at Guadalcanal*. Annapolis, Md.: Naval Institute Press, 1996.

Bryan, Joseph III, and Philip Reed. *Mission Beyond Darkness*. New York: Duell, Sloan and Pearce, 1945.

Buell, Harold L. *Dauntless Helldivers: A Dive-Bomber Pilot's Epic Story of the Carrier Battles*. New York: Orion, 1991.

Burns, Eugene. *Then There Was One: The U.S.S. Enterprise and the First Year of War*. New York: Harcourt, Brace, 1944.

Burt, Ron. *Kamikaze Nightmare*. Corpus Christi, Tex.: Alfie Publishing, 1995.

Carl, Marion E. *Pushing the Envelope: The Career of Fighter Ace and Test Pilot Marion Carl*. Annapolis, Md.: Naval Institute Press, 1994.

Caron, George R., and Charlotte E. Meares. *Fire of a Thousand Suns: The George R. "Bob" Caron Story—Tail Gunner of the Enola Gay*. Westminster, Colo.: Web, 1995.

Cheshire, Leonard. *Bomber Pilot*. London: Hutchinson, 1943.

———. *The Face of Victory*. London: Hutchinson, 1961.

Clausen, Walter B. *Blood for the Emperor: A Narrative History of the Human Side of War in the Pacific*. New York: D. Appleton-Century, 1943.

Coffey, Thomas M. *Iron Eagle: The Turbulent Life of General Curtis LeMay*. New York: Crown, 1986.

Cortesi, Lawrence. *The Deadly Skies*. New York: Zebra Books, 1982.

Cox, Bryan. *Too Young to Die: The Story of a New Zealand Fighter Pilot in the Pacific War*. Ames: Iowa State University Press, 1989.

Cundiff, Michael J. *Ten Knights in a Bar Room: Missing in Action in the Southwest Pacific, 1943*. Ames: Iowa State University Press, 1990.

Davis, Burke. *Get Yamamoto*. New York: Random House, 1969.

Dickinson, Clarence E. *The Flying Guns*. New York: Scribner's, 1942.

Doolittle, James H., with Carroll V. Glines. *I Could Never Be So Lucky Again*. New York: Bantam [hardcover], 1991.

Dugger, Ronnie. *Dark Star: Hiroshima Reconsidered in the Life of Claude Eatherly of Lincoln Park, Texas*. Cleveland, Ohio: World, 1967.

Dyess, William E. *The Dyess Story*. New York: Putnam's, 1944.

Eatherly, Claude, with Gunther Anders. *Burning Conscience*. New York: Monthly Review Press, 1962.

Ferguson, Kathy E., and Phyllis Turnbull. *Oh, Say, Can You See? The Semiotics of the Military in Hawai'i*. Minneapolis: University of Minnesota Press, 1999.

Finney, Ben. *Feet First*. New York: Crown, 1971.

Forsyth, John F. *Hell Divers: U.S. Navy Dive-Bombers at War*. Osceola, Wis.: Motorbooks, 1991.

Foss, Joe, with Donna Wild Foss. *A Proud American: The Autobiography Joe Foss*. New York: Simon & Schuster, 1992.

Foss, Joe, with Walter Simmons. *Joe Foss, Flying Marine*. New York: Dutton, 1943.

Fuchida, Mitsuo, and Masatake Okumiya. *Midway: The Battle That Doomed Japan*. Annapolis, Md.: U.S. Naval Institute, 1955.

Furey, Charles. *Going Back: A Navy Airman in the Pacific War*. Annapolis, Md.: Naval Institute Press, 1997.

Gailey, Harry A. *The War in the Pacific: From Pearl Harbor to Tokyo Bay*. Novato, Calif.: Presidio Press, 1995.

Gamble, Bruce. *The Black Sheep: The Definitive Account of Marine Fighting Squadron 214 in World War II.* Novato, Calif.: Presidio Press, 1998.

———. *Black Sheep One: The Life of Greg "Pappy" Boyington.* Novato, Calif.: Presidio Press, 2000.

Gaskill, William M. *Fighter Pilot: World War II in the South Pacific.* Manhattan, Kans.: Sunflower University Press, 1997.

Gay, George. *Sole Survivor: A Personal Story About the Battle of Midway.* Dallas: Midway Publishers, 1986.

Glines, Carroll V. *Attack on Yamamoto.* New York: Orion, 1990.

———. *The Doolittle Raid: America's Daring First Strike Against Japan.* New York: Crown, 1988.

———. *Four Came Home: A Pictorial History of Doolittle's Tokyo Raid, April 18, 1942.* Missoula, Mont.: Pictorial Histories Publishing, 1983.

Greene, Bob. *Duty.* New York: William Morrow/HarperCollins, 2000.

Greenlaw, Olga. *The Lady and the Tigers.* New York: Dutton, 1943.

Gurney, Gene. *Journey of the Giants.* New York: Coward-McCann, 1961.

Guyton, Boone. *Air Base.* New York: Whittlesey House/McGraw-Hill, 1941.

Hall, R. Cargill. *Lightning Over Bougainville: The Yamamoto Mission Reconsidered.* Washington, D.C.: Smithsonian Institution Press, 1991.

Hardison, Priscilla. *The Suzy-Q.* Boston: Houghton Mifflin, 1943.

Harmon, Tom. *Pilots Also Pray.* New York: Crowell, 1944.

Harwit, Martin. *An Exhibit Denied: Lobbying the History of Enola Gay.* New York: Copernicus/Springer-Verlag, 1996.

Hersey, John. *Hiroshima.* New York: Knopf, 1946.

Horikoshi, Jori. *Eagles of Mitsubishi: The Story of the Zero Fighter.* Seattle: University of Washington Press, 1981.

Hoyt, Edwin P. *Blue Skies and Blood: The Battle of the Coral Sea.* New York: Paul S. Eriksson, 1975.

———. *The Kamikazes.* New York: Arbor House, 1983.

———. *McCampbell's Heroes: The Story of the U.S. Navy's Most Celebrated Carrier Fighters of World War II.* New York: Van Nostrand Reinhold, 1983.

———. *Yamamoto: The Man Who Planned Pearl Harbor.* New York: McGraw-Hill, 1990.

Huie, William Bradford. *The Hiroshima Pilot.* New York: Putnam's, 1964.

Hunt, E. Howard. *Limit of Darkness.* New York: Random House, 1944.

Hyams, Joe. *Flight of the Avenger: George Bush at War.* San Diego: Harcourt Brace Jovanovich, 1991.

Hynes, Samuel. *Flights of Passage: Reflections of a World War II Aviator.* New York: Frederic C. Beil, 1988.

Inoguchi, Rikihei, Tadashi Nakajima, and Roger Pineau. *The Divine Wind.* Annapolis, Md.: United States Naval Institute, 1958.

Johnston, Stanley. *The Grim Reapers.* New York: Dutton, 1943.

———. *Queen of the Flat-Tops: The U.S.S. Lexington and the Coral Sea Battle.* New York: Dutton, 1942.

Karig, Walter, and Welbourn Kelley. *Battle Report: Pearl Harbor to Coral Sea.* New York: Farrar and Rinehart, 1944.

Kawato, Masajiro. *Flight Into Conquest.* Anaheim, Calif.: KNI Inc., 1978.

Kenney, George C. *Dick Bong: Ace of Aces.* New York: Duell, Sloan and Pearce, 1960.

———. *The Saga of Pappy Gunn.* New York: Duell, Sloan and Pearce, 1959.

Kinney, John F., with James M. McCaffrey. *Wake Island Pilot: A World War II Memoir.* Washington, D.C.: Brassey's, 1995.

Klinkowitz, Jerome. *Their Finest Hours: Narratives of the RAF and Luftwaffe in World War II.* Ames: Iowa State University Press, 1989.

———. *With the Tigers Over China, 1941–1942.* Lexington: University Press of Kentucky, 1999.

———. *Yanks Over Europe: American Flyers in World War II.* Lexington: University Press of Kentucky, 1996.

Kurtz, Margo. *My Rival, The Sky.* New York: Putnam's, 1945.

Kuwahara, Yasuo, and Gordon T. Allred. *Kamikaze.* New York: Ballantine Books, 1957.

Lamont-Brown, Raymond. *Kamikaze: Japan's Suicide Samurai.* London: Arms and Armour, 1997.

Lawson, Ted W. *Thirty Seconds Over Tokyo.* New York: Random House, 1943.

Lay, Beirne, Jr., and Sy Bartlett. *Twelve O'Clock High.* New York: Dodd, Mead, 1948.

LeMay, Curtis, with MacKinlay Kantor. *Mission with LeMay.* Garden City, N.Y.: Doubleday, 1965.

LeMay, Curtis, and Bill Yenne. *Superfortress: The Story of the B-29 and American Air Power.* New York: McGraw-Hill, 1988

Lord, Walter. *Day of Infamy.* New York: Henry Holt, 1957.

———. *Incredible Victory.* New York: Harper and Row, 1967.

Lundstrom, John B. *The First Team: Pacific Naval Air Combat From Pearl Harbor to Midway.* Annapolis, Md.: Naval Institute Press, 1984.

McClendon, Dennis E., and Wallace F. Richards. *The Legend of Colin Kelly.* Missoula, Mont.: Pictorial Histories Publishing, 1994.

McEniry, John Howard, Jr. *A Marine Dive-Bomber Pilot at Guadalcanal.* Tuscaloosa: University of Alabama Press, 1987.

McGregor, Carter, Jr. *The Kagu-Tsuchi Bomb Group.* Wichita Falls, Tex.: Nortex Press, 1981.

McWhorter, Hamilton III, with Jay A. Stout. *The First Hellcat Ace.* Pacifica, Calif.: Pacifica Military History, 2000.

Markey, Morris. *Well Done! An Aircraft Carrier in Action.* New York: D. Appleton-Century, 1945.

Mears, Frederick. *Carrier Combat*. Garden City, N.Y.: Doubleday, Doran, 1944.

Michener, James. *Tales of the South Pacific*. New York: Macmillan, 1947.

Mikesh, Robert C. *Broken Wings of the Samurai: The Destruction of the Japanese Airforce*. Annapolis, Md.: Naval Institute Press, 1993.

Millott, Bernard. *Divine Thunder: The Life and Death of the Kamikazes*. New York: McCall, 1971.

Moore, Thomas, Jr. *The Sky Is My Witness*. New York: Putnam's, 1943.

Morehead, James B. *In My Sights: The Memoir of a P-40 Ace*. Novato, Calif.: Presidio Press, 1998.

Nagatsuka, Ryuji. *I Was a Kamikaze*. New York: Macmillan, 1972.

Naito, Hatshuho. *Thunder Gods: The Kamikaze Pilots Tell Their Stories*. New York: Dell, 1990.

Okumiya, Masatake, and Jiro Horikoshi. *Zero!* New York: Dutton, 1956.

Okumiya, Masatake, and Jiro Horikoshi, with Martin Caidin. *The Zero Fighter*. London: Cassell, 1958.

Olds, Robert. *Helldiver Squadron: The Story of Carrier Bombing Squadron 17 with Task Force 58*. New York: Dodd, Mead, 1944.

Park, Edwards. *Angels Twenty: A Young American Flyer a Long Way from Home*. New York: McGraw-Hill, 1997.

Porter, R. Bruce, with Eric Hammel. *Ace! A Marine Night-Fighter Pilot in World War II*. Pacifica, Calif.: Pacifica Military History, 1985.

Potter, John Deane. *Yamamoto: The Man Who Menaced America*. New York: Viking, 1965.

Prange, Gordon W., with Donald M. Goldstein and Katherine V. Dillon. *At Dawn We Slept: The Untold Story of Pearl Harbor*. New York: Viking-Penguin, 1991.

———. *God's Samurai: Lead Pilot at Pearl Harbor*. Washington, D.C.: Brassey's, 1990.

Rothgeb, Wayne. *New Guinea Skies: A Fighter Pilot's View of World War II*. Ames: Iowa State University Press, 1992.

Sakai, Saburo, with Martin Caiden and Fred Saito. *Samurai!* New York: Dutton, 1957.

Sakaida, Henry. *Winged Samurai: Saburo Sakai and the Zero Fighter Pilots*. Mesa, Ariz.: Champlin Fighter Museum, 1985.

Sakamaki, Kazuo. *I Attacked Pearl Harbor*. New York: Association Press, 1949.

Sheehan, Susan. *A Missing Plane*. New York: Putnam's, 1986.

Slackman, Michael. *Target: Pearl Harbor*. Honolulu: University of Hawaii Press, 1990.

Smith, John F. *Hellcats Over the Philippine Deep*. Manhattan, Kans.: Sunflower University Press, 1995.

Smurthwaite, David. *The Pacific War Atlas, 1941–1945*. New York: Facts on File, 1995.

Snyder, Earl. *General Leemy's Circus: A Navigator's Story of the 20th Air Force in World War II*. New York: Exposition Press, 1955.

Spector, Ronald H. *Eagle Against the Sun: The American War with Japan.* New York: Random House, 1985.

Spurdle, Bob. *The Blue Arena.* London: William Kimber, 1986.

Stinnett, Robert B. *George Bush: His World War II Years.* Missoula, Mont.: Pictorial Histories Publishing, 1991.

Thomas, Gordon, and Max Morgan Witts. *Enola Gay.* New York: Stein and Day, 1977.

———. *Ruin from the Air: The Enola Gay's Atomic Mission to Hiroshima.* London: Hamish Hamilton, 1977 [includes material added to the American edition, *Enola Gay*].

Thomas, Rowan T. *Born in Battle: Round the World Adventures of the 513th Bombardment Squadron.* Philadelphia: John C. Winston, 1944.

Tibbets, Paul W., with Clair Stebbins and Harry Franken. *The Tibbets Story.* New York: Stein and Day, 1978.

Toll, Henry C. *Tropic Lightning.* Manhattan, Kans.: Sunflower University Press, 1987.

Tregaskis, Richard. *Guadalcanal Diary.* New York: Random House, 1943.

Twining, Merrill B. *No Bended Knee: The Battle for Guadalcanal.* Novato, Calif.: Presidio Press, 1996.

Walker, Samuel I. *Up the Slot.* Oklahoma City, Okla.: Walker, 1984.

Walton, Frank E. *Once They Were Eagles: The Men of the Black Sheep Squadron.* Lexington: University Press of Kentucky, 1986.

Watry, Charles A., and Duane L. Hall. *Aerial Gunners: The Unknown Aces of World War II.* Carlsbad: California Aero Press, 1986.

Watson, C. Hoyt. *DeShazer: The Doolittle Raider Who Turned Missionary.* Winona Lake, Ind.: Light and Life Press, 1950.

White, W. L. *Queens Die Proudly.* New York: Harcourt, Brace, 1943.

Williams, Ted, with John Underwood. *My Turn at Bat.* New York: Simon and Schuster, 1969.

Winston, Robert A. *Dive Bomber.* New York: Holiday House, 1939.

———. *Fighting Squadron: A Sequel to Dive Bomber.* New York: Holiday House, 1946.

Winters, T. Hugh. *Skipper: Confessions of a Fighter Squadron Commander.* Mesa, Ariz.: Champlin Fighter Museum, 1985.

Wolfert, Ira. *Torpedo 8: The Story of Swede Larsen's Bomber Squadron.* Boston: Houghton Mifflin, 1943.

Wyper, William W. *The Youngest Tigers in the Sky.* Palos Verdes, Calif.: privately published, 1980.

Yellin, Jerry. *Of War and Weddings: A Legacy of Two Fathers.* Fairfield, Iowa: Sunstar, 1995.

Yoshimura, Akira. *Zero Fighter.* Westport, Conn.: Praeger, 1996.

INDEX